CONTROVERSIES IN PHILOSOPHY

General Editor: A. G. N. Flew

Each volume in this series deals with a topic that has been, and still is, the subject of lively debate among philosophers. The sort of issues that they embrace are only partially covered, if covered at all, by the usual collections of reprinted work.

The series consists largely but not entirely of material already published elsewhere in scattered sources. It is a series distinguished by two guiding ideas. First, the individual editors of the various constituent volumes select and collect contributions to some important controversy which in recent years has been, and which still remains, alive. The emphasis is thus upon controversy, and upon the presentation of philosophers in controversial action. Second, the individual editors are encouraged to edit extensively and strongly. The idea is that they should act as firm, fair and constructive chairmen. Such a chairman gives shape to a discussion and ensures that the several contributors are not merely heard, but heard at the moment when their contributions can be most relevant and most effective. With this in mind the contributions as they appear in these volumes are arranged neither in the chronological order of their first publication nor in any other possibly arbitrary sequence, but in such a way as to provide and to reveal some structure and development in the whole argument. Again, and for similar reasons, the editorial introductions are both substantial and forthcoming.

Although most of the contributions in each volume have been published before as articles in journals, the editors are asked not to confine themselves to this source. There will be a fair element of previously unpublished material and, even more frequently, extracts will be taken from books.

The Private Language Argument

EDITED BY

O. R. Jones

CONTRIBUTORS

A. J. Ayer, Hector-Neri Castañeda, V. C. Chappell, Newton Garver, Helen Hervey, L. C. Holborow, Anthony Kenny, Norman Malcolm, C. W. K. Mundle, Rush Rhees, P. F. Strawson, J. F. Thomson, Judith Jarvis Thomson, L. Wittgenstein

MACMILLAN

ST MARTIN'S PRESS

First published 1971 by
MACMILLAN AND CO LTD
London and Basingstoke
Associated companies in New York Toronto
Dublin Melbourne Johannesburg and Madras

Library of Congress catalog card no. 76-124949

SBN 333 10510 9 (hard cover)

Printed in Great Britain by
WESTERN PRINTING SERVICES LTD
Bristol

Foreword by the General Editor

The series, of which the present volume is the third member, consists largely but not entirely of material already published elsewhere in scattered sources. It is as a series distinguished by two guiding ideas. First, the individual editors of the various constituent volumes select and collect contributions to some important controversy which in recent years has been, and which still remains, alive. The emphasis is thus upon controversy, and upon the presentation of philosophers in controversial action. Second, the individual editors are encouraged to edit extensively and strongly. The idea is that they should act as firm, fair, and constructive chairmen. Such a chairman gives shape to a discussion and ensures that the several contributors are not merely heard, but heard at the moment when their contributions can be most relevant and most effective. With this in mind the contributions as they appear in these volumes are arranged neither in the chronological order of their first publication nor in any other arbitrary sequence, but in such a way as to provide and to reveal some structure and development in the whole argument. Again, and for similar reasons, the editorial introductions are both substantial and forthcoming.

The controversy presented in this third volume was, as Dr O. R. Jones in his systematic Editor's Introduction is careful to explain, provoked by the posthumous publication in 1953 of Wittgenstein's *Philosophical Investigations*. It concerns the possibility of a language which might be in some way essentially and irredeemably private to its sole user, rather than that of a method of encoding or encyphering which, whether by chance or by design, just happens to be familiar only to a single person. This second and unproblematic possibility can be aptly illustrated by referring to John Locke, who successfully employed such a system to conceal the meaning of his private papers from prying contemporaries, although modern scholarship has become at last able to render these into public English. What makes such a reference to Locke particularly apt is that he also provided what is perhaps the clearest statement in any classical philosopher of the view that, in another interpretation of the term 'private', not just some but all language is not merely contingently but essentially private. Thus in his *Essay Concerning Human Understanding* Locke says that 'words, in their primary or immediate signification, stand for nothing but the ideas in the mind of him that uses them, however imperfectly soever or carelessly these ideas are collected from the things which they are supposed to represent. . . . That then which words are the marks of are the ideas of the speaker: nor can anyone apply them as marks, immediately to anything else but the ideas which he himself hath . . .' (III. ii. 2; cf. III. ii. 8 and III. i. 2).

Two more volumes in this series are already under construction, and some others are less definitively on the way. As General Editor I shall be glad to consider other possibilities, whether the suggestions come from colleagues who would like to do the editorial work themselves or whether they are made by others who as teachers feel a need which they would like someone else to fill.

ANTONY FLEW

University of Keele,
Staffordshire,
England

Contents

8   *Contents*

Acknowledgements

The kindness of authors, literary executors, editors and publishers who gave permission for the inclusion of material in this book is gratefully acknowledged.

Chapter I(i) is a section from 'Critical Notice: *Philosophical Investigations*', *Mind*, LXIII (1954) pp. 70–99. Reprinted by permission of the author and editor.

Chapter I(ii) consists of sections from 'Wittgenstein's *Philosophical Investigations*' as printed in *Knowledge and Certainty: Essays and Lectures* (Englewood Cliffs, N.J., 1963) pp. 96–129. Reprinted by permission of the author and Prentice-Hall Inc., Englewood Cliffs, N.J. This essay originally appeared in *Philosophical Review*, LXIII (1954) pp. 530–59, and was revised for *Knowledge and Certainty*.

Chapter II(i) and (ii) is the symposium entitled 'Can There Be a Private Language?' published in the *Aristotelian Society Proceedings*, supplementary vol. XXVIII, pp. 63–94. Copyright © 1954 The Aristotelian Society. Reprinted by courtesy of the authors and the editor of the Aristotelian Society. Professor Ayer's contribution has been reprinted, with additional notes, in his book *The Concept of a Person* (Macmillan, 1963). The notes are reprinted here with the permission of the author, Macmillan & Co. Ltd, and Doubleday & Co. Inc., New York.

Chapter III(i) is 'The Private Language Problem', from *Philosophical Quarterly*, VII (1957) pp. 63–79. Peprinted by permission of the author and editor.

Chapter III(ii) is 'Wittgenstein on Private Language', from *Philosophy and Phenomenological Research*, XX (1959–60) pp. 389–396. Reprinted by permission of the author and editor.

Chapter IV(i) is ' "Private Language" and Wittgenstein's Kind of Behaviourism', from *Philosophical Quarterly*, XVI (1966) pp. 35–46. Reprinted by permission of the author and editor.

Chapter IV(ii) is 'Wittgenstein's Kind of Behaviourism?', from *Philosophical Quarterly*, XVII (1967) pp. 345–57. Reprinted by permission of the author and editor.

Chapter V(i), (ii), (iii) and (iv) is the symposium 'The Private Language Argument', from *Knowledge and Experience: Proceedings of the 1962 Oberlin Colloquium in Philosophy*, ed. C. D. Rollins (University of Pittsburgh Press) pp. 88–132. Reprinted by permission of the authors, editor and the Provost of Oberlin College. Professor Castañeda's contributions have been revised, and his preface was prepared for this volume.

Chapter VI(i) is 'Private Languages', from *American Philosophical Quarterly*, 1 (1964) pp. 20–31. Reprinted with a few changes by permission of the author and editor.

Chapter VI(ii) has not been previously printed.

Chapter VII is 'Wittgenstein's Notes for Lectures on "Private Experience" and "Sense Data"', ed. Rush Rhees, from *Philosophical Review*, LXXVII (1968) pp. 271–320. Reprinted by permission of Wittgenstein's literary executors (Professor G. E. M. Anscombe, Mr Rush Rhees and Professor G. H. von Wright) and the editors of the *Philosophical Review*.

List of Abbreviations

Abbreviations used to refer to Wittgenstein's works:

NB   *Notebooks, 1914–1916*, ed. G. H. von Wright and G. E. M Anscombe, trans. G. E. M. Anscombe (Oxford: Blackwell, 1961). (Contains also letters to Russell, 1912–20, and 'Notes on Logic', 1913.)

TLP   *Tractatus Logico-Philosophicus* (*Logisch-Philosophische Abhandlung*), trans. D. F. Pears and B. F. McGuinness (London: Routledge & Kegan Paul, 1961). (Dates from 1916–19.)

LF   'Some Remarks on Logical Form', *Proceedings of the Aristotelian Society*, supp. vol. IX (1929).

WWK   *Ludwig Wittgenstein und der Wiener Kreis*, shorthand notes recorded by F. Waismann, B. F. McGuinness (Oxford: Blackwell, 1967). (Dates from 1929–32.)

PB   *Philosophische Bemerkungen*, ed. Rush Rhees (Oxford: Blackwell, 1964). (Dates from 1930.)

ML   'Wittgenstein's Lectures in 1930–33', in Moore, *Philosophical Papers* (London: Allen & Unwin, 1959).

BB   *The Blue and Brown Books* (Oxford: Blackwell, 1958). (Blue Book dates from 1933–4, Brown Book 1934–45.)

RFM   *Remarks on the Foundations of Mathematics*, ed. by G. H. von Wright, R. Rhees and G. E. M. Anscombe, trans. G. E. M. Anscombe (Oxford: Blackwell, 1956). (Dates from 1937–42.)

Z   *Zettel*, ed. G. E. M. Anscombe and G. H. von Wright, trans. G. E. M. Anscombe (Oxford: Blackwell, 1967). (Dates principally from 1945–8.)

Inv.   *Philosophical Investigations*, ed. G. E. M. Anscombe and R. Rhees, trans. G. E. M. Anscombe (Oxford: Blackwell, 1953). (Dates from 1945–9.) References to paragraph numbers in Part I will be by numbers, thus *Inv.* 302, and references to Part II will be by II followed by roman numerals for sections, thus *Inv.* II iv, and by page numbers for pages, thus *Inv.* II, p. 246.

Note: All references to work reprinted in this book will be by number of the page in this book.

Editor's Introduction[1]

O. R. Jones

The question whether there could be a private language has become the subject of voluminous and sometimes quite abstruse discussion ever since Wittgenstein's remarks on the topic were published in his *Philosophical Investigations.* After wading through the literature, one might well concur in despair with Professors Hector-Neri Castañeda and J. F. Thomson that, to quote the latter, 'it is not clear at all what the Private Language Argument is supposed to come to or what its assumptions and reasonings are' (p. 168 below). The present collection of articles is only a small sample of the sometimes tortuous attempts that have been made to come to grips with Wittgenstein's investigations, so one cannot help asking why those investigations should prove so terribly difficult to fathom. It could be due to the complexity and profundity of the issues raised, of course, but I suspect that there is another reason as well. There seems to be a significant difference between Wittgenstein and many of his readers in their view of what it is to philosophise. The point emerges in Mrs J. J. Thomson's contribution towards the end of this collection, and it is a point to which I shall return later.

What is the significance of the private language controversy in the context of the development of contemporary philosophy? It pertains especially to two fields of philosophical study. The first is philosophy of mind, or philosophical psychology as it is often called, and the second is philosophy of language. Wittgenstein was himself primarily concerned with the second of these two themes, as the opening sections of the *Inv.* show. His concern with philosophy of mind is a part of his wider concern with the philosophy of language. It was as a result of his reflections on language that he came to question a well-established and widely held view about such things as sensations, feelings, and thoughts. The view which he challenged goes back to Descartes, as some of our contributors point out (for example, Malcolm, p. 41 below, and Garver, p. 99 below, who describe the private language argument as a *reductio ad absurdum* of the Cartesian position). However, as both Malcolm and Anthony Kenny[2] have made clear, the particular feature of Cartesian dualism which is the subject of Wittgenstein's criticism is not something peculiar to Descartes. It began with Descartes, but it is a feature which has subsequently pervaded the thinking of the British Empiricists – Locke, Berkeley and Hume – and has become a heritage which many later philosophers and psychologists have accepted without question. It is worth noting that even so-called behaviourist psychologists are not always as behaviourist in their outlook as their work in the laboratories might lead one to expect. For example, D. O. Hebb, who is an out-and-out behaviourist in his psychological methods, is prepared to pay more than lip-service to Cartesian dualism in his non-professional moments. Descartes would be happy to agree with Hebb when he says that '*private,* or *subjective,* or *introspective evidence* concerns events within the observer himself, and by the nature of things available to that one observer only', and that 'all that we can know about the conscious processes of another . . . is *an inference from behaviour,* verbal or non-verbal' (*A Textbook of Psychology* (Philadelphia and London, 1958) p. 4).

THE CARTESIAN VIEW

It will be worth setting out the essence of the Cartesian position in more detail before attempting to show how the private language argument bears upon it. According to the Cartesian view, sensations and feelings are only contingently related to the manifest behaviour and circumstances of the person who has the experience in question. That is to say, if the behaviour and circumstances normally associated with toothache, for example, had generally been quite different, our concept of toothache could have remained the same. Perhaps the point could be brought out by considering the following example. It is a contingent matter that rats happen to occupy the position they do at a particular time. If they happened to occupy quite different positions, some being on the moon even, this would make no difference to our concept of rat. We would not cease to call an animal a rat merely because we found it in one place rather than another. Contrast this with the fact that rats have incisor teeth. This is not a contingent matter at all. A rat is defined as a rodent and a rodent is defined as having incisor teeth. If we were quite generally prepared to call an animal a rat without regard for the fact that it had no incisor teeth, then the word 'rat' would take on a different meaning; in other words, we would have a different concept. Of course, it may be allowed that rats lose their incisor teeth or that an occasional rat may fail to grow them. The point is that if a certain kind of animal which we called a rat did not as a rule have incisor teeth, then the word 'rat' would not mean what it does now.

According to the Cartesian view, the behaviour that we normally associate with toothache is not comparable to the rat's incisor teeth in the respect just described. It is like the rat's position. A rat is a rat no matter what positions rats may have taken from time to time, and the Cartesian holds that a toothache is a toothache no matter how sufferers might behave at various times. It is held that, though it so happens that people are inclined to grimace, complain and seek a dentist when they have toothache, it could have been quite otherwise without it making any difference to our concept of toothache.

A rat's incisor teeth are such that anyone could have a look at them, feel them (if he would care to try) or even have them X-rayed. In this sense they are public features, or properties, of a rat, and as we have just seen, our concept of rat requires that they are features which a creature must, as a rule, have if it is to be correctly called a rat. This point could be expressed by saying that possession of these particular features is a criterion by which we may judge whether or not a particular animal is a rat. Since these features are public in the sense specified, we could call rats public objects, though it should be borne in mind that this does not mean that rats are public in *every* sense of that word. But the Cartesian position with respect to things like toothache is that they need never be accompanied by any of the public features we normally associate with toothache; in other words, all public manifestations of toothache are purely contingent. Everything essential to toothache, everything that makes a pain count as toothache, is assumed to be private to the individual who has it. Another way of expressing this point is to say that toothache is a private object. According to the Cartesian view all sensations, feelings and other psychological states are private in this sense.

The Cartesian assumes that words for sensations and feelings come to have the meaning they do in much the same way as words for things like chairs and tables acquire their meaning. There is just one difference. In the case of sensations and feelings all public features, including the behaviour and observable circumstances of the person who has the sensations or feelings in question, will be irrelevant so far as the meaning of the word is concerned. The relevant features will all be private. The Cartesian assumes that this presents no problems, for he thinks that just as you can have public acquaintance with a public object, so also you can have a private acquaintance with a private object such as your own toothache. That is how there can be words for private, just as there are words for public, objects.

Wittgenstein, with incredulity, asks: But how could it be like that? The question arises out of his reflections on language. He finds that his understanding of what language is comes into conflict with the Cartesian view which I have outlined, and it is this conflict that is expressed in his remarks on the impossibility of a private language. These are the remarks that have came to be known as the private language argument. The fact that it challenges a view that has been held by so many, and for so long, is one good reason why the argument is worth studying.

The Argument

It may be useful at the beginning to distinguish between three notions of a private language, not two as is sometimes done. Firstly, there is the notion of a language which is private in the sense that only the speaker can, as it happens, speak it, though the language could be taught to others in any of the various normal ways we have of teaching a new language to someone who does not know it already. An example of such a language would be a private code straightforwardly translatable into English. This presents no problem, and can be put aside (see, for example, Ayer, on p. 50 below, and Garver on p. 95 below). Secondly, there is the notion of a language such that no one other than the speaker could understand it even if all the experiences of the speaker were available to others. This would be a language some feature or other of which, irrespective of what the language is about, would make it logically impossible that anyone other than the speaker should understand it, or follow its rules. No case for such a notion of a private language has been made to my knowledge, and it is indeed hard to see how a language could possibly be such as to determine logically who should be capable of understanding it, and do that irrespectively of what a person's experiences were. This notion may be what Dr Hervey is rejecting when she throws out the notion of a language that is *in principle* incapable of being understood by anyone other than the speaker (p. 85 below). She points out that this would not qualify as a language at all, private or otherwise. This notion of a private language may also be dismissed. Thirdly, one might consider the possibility of a language which cannot be taught to, or learnt by, anyone other than the speaker because it is a language which is used to talk about objects which are private in the sense already explained earlier. This last alternative is the one worth considering, as several of the contributors take pains to show in their various ways (Malcolm, pp. 41 f. below; Ayer p. 51 below; Mundle, pp. 104 ff. below; Garver, pp. 95 f. below).

Now let us look at the steps of the argument, beginning with points on which there seems to be fairly general agreement among the contributors to the controversy. Firstly, it is fairly generally agreed that the existence of a language involves the following of rules in some sense or other, though Mrs J. J. Thomson rightly raises some important questions about what precisely is involved in rule-following in this context (pp. 187 ff. below). Whatever this rule-following amounts to, we may safely say that at the very least it requires that the same word be used regularly for the same thing. Secondly, it is agreed that rule-following presupposes the possibility of checking on the application of words, thereby making sure that the rule is being correctly followed. The point is not that one needs to carry out the check, nor even that it should be possible in practice to carry it out. The point is that there must be some procedure which would count as checking if it were carried out. The point is argued by Malcolm on pp. 42 f. below, but seems to be admitted by critics of the private language argument as well. Ayer and Mundle, for example, do not deny that checking must be possible; what they deny is that a Robinson Crusoe would be without resources for carrying out checks (see p. 54 with note, and p. 108 below). Similarly Castañeda argues that the speaker of Privatish would have checks available, but agrees from the start that 'one thing, however, is definitely clear, namely, *that a person possesses a language only inasmuch as he is capable of self-correction*' (p. 147 below). Thirdly, no one disputes that it is possible to check on the application of words used to refer to public objects like tables and chairs. If you think you are using the word 'chair' regularly to refer to the same kind of thing on various occasions, someone else could soon tell you if you are or not. Anyone who reads the contributions to this volume will realise that a certain amount of oversimplification is inevitable in this Introduction, but I do not think we shall go far wrong in regarding these three points as matters on which the disputants are more or less agreed.

Now I come to a point in the argument which is the crucial bone of contention between the different sides in the controversy. Could there be any possible check on the application of words used to refer to private objects such as the Cartesians take sensations and feelings to be? Wittgenstein, I think, is suggesting that it would not be possible if the objects were private in the sense explained earlier. There are some who agree with him and some who do not. This is the basic cleavage in the whole debate. I will return to it in a moment.

If there is no possible check on the application of words for private objects, then it seems to follow in accordance with the second point mentioned above that there cannot be any rule-following in the case of such words. But that means, according to the first step of the argument, that such words could not be part of a language; which means that they could not be genuine words at all. A private language is impossible.

The implication for the Cartesian viewpoint should be clear. Sensations, feelings and so forth are not private in the way supposed in the Cartesian view. If they were, then only a private language involving private rules would be possible to talk about them. But such a language is impossible. Conversely, since we are able to talk about our sensations and feelings, they are not Cartesian private objects.

PRIVATE RULE-FOLLOWING

The first chapter of this collection consists of two critical expositions of those sections of Wittgenstein's *Inv.* which deal with the private language problem. Strawson is prepared to accept that naming a sensation involves the formation of, and adherence to, a customary practice in the use of the name, but he thinks that an individual could do this privately. So far as checking goes he suggests that, though memory may be fallible, it is in general sufficiently reliable to enable us to carry out a measure of checking. This, he thinks, would be good enough to enable us to set up the kind of customary practice that is necessary for a language to get going. Malcolm draws on the text of the *Inv.* to show that setting up a customary practice, or following a rule in the way we apply a word, is not as simple as Strawson thinks it is. For example, you could not claim to be following a rule simply on the ground that you have called a certain sensation a 'thrill' and keep on applying that word to the *same* sensation regularly. This claim is not as substantial as it looks; in particular the word 'same' conveys so little as to be useless in this context. Malcolm's discussion shows that it is no easy matter to explain precisely what it is to follow a rule in the application of a word, but on one thing he is quite definite. One must be able to distinguish between following a rule and merely being under the impression that one is following a rule. This is where checks become relevant, but memory checks alone will not do. The reason is that one must also be able to distinguish between remembering and being under the impression that one remembers.

Strawson would no doubt agree that the case for the possibility of private rule-following and private checking deserves a fuller statement than he gave it, for he concedes that his outline is 'extremely crude' (p. 32 below). We have an amplified statement of the case given by Ayer in Chapter II, where he brings in the well-known example of a Robinson Crusoe forming a language on his own. He argues for the validity of private recognitions on the ground that we cannot go beyond a bedrock of recognitions even in our naming of public objects. Each individual recognition may be questioned, but there is no reason why several of them should not corroborate each other.

Rush Rhees is not convinced by Ayer's arguments. Rhees points out that the things done by a Robinson Crusoe – inventing names, defining things or calling things by a certain name, finding corroboration for a recognition – already presuppose language. On Rhees's view the rule-following which is crucial for language is not a rule-following which is made possible by language, but a rule-following which makes language itself possible. He thinks that this rule-following could not take place privately. This is not so much because memory cannot be trusted in seeking confirmation for the correctness of the reapplication of a word, but because there is no room for the notion of correctness or incorrectness in a case like this.

I will venture to offer two examples of my own in an effort to bring the issue into sharper focus. Suppose my friend claims that he can recognise a certain property of an iron bar simply by grasping it with his hand. I am told, however, that what he recognises is not one of the well-known properties like roughness or shape, but something which he calls 'ponk'. The first difficulty here is not the difficulty about knowing if my friend is right when he says that a particular bar of iron is ponk. There is a more fundamental difficulty that comes before that. The difficulty is that one cannot make any sense of the notion of his being right or wrong; one does not know what it would be to say that he was right or to say that he was wrong. Consequently one does not know what it would be to say that he was following a rule, even though he makes a show of sorting out iron bars into those which are ponk and those which are not. It does not help at all at this stage if my friend says he can tell if a piece of iron is ponk by recognising something else about the iron. Suppose he calls this 'tonk', and tonk is something which eludes everybody else's notice in just the same way as ponk does. This does not help, for tonk is puzzling in precisely the same way as that whose obscurity already needs dispelling.

Contrast this with a different case where my friend says that a good way of telling if an iron bar is ponk is to place it amidst some iron filings and see whether it produces a characteristic pattern. The pattern could be the one we are familiar with where an iron bar is magnetised. Suppose my friend says that it is not simply that the formation of the pattern of iron filings is a good indication that the iron is ponk; it is not simply that ponk is often accompanied by a certain formation of iron filings. On the contrary, he says that part of what he *means* by saying that the iron is ponk is simply that it normally produces the characteristic pattern of iron filings in the appropriate circumstances. If ponk is like this, then there is no insuperable difficulty about regarding claims about ponk as being correct or incorrect. My friend's use of the word 'ponk' will in fact be very like our ordinary use of the word 'magnetised'.

In this second case claims about ponk can be taken to be either correct or incorrect, and that enables us to regard our friend's use of the word 'ponk' as a case of rule-following. As we have already seen, it is generally agreed that this is necessary if 'ponk' is to qualify as a word in a language. In the first case which I described we have no idea what it would be for claims about ponk to be either correct or incorrect. Consequently, it was impossible for us to regard our friend's use of 'ponk' as a case of rule-following. That, in turn, means that we could not regard 'ponk' as a word in a language.

These two examples leave some questions unasked, let alone answered, but they may help to pin-point the kind of difficulty that the proponents of the private language argument were trying to raise. Ponk as introduced in my first example would purport to be a private object in the sense I described earlier, whereas the ponk of my second example would be public. If we say that all the public behaviour of a toothache sufferer is only contingent in the sense I described earlier, then we construe 'toothache' like 'ponk' in my first example. The implication of the private language argument is that 'toothache', on that account, does not get going as a word in the language any more than 'ponk' gets going as a word in my first example. But if it is allowed that the public, observable behaviour usually associated with toothache is not just contingent, then 'toothache' becomes like 'ponk' in our second example, and clearly qualifies as a word in the language.

BEHAVIOURISM

The two contributors who write in Chapter III have had the benefit of reflecting on the arguments of Ayer and Rhees, and have some comments to make on their remarks, but they come to opposite conclusions. According to Dr Harvey, Wittgenstein is out to eliminate the notion of private experiences, but she is not convinced by the private language argument. Taking up Ayer's example, she deploys further arguments to show that Robinson Crusoe could produce a private language. Garver thinks differently. Using Wittgenstein's example of the private diarist, he argues that Wittgenstein succeeds in producing a *reductio ad absurdum* of Cartesian dualism. What are we to make of this? Many philosophers think that if we turn our backs on dualism the only alternative we have left to us is behaviourism. This is the view that any statements about human experience can be reduced to statements about observable behaviour, or about disposition to such behaviour. To say that someone has toothache, on this view, is to say that he behaves, or is inclined to behave, in certain specific ways, to produce grimaces and so forth. The experience of toothache seems to drop out of the picture. Many philosophers are very reluctant to embrace such a view, and cannot believe it is true to the facts. Basically, Dr Hervey's complaint against Wittgenstein is that he is moving in this behaviourist direction, and she is not the only one to lodge such a complaint. Nor is she alone in thinking that a behaviourist view is quite unacceptable. Mundle, in the next chapter, explicitly develops the charge that Wittgenstein's view is behaviourist, and attempts to undermine Wittgenstein's alleged behaviourism by attacking the private language argument.

How is it that people come to think that the private language argument leads straight into behaviourism? It is easy to see this if we consider again the examples of my friend and the word 'ponk'. I suggested that 'ponk' could be accepted as a genuine word in the language provided the man stood consistently by the public test of the pattern of iron filings, but then it is tempting to think that by calling the iron 'ponk' he simply means that it will produce the specified pattern of iron filings in the appropriate circumstances. On this view, claims about ponk are reducible to claims about producing a pattern of iron filings. Similarly, it is felt that Wittgenstein is putting forward a reductionist programme according to which claims about experiences are to be understood as amounting to no more than claims about various patterns of behaviour. In other words, Wittgenstein would appear to be a behaviourist.

If Wittgenstein is a behaviourist, then he is certainly not a consistent one. Consider what he says about knowing that one is in pain, for instance. He holds that to say that one knows that one is in pain is simply to say that one is in pain, for the claim to know has substance only where doubt can be denied, and he claims that it makes no sense to say that a person doubts whether he is in pain. So the claim to know that one is in pain, considered as distinct from the claim that one is in pain, is empty – in other words, not a claim at all. But if having pain were simply a matter of behaving in a certain way, then of course it would make sense to say that we were mistaken about it, for it does make sense to say that we are mistaken about the way we behave. It sometimes takes a mirror to tell you how worried you look. Suppose you were as determined as you could be to keep a straight face for five minutes and were quite convinced that you had succeeded; still if you were confronted with the contrary testimony of a number of people who had watched you, and with the evidence of a movie taken of your face over that period, then you would have to give precedence to this evidence over your own previous conviction. So it does make sense to say that a person is mistaken about his own behaviour, but if one cannot be said to know or be mistaken as regards one's sensations and feelings, then they cannot simply amount to patterns of behaviour. Thus Wittgenstein could not consistently maintain what he does about knowing that one is in pain and be an out-and-out behaviourist at the same time.

There are, as Mundle himself points out, other passages in the *Inv.* which are inconsistent with a behaviourist position. But whereas Mundle argues that Wittgenstein is indeed inconsistent, Holborow comes to Wittgenstein's defence. Holborow detects an ambivalence in the use of the word 'private', and suggests that we distinguish between what is private and what is radically private. I may well have toothache without behaving in the way people often do when they have toothache. The toothache in my case may happen to be

slight, and I may have other, happier things to think of, or I may
have a good reason to hide the fact that I have toothache. Furthermore, I am never in the position of having to find out if I have
toothache by watching my own behaviour. For these two reasons
we may quite properly call toothache a private experience. It could
remain true, however, that the word 'toothache' would not have
the meaning it does if the usual behaviour and circumstances associated with toothache were quite irrelevant for the application of
the word. If they were irrelevant, then toothache would be radically
private, and the language used to talk about it would be radically
private. When Wittgenstein allows that experiences are private, he
means 'private' in the first sense just mentioned, but what his private language argument denies is radical privacy. Therefore he is
not inconsistent.

Castañeda, in Chapter V, pursues further the task of distinguishing different senses of 'private'. He tables six different senses, with
further subdivision for good measure (p. 137 below). Professor J. F.
Thomson, in his comment on Castañeda's contribution, also thinks
that the sense of the word 'private' is very much at issue (pp. 169
and 172 below). But there are other points arising from the discussion in Chapter V to which I now wish to draw attention.

INTERPRETING WITTGENSTEIN

Castañeda interprets the private language argument as a *reductio
ad absurdum* which should be capable of being set out clearly in the
form of precise premisses which lead inexorably to a conclusion. On
this view the task of the critic is to examine the premisses and test the
validity of the inferences. But on turning to Malcolm's text to trace
the steps in the argument, Castañeda finds an odd assortment of
questions where one might expect reasons, a conclusion half-way
down the line where premisses should appear, and he finds the sup-
porting premisses themselves appearing later on coupled with an
analogy posing as a reason. Obviously, Malcolm's style of philosophising is very different from Castañeda's, and it is much more
reminiscent of the *Inv.* itself. Incidentally, this comment is true of
Rush Rhees's contribution as well, and it is noteworthy that both
he and Malcolm knew Wittgenstein and had first-hand acquaintance
with his way of philosophising. The question arises whether Malcolm
was trying to do the sort of thing that Castañeda is doing, and in so

far as Malcolm reflects Wittgenstein we may ask if Wittgenstein himself ever intended to produce an argument which could be set out in distinct premisses leading to a conclusion which is to be taken as proved by the argument. But there is something quite paradoxical here, for it is Malcolm himself who started the habit of taking Wittgenstein's discussion as an argument by calling it a *reducto ad absurdum*. J. F. Thomson has spotted the paradox and he suggests that perhaps Malcolm himself never took that claim very seriously (p. 172 below).

Mrs J. J. Thomson, in Chapter VI, gives a different verdict. She thinks that Malcolm did put forward an argument, an argument which she regards as nothing other than the discredited Principle of Verification in disguise. But she does not think that this argument, or any other, should be associated with the name of Wittgenstein. Wittgenstein repeatedly denied that it was his business to put forward theses; he was not out to *prove* that something or other is right or wrong (*Inv.* 109, 126, 128). Mrs Thomson is convinced that we have not taken Wittgenstein's disclaimers about putting forward theses seriously enough.[3] Other philosophers will no doubt take a different view. Some suggest that we should not take Wittgenstein too seriously at his own word, which is precisely what J. F. Thomson suggested we do with Malcolm. This is what A. M. Quinton, for example, does, and he adds 'in practice, even the most loyal of his [Wittgenstein's] disciples ... treat his passionate revulsion from the idea of himself as a philosophical theorist as the aberration which those who admire the rest of his work openly proclaim it to be' (see 'Contemporary British Philosophy', in *A Critical History of Western Philosophy*, ed. D. J. O'Connor (London, 1964) p. 541). There is an issue here which is ripe for further discussion, not only as a matter of interpreting Wittgenstein, but as a matter of deciding what philosophy is.

In the second part of Chapter VI it soon becomes evident that Kenny cannot agree that there is no argument in the *Inv.*[4] He takes the view that the possibility of a private language is disproved, and he comes back to the crux of the issue by giving a detailed discussion of the reason why memory could not play the role which would make private rule-following possible. In the course of developing the argument and drawing out its implications for Cartesianism, Kenny clarifies several of the issues raised in the earlier discussions. On one thing, however, Kenny can agree with Mrs Thomson. He agrees that the Verification Argument which she mentions is not in Wittgenstein. Wittgenstein's private language argument, he points out, derives not from the verificationism of the 1930s but from the picture theory which dates back to the early material of Wittgenstein's *Notebooks* (pp. 221 f. below). This suggestion is developed in a novel way towards the end of Kenny's contribution, and it is no doubt a suggestion that will come in for further discussion in future as more people take interest in the unity and continuity of Wittgenstein's philosophy.[5]

Chapter VII consists of Wittgenstein's notes for lectures on 'Private experience' and 'Sense data', which are highly relevant to the controversy over the private language argument. The remarks about distinguishing between 'mere behaviour' and 'experience + behaviour (p. 273 below), for example, are clearly addressed to the problem of behaviourism which I have already mentioned. Wittgenstein's interest in the topic of philosophical psychology is evident, but it is equally clear that the dominant question is about language (see the point about language games, p. 258 below). It is a question cf the form: 'What is it to say this, that or the other?' It should of course be remembered that these are notes for lectures, but they give a good impression of what doing philosophy was like for Wittgenstein; the reader may decide for himself whether it is a matter of putting forward theses and advancing arguments. Finally, remembering Kenny's suggested link between the private language argument and the picture theory, we should look at the use which Wittgenstein makes of the notion of picturing in these notes, (pp. 237, 242, 257, 260, 263, 266, and 274).

OTHER ISSUES

It is impossible in a short introduction to give a full indication of the wealth of issues raised in these discussions of the private language argument. There is, for instance, the question of the ownership of experiences which is raised by Ayer (pp. 59 f. below). He argues that it is conceivable that people should share a common pain, but he thinks that as a matter of fact two toothache-sufferers, for instance, have each his own toothache. Mundle assumes this too (pp. 104 ff. below), and makes it a basis for arguing that language about experience is private in that it has a private reference.[6] Kenny sorts out the difficulties of this issue by distinguishing between 'incommunicable' and 'inalienable' privacy (pp. 211 ff. below).

Another question that is intimately linked up with the private language argument arises from Wittgenstein's suggestion that saying 'I know that I am in pain' is no different from saying 'I am in pain' since 'it means nothing to doubt whether I am in pain' (*Inv.* 288). Holbrow thinks this is a mistake (p. 126 below) and produces examples intended to show that one can be in doubt about the precise details of one's own sensation. The same question is taken up, but dealt with differently, by Kenny (p. 226 below), who ends up with a distinction between four senses, or would-be senses, of 'I know I am in pain'.

The private language controversy ranges over a cluster of inter-related problems. The point of going over it and studying it is not so much to find a 'Yes' or 'No' answer to one question, but to get a better understanding of many questions and their answers.

I Exposition and criticism of Wittgenstein's *Investigations*

(i) *P. F. Strawson*

PAIN AND PERSONS

(See *Inv.* 142, 243–315, 350–1, 384, 390, 398–421, II. iv, II. v.) Studying the sections in which Wittgenstein deals with sensations, one may well feel one's capacity to learn coming to an end. Wittgenstein's case against saying that the phrases 'meaning/understanding something by an expression' stand for or name special experiences seems to me thoroughly made out. But even the significance of this denial comes into question if it then appears that no word whatever stands for or names a special experience. (Experiences which characteristically accompany 'I understand!' are not to be identified with understanding. Try substituting 'I am in pain' and 'pain' in the appropriate places here.) Wittgenstein seems to me to oscillate in his discussion of this subject between a stronger and a weaker thesis, of which the first is false and the second true. These may be described, rather than formulated, as follows. (I attach no importance to their descriptions: their significance must emerge later.) The stronger thesis says that no words name sensations (or 'private experiences'); and in particular the word 'pain' does not (cf. *Inv.* 293). The weaker thesis says that certain conditions must be satisfied for the existence of a common language in which sensations are ascribed to those who have them; and that certain confusions about sensations arise from the failure to appreciate this, and consequently to appreciate the way in which the language of sensations functions. The oscillation between the two theses is to be explained by the fact that the weaker can be made to yield to the stronger by the addition of a certain premise about language, viz. that all there is to be said about the descriptive meaning of a word is said when it is indicated what *criteria* people can use for employing it or for deciding whether or not it is correctly employed.

The stronger thesis is first developed by an attack on the idea of a private language (*Inv.* 243 ff.). By a 'private language' we are here to understand a language of which the individual names (descriptive words) refer solely to the sensations of the user of the language. He may be imagined as keeping a record of the occurrence of certain sensations. The main point of the attack is that the hypothetical user of the language would have no check on, no criterion of, the *correctness* of his use of it. We might be inclined to say that his memory provides a check. But what check has he on his memory? Suppose in the case of one particular word he keeps on misremembering its use. What difference will it make? There will be no way in which he can distinguish between a correct and an incorrect use. So the idea of a correct use is empty here: and with it the idea of such a language. Now the interesting thing about the attack is that Wittgenstein presents it as if it applied only or peculiarly to the idea of a private language in which all the descriptive words were supposed to stand for sensations. But of course, if it has any validity at all, it has an equal validity for the case of a private language (here this means 'a language used by only one individual') in which the words stand not for sensations at all, but for things like colours or material objects or animals. Here again the individual will have no external check on the correctness of his use of the names. (It is no good saying that he can, in this case, though not in the case of the sensation-language, make himself a physical dictionary, e.g. a table with names opposite pictures. Wittgenstein's own arguments in other places are here decisive. The interpretation of the table depends on the use that is made of it). But if this is so, then Wittgenstein's arguments would at most tend to show that the idea of a language *of any kind* used only by one person was an absurdity: and this conclusion would have no special immediate relevance to the case of sensation.

But it is clear that Wittgenstein intends his arguments to have special relevance to this case. So let us look at the differences between the two supposed private languages. We may suppose (following Wittgenstein) that in the case of the first private language, the one for sensations only, there are no particular characteristic overt expressions of the sensations, manifested by the hypothetical user of the language. Now we introduce observers, studying the behaviour and surroundings of the language users. The observer (B) of the user of the second language observes a correlation between the use of its words and sentences and the speaker's actions and environment. The observer of the user of the first language does not. Observer B is thus able to form hypotheses about the meanings (the

regular use) of the words of his subject's language. He might in time
come to be able to speak it: then the practice of each serves as a
check on the correctness of the practice of the other. But shall we
say that, before this fortunate result was achieved (before the use of
the language becomes a *shared* 'form of life'), the words of the
language had no meaning, no use? And if we do not say this of
the case where this result can be achieved, why should we say it of
the hypothetical case where it cannot? In each case, while the language is used by one person alone (let us say as in one of Wittgenstein's examples, to record occurrences), the meaning of the words
is a matter of the customary practice of the user: in each case the
only check on this customary practice is memory. But (it might be
said), the hypothesis that someone was using a language of the first
kind could never be tested. But what is to count as a test here? Suppose he also mastered the ordinary common language, and then
told us that he had been (or was still) using a private language. It is
also *just* worth asking, in connection with some of Wittgenstein's
arguments here: Do we ever in fact find ourselves misremembering
the use of very *simp*le words of our common language, and having
to correct ourselves by attention to others' use? – Wittgenstein gives
himself considerable trouble over the question of how a man would
introduce a name for a sensation into this private language. But we
need imagine no special ceremony. He might simply be struck by
the recurrence of a certain sensation and get into the habit of
making a certain mark in a different place every time it occurred.
The making of the marks would help to impress the occurrence on
his memory. One can easily imagine this procedure being elaborated
into a system of dating. (The purpose of these remarks is to indicate
the place the sensation-name might play in the private language-
game.)

Another of Wittgenstein's main arguments is basically a variant
on the first. He notes two associated points, which one is not inclined
to dispute: (1) 'the expression of doubt has no place in the language-
game' (*Inv.* 288), i.e. in the language-game with 'I am in pain';[1]
and (2) 'what I do (when I say 'I am in pain') is not to identify
my sensation by criteria' (*Inv.* 290). Wittgenstein seems to think that
these facts can only be accommodated if we regard 'I am in pain'
as an *expression* or manifestation of pain, alongside such natural
expressions as crying or groaning, but of course, one which, unlike
these, is the result of training (*Inv.* 244, 288, etc.). So regarded,
'pain' ceases to appear as the name or the description of a sensation.
If we do *not* so regard it, then we shall require criteria of identity

for the sensation; and with these there would enter the possibility of
error (*Inv.* 288). (Here one is, of course, reminded of the discussion
of understanding. There are criteria of understanding, as of pain,
which we apply in the case of others. But a man does not apply
them to himself when he says 'I understand' – and his saying this
is to be compared with an exclamation, a glad start, not a report of
a mental occurrence.) Wittgenstein here seems to me to be in a
muddle: the weaker thesis is being muddled with the stronger. What
he has committed himself to is the view that one cannot sensibly be
said to recognise or identify anything, unless one uses *criteria*; and,
as a consequence of this, that one cannot recognise or identify sensations. But of course this is untrue. Consider cases where the rival
pull of 'expression' or 'manifestation' is weaker or non-existent.
Consider, for example, tastes; and such phrases as 'the taste of
onions', 'a metallic taste'. Here we have one thing (a taste) associated with another (a material substance), but quite certainly recognisable and identifiable in itself. Only, of course, one does not use
criteria of identity for *the taste*. If the question 'What is the criterion
of identity here?' is pushed, one can only answer: 'Well, the taste
itself' (cf. 'the sensation itself'). Of course, the phrases by which we
refer to such tastes involve allusions to what can be seen and
touched; for we speak a common language. But we do not identify
the taste by means of the associated substance by allusion to which
we name it. Consider also that we discriminate and recognise different particular pains (I do not mean pains in different places) –
aches and throbs, searing and jabbing pains, etc. In many cases,
there are not, or not obviously different characteristic natural expressions of pain to correspond to these differences in quality. The
phrases by which we name these particular pain-experiences are
commonly analogical; and this too for the reason that we want a
common language.[2] All the time here Wittgenstein is driving at the
conditions that are necessary for a common language in which pain
can be ascribed to persons, the consequent need for *criteria for the
ascription* of pain, and the effects of this upon the use of the word
'pain' of our common language. Hence his obsession with the *expression* of pain. But he errs through excess of zeal when this leads
him to deny that sensations can be recognised and bear names.
Rather the case is that these names must always contain in a more
or less complex way, within their logic, some allusion to what is not
sensation, to what can be seen and touched and heard.

   Why is this? The answer illuminates the nature of Wittgenstein's
mistake, and also the great extent to which he is right.

(1) To deny that 'pain' is the name of a (type of) sensation is comparable with denying that 'red' is the name of a colour.

(2) It is just the difference between the ways colours and pains enter into our lives that accounts for the fact (i) that we call the latter and not the former sensations (or, alternatively, that accounts for the very special status we assign to sensations); it is just this difference that accounts for the fact (ii) that we *ascribe* pains to those who suffer them and not colours to those who see them; and which accounts for the fact (iii) that *without* criteria for ascribing pains to persons, we could have no common language of pain. Finally, it is because our common language-game must be that of ascribing pains to persons that symptoms, expressions, of pain assume such overwhelming importance.

(3) Fact (iii), misunderstood, is reflected (upside down) in all the usual philosophers' confusions about sensations, and, over-emphasised, is reflected (rightside up, but obscuring the rest of the picture) in Wittgenstein's.

To understand at least part of what is meant by 'the difference between the ways colours and pains enter our lives', it will be helpful to consider some unrealised possibilities. Let us suppose first that we feel pain only and always under the condition that our skin is in contact with the surfaces of certain bodies. (Cf. Wittgenstein's 'pain-patches', *Inv.* 312. But he does not exploit this fully.) The pain begins and ends with the contact. Then our pain-language might have a logic wholly different from that which it does have. Instead of ascribing pains to sufferers, we might ascribe painfulness to surfaces, much as we at present call them rough, smooth, hard, soft, etc. Another possibility is this. We say things like 'It's hot in here', 'It's cold out there', and so on, ascribing temperatures (I do not mean in degrees Fahrenheit or Centigrade) to regions. Let us suppose that any person felt pain if and only if every other normal person in the same region (which could be the size of a room or a continent) at the same time also felt pain. Then we might ascribe painfulness to regions instead of pain to persons; saying, e.g., 'It's painful today', or 'It's painful in here'. The point of both examples is that in each case we should have as *impersonal* a way of describing pain-phenomena as we have of describing colour-phenomena. But of course the incidence of physical pain is not like this. The causes of pain are often internal and organic. Even when pain is caused by contact, it generally requires a special kind of contact rather than contact with any special kind of thing; and it generally does not cease when contact ceases. If you have a pain and I come to the

place where you are, or touch or look at what you are touching or
looking at, this will not in general result in my having a pain. As
Wittgenstein not infrequently points out, it is such very obvious
general facts of nature which determine the logic of our concepts. I
may put the point very roughly as follows. A set of people together
in certain surroundings will be in general agreement on 'what it looks
like here, what it feels like (to the touch) here, what it sounds like
here'. In this possibility of a general agreement in judgments lies
the possibility of a common impersonal language for describing what
we see and hear and touch (cf. *Inv.* 242). But there is no such
general agreement as to whether or not 'it's painful here', as to what
it feels like (as we misleadingly say) *within*. In the absence of general
agreement in judgment, a common language is impossible; and this
is why a common impersonal pain-language is impossible. But if (to
speak absurdly) we are prepared to make our pain-language a language for ascribing pain to persons, then we have something (i.e.
people's pain-behaviour) which we see and hear, and on which, in
consequence, general agreement in judgment is possible. Because of
certain general facts of nature, therefore, the only possible common
pain-language is the language in which pain is ascribed to those who
talk the language, the criteria for its ascription being (mainly) pain-
behaviour. And because of *this* fact it is necessarily empty and pointless (I will *not* say meaningless) either (*a*) to speculate about the
ascription of pain to anything which does not exhibit behaviour
comparable in the relevant respects with human behaviour (i.e. the
behaviour of those who use the concept), or (*b*) to raise generalised
doubts about other people's experience of pain, or about one's own
knowledge of this. It is the above points which I take Wittgenstein
essentially to be making. (He sees (*Inv.* 142) that, as things are, the
possibility of the language-game rests on there being characteristic
expressions of pain.) But the way in which he makes them is, in part
at least, misleading. For from none of these facts does it follow that
'pain' is not the name of a sensation. On the contrary. It is only
in the light of the fact that 'pain' is the name of a sensation that
these facts are intelligible; or, better, to say that 'pain' is the name
of a sensation is (or ought to be) just to begin to draw attention to
these facts. One could say: that pain is a sensation (or, that sensations have the special status they have) is a *fact of nature* which
dictates the logic of 'pain'.

This outline is of course extremely crude. What a proper treatment
of the topic above all requires is extensive and detailed *comparisons*
between the different types of sensible experience we have.

(ii) *Norman Malcolm*

STRAWSON'S CRITICISM

Peter Strawson's critical notice[3] of the *Investigations* contains misunderstandings that might obtain currency. To Strawson it appears that, for Wittgenstein, 'no word whatever stands for or names a special experience' (p. 27 above), 'no words name sensations (or "private experiences"); and in particular the word "pain" does not' (p. 27 above). Wittgenstein 'has committed himself to the view that one cannot sensibly be said to recognise or identify anything, unless one uses *criteria*; and, as a consequence of this, that one cannot recognise or identify sensations' (p. 30 above). His 'obsession with the *expression* of pain' leads him 'to deny that sensations can be recognised and bear names' (p. 30 above). Wittgenstein is hostile to 'the idea of what is not observed (seen, heard, smelt, touched, tasted), and in particular to the idea that what is not observed can in any sense be recognised or described or reported' (*Mind* LXIII (1954) p. 90) – although at one place in the book (*Inv.* II, p. 189) 'it looks as if he were almost prepared to acknowledge' that 'I am in pain' 'may be just a report of my sensations' (*Mind*, LXIII (1954) p. 94). His 'prejudice against "the inner"' leads him to deny that it is possible for a person to report the words that went through his mind when he was saying something to himself in his thoughts (*Mind*, LXIII (1954) p. 91). Strawson attributes Wittgenstein's errors not only to prejudice and, possibly, to 'the old verificationist horror of a claim that cannot be checked' (*Mind*, LXIII (1954) p. 92), but also to various confusions and muddles (p. 30 above), and *Mind*, LXIII (1954) p. 98).

It is important to see how very erroneous is this account of Wittgenstein. The latter says, 'Don't we talk about sensations every day, and give them names?' and then asks, 'How does a human being learn the names of sensations? – of the word "pain" for example?' (*Inv.* 244). So Wittgenstein does not deny that we *name* sensations. It is a howler to accuse Wittgenstein of 'hostility to the idea of what is not observed' ('observed' apparently means 'perceived by one of the five senses') and of 'hostility to the idea that what is not observed can in any sense be recognised or described or reported' (*Mind*, LXIII (1954) p. 90). Dreams and mental pictures are not observed, in Strawson's sense; yet Wittgenstein discusses *reports* of dreams (*Inv.* II, p. 222; also p. 184) and *descriptions* of mental pic-

tures (e.g. *Inv.* 367). Consider this general remark: 'Think how
many different kinds of things are called "description": description of a body's position by means of its co-ordinates, description
of a facial expression; *description of a sensation of touch*; of a mood'
(*Inv.* 24, my italics). And at many places in the *Investigations*, Wittgenstein *gives* descriptions of various sensations, although sensations are not osberved, in Strawson's sense. Strawson's belief that
Wittgenstein thinks that 'one cannot sensibly be said to recognise
or identify anything, unless one uses criteria' (p. 30 above), is
proved false by the remarks about mental images: I have *no*
criterion for saying that two images of mine are the same (*Inv.* 377);
yet there is such a thing as *recognition* here, and a correct use of
'same' (*Inv.* 378). How can it be maintained that Wittgenstein has
a prejudice against 'the inner' when he allows that in our ordinary
language a man *can* write down or give vocal expression to his
'inner experiences – his feelings, moods, and the rest – for his private
use'? (*Inv.* 243). Wittgenstein does not deny that there are *inner*
experiences any more than he denies that there are *mental* occurrences. Indeed, he gives examples of things that he calls '*seelische
Vorgänge*', e.g. 'a pain's growing more or less', and in contrast with
which a thing like *understanding a word* is not, he argues, a '*seel-
ischer Vorgang*' (*Inv.* 154). Either to deny that such occurrences
exist or to claim that they cannot be named, reported, or described
is entirely foreign to Wittgenstein's outlook. For what would the
denial amount to other than an attempt to 'reform language', which
is not his concern? It may *look* as if he were trying to reform language, because he is engaged in 'giving prominence to distinctions
which our ordinary forms of language easily make us overlook'
(*Inv.* 132). For example, Wittgenstein suggests that when we think
about the philosophical problem of sensation the word 'describe'
tricks us (*Inv.* 290). Of course he does not mean that it is a mistake
to speak of 'describing' a sensation. He means that the similarity in
'surface grammar' (*Inv.* 664) between 'I describe my sensations'
and 'I describe my room' may mislead, may cause us to fail 'to call
to mind the differences between the language-games' (*Inv.* 290).

Strawson rightly avers, 'To deny that "pain" is the name of a
(type of) sensation is comparable to denying that "red" is the name
of a colour' (p. 31 above). I suppose that, conversely, to affirm that
'pain' is the name of a sensation is like affirming that 'red' is the
name of a colour, and also that 'o' is the name of a number. This
classification tells us nothing of philosophical interest. What we
need to notice is the *difference* between the way that 'o' and '2',

say, function, although both are 'names of numbers' (think how
easily one may be tempted to deny that o is a number), and the
difference between the way 'red' and 'pain' function, although both
are 'names'. 'We call very different things "names"; the word
"name" is used to characterise many different kinds of use of a
word, related to one another in many different ways' (*Inv.* 38). To
suppose that the uses of 'pain' and 'red', as *names,* are alike is just
the sort of error that Wittgenstein wants to expose. If one thinks
this, one will want to by-pass the *expression* of pain and will wonder
at Wittgenstein's 'obsession' with it. Not that Strawson does by-pass
it, but he seems to attach the wrong significance to it. He appears
to think that the fact that there is a characteristic pain-behaviour
is what makes possible a *common* 'language of pain', and he seems
to imply that if we did not care to have a *common* language of pain
each of us would still be able to name and describe his pains in 'a
private language-game', even if there were no characteristic pain-
behaviour (pp. 27–32 above). It looks as if he thinks that with his
private language he could step between pain and its expression, and
apply names to the bare sensations themselves (cf. *Inv.* 245).

For Strawson the conception of a private language possesses
no difficulty. A man 'might simply be struck by the recurrence
of a certain sensation and get into the habit of making a certain
mark in a different place every time it occurred. The making of
the marks would help to impress the occurrence on his memory'
(pp. 28–9 above). Just as, I suppose, he might utter a certain sound
each time a cow appeared. But we need to ask, what makes the
latter sound a *word,* and what makes it the word for *cow*?
Is there no difficulty here? Is it sufficient that the sound is
uttered when and only when a cow is present? Of course not.
The sound might refer to anything or nothing. What is necessary
is that it should play a part in various activities, in calling,
fetching, counting cows, distinguishing cows from other things
and pictures of cows from pictures of other things. If the sound
has no fixed place in activities ('language-games') of this sort,
then it isn't a word for *cow.* To be sure, I can sit in my chair and
talk about cows and not be engaged in any of those activities
– but what makes my words *refer* to cows is the fact that I have
already mastered those activities; they lie in the background. The
kind of way that 'cow' refers is the kind of language-game to which
it belongs. If a mark or sound is to be a word for a *sensation* it, too,
must enter into language-games, although of a very different sort.
What sort? Well, such things as showing the location of the sensa-

tion, exhibiting different reactions to different intensities of stimulus, seeking or avoiding causes of the sensation, choosing one sensation in preference to another, indicating the duration of the sensation, and so on. Actions and reactions of that sort constitute the sensation-behaviour. They are the 'outward criteria' (*Inv.* 580) with which the sign must be connected if it is to be a sign for a sensation *at all*, not merely if it is to be a sign in a *common* language. In the mere supposition that there is a man who is 'struck by the recurrence of a certain sensation' and who gets into the habit of 'making a certain mark in a different place every time it occurred', no ground *whatever* has been given for saying that the mark is a sign for sensation. The necessary surroundings have not been supplied. Strawson sees no problem here. He is surprised that 'Wittgenstein gives himself considerable trouble over the question of how a man would *introduce* a name for sensation into this private language' (p. 29 above). It is as if Strawson thought: There is no difficulty about it; the man just *makes* the mark refer to a sensation. How the man does it puzzles Strawson so little that he is not even inclined to feel that the connection between the name and the sensation is queer, occult (cf. *Inv.* 38) – which it would be, to say the least, if the name had no fixed place in those activities and reactions that constitute sensation-behaviour, for that, and not a magical act of the mind, is what *makes* it refer to a sensation.

The conception of private language that Wittgenstein attacks is not the conception of a language that only the speaker does understand, but of a language that no other person *can* understand (*Inv.* 243). Strawson thinks that Wittgenstein has not refuted the conception of a private language but has only shown that certain conditions must be satisfied if a common language is to exist. Strawson appears to believe (I may misunderstand him) that each of us not only can have but does have a private language of sensations, that if we are to understand one another when we speak of our sensations there must be criteria for the use of our sensation-words, and that therefore the words with which we *refer* to our sensations must, in addition, contain 'allusions' either to behaviour or to material substances that are 'associated' with the sensations (p. 30 above). The allusions must be to things that can be perceived by us all. By virtue of this the use of sensation-words can be taught and misuses corrected, and so those words will belong to a common language. There is another feature of their use (namely, their reference) that cannot be taught. Thus sensation-words will have both a public and a private meaning. Strawson's view appears to be accurately characterised by Wittgenstein's mock conjecture: 'Or is it like this: the word "red" means something known to everyone; and in addition, for each person, it means something known only to him? (Or perhaps rather: it *refers* to something known only to him.)' (*Inv.* 273.)

But if my words, *without* these allusions, can refer to my sensations, then what is alluded to is only *contingently* related to the sensations. Adding the 'allusions to what can be seen and touched' (p. 30 above) will not help one little bit in making us understand one another. For the behaviour that is, for me, contingently associated with 'the sensation of pain' may be, for you, contingently associated with 'the sensation of tickling'; the piece of matter that produces in you what you call 'a metallic taste' may reproduce in me what, if you could experience it, you would call 'the taste of onions'; my 'sensation of red' may be your 'sensation of blue'; we do not know and cannot know whether we are talking about the same things; we cannot *learn* the essential thing about one another's use of sensation-words – namely, their reference. The language in which the private referring is done cannot be turned into a common language by having something grafted on to it. Private language cannot be the understructure of the language we all understand. It is as if, in Strawson's conception, the sensation-words were supposed to perform two functions – to refer and to communicate. But if the reference is incommunicable, then the trappings of allusion will not communicate it, and what they do communicate will be irrelevant.

Strawson's idea that expressions like 'jabbing pain', 'metallic taste', mean something known to everyone and, in addition, for each person, refer to something known only to him, is responsible, I believe, for his failure to understand Wittgenstein on the topic of recognising and identifying sensations. There is *a* sense of 'recognise' and 'identify' with respect to which Wittgenstein does deny that we can recognise or identify our own sensations, feelings, images. Consider, for example, that although a man understands the word 'alcohol' he may fail to identify the alcohol in a bottle as alcohol, because the bottle is marked 'gasoline' or because the cork smells of gasoline; or, although he understands 'rabbit' and is familiar with rabbits, he may fail to recognise a rabbit as a rabbit, taking it for a stump instead; or, he may be in doubt and say, 'I don't know whether this is alcohol', 'I'm not sure whether that is a rabbit or a stump'. But can a man who understands the word 'pain' be in doubt as to whether he has pain? Wittgenstein remarks:

If anyone said 'I do not know if what I have got is a pain or

something else', we should think something like, he does not know
what the English word 'pain' means; and we should explain it
to him. – How? Perhaps by means of gestures, or by pricking him
with a pin and saying: 'See, that's what pain is!' This explanation, like any other, he might understand right, wrong, or not at
all. And he will show which he does by his use of the word, in this
as in other cases.

If he now said, for example: 'Oh, I know what "pain" means;
what I don't know is whether *this*, that I have now, is pain' – we
should merely shake our heads and be forced to regard his words
as a queer reaction which we have no idea what to do with (*Inv.*
288).

That a man wonders whether what he has is pain can only mean
that he does not understand the word 'pain'; he cannot both understand it and have that doubt. Thus there is a sense of 'identify' that
has no application to sensations. One who understands the word
'alcohol' may fail to identify *this* as alcohol or may be in doubt as
to its identity or may correctly identify it. These possibilities have
no meaning in the case of pain. There is not over and above (or
underneath) the understanding of the word 'pain' a further process
of correctly identifying or failing to identify *this* as pain. There
would be if Strawson's conception was right. But there is not, and
this is why 'That expression of doubt ['Oh, I know what "pain"
means; what I don't know is whether *this*, that I have now, is pain]
has no place in the language-game' (*Inv.* 288). (Strawson does not
have, but in consistency should have, an inclination to dispute this
last remark of Wittgenstein's (see p. 29 above).) The fact that there
is no *further* process of identifying a particular sensation is a reason
why 'the object drops out of consideration as irrelevant' when 'we
construe the grammar of the expression of sensation on the model of
"object and name" ' (*Inv.* 293 – a remark that Strawson misunder-
stands as the thesis that 'no words name sensations' (p. 27 above). If
my use of a sensation-word satisfies the normal outward criteria and
if I truthfully declare that I have that sensation, then I *have* it –
there is not a further problem of my applying the word right or
wrong within myself. If a man used the word 'pain' in accordance
with 'the usual symptoms and presuppositions of pain' then it would
have no sense to suppose that perhaps his memory did not retain
what the word 'pain' refers to, 'so that he constantly called different
things by that name' (*Inv.* 271). If my use of the word fits those
usual criteria there is not an added problem of whether I accurately

pick out the objects to which the word applies. In this sense of 'identify', the hypothesis that I identify my sensations is 'a mere ornament, not connected with the mechanism at all' (*Inv.* 270).

It does not follow nor, I think, does Wittgenstein mean to assert that there is *no* proper use of 'identify' or 'recognise' with sensations. He acknowledges a use of 'recognise' with mental images, as previously noted. It would be a natural use of language, I believe, if someone who upon arising complained of an unusual sensation were to say, 'Now I can identify it! It is the same sensation that I have when I go down in an elevator.' Wittgenstein, who has no interest in reforming language, would not dream of calling this an incorrect use of 'identify'. He attacks a philosophical use of the word only, the use that belongs to the notion of the private object. In this example of a non-philosophical use, if the speaker employed the rest of the sensation-language as we all do, and if his behaviour in this case was approximately what it was when he was affected by the downward motion of an elevator, then his declaration that he was feeling the elevator-sensation would be decisive; and also his declaration that it was *not* the elevator-sensation would be decisive. It is *out of the question* that he should have made a mistake in identifying the sensation. His identification of his sensation is an *expression* of sensation (in Wittgenstein's extended sense of this phrase). The identification is 'incorrigible'. We have here a radically different use of 'identify' from that illustrated in the example of alcohol and rabbit.

The philosophical use of 'identify' seems to make possible the committing of *errors* of identification of sensations and inner experiences. The idea is that my sensation or my image is an object that I cannot show to anyone and that I identify it and from it derive its description (*Inv.* 374). But if this is so, why cannot my identification and description go wrong, and not just sometimes but always? Here we are in a position to grasp the significance of Wittgenstein's manœuvre: 'Always get rid of the idea of the private object in this way: assume that it constantly changes, but that you do not notice the change because your memory constantly deceives you' (*Inv.* II, p. 207). We are meant to see the *senselessness* of this supposition: for what in the world would *show* that I was deceived constantly or even once? Do I look again – and why can't I be deceived that time, too? The supposition is a knob that doesn't turn anything (cf. *Inv.* 270). Understanding this will perhaps remove the temptation to think that I have something that I cannot show to you and from which I derive a knowledge of its identity. This is what Wittgenstein means in saying that when I related to another what I just said to myself in my thoughts ' "what went on within me" is not the point at all' (*Inv.* II, p. 222). He is not declaring, as Strawson thinks, that I cannot report what words went through my mind (*Mind*, LXIII (1954) pp. 90–1). He is saying that it is a report 'whose truth is guaranteed by the special criteria of truthfulness' (*Inv.* II, p. 222). It is *that* kind of report. So it is not a matter of trying faithfully to observe something within myself and of trying to produce a correct account of it, of trying to do something at which I might unwittingly fail.

The influence of the idea of the private object on Strawson's thinking is subtly reflected, I believe, in his declaration that a metallic taste is 'quite certainly recognisable and identifiable in itself' and in his remark that 'if the question "What is the criterion of identity here?" is pushed, one can only answer: "Well, the taste itself" (cf. "the sensation itself")' (p. 30 above). Strawson realises that we don't identify a sensation by means of criteria (e.g. a metallic taste by means of the metallic material that produces it). He is inclined to add that we identify it by 'the sensation itself'. This seems to me to misconstrue the 'grammar' of 'identify' here. It may be to the point to consider again the comparison of colours and sensations. Wittgenstein says, 'How do I know that this colour is red? – It would be an answer to say "I have learned English" ' (*Inv.* 381). One thing this answer does is to deny that I have *reasons* for saying that this colour before me is red. We might put this by saying that I identify it as red by 'the colour itself', not by anything else. The cases of red and pain (or metallic taste) so far run parallel. Equally, I don't have reasons for saying that this colour is red or that this sensation is pain. But it *can* happen that I should fail to identify this colour correctly, even though I have learned English (e.g. the moonlight alters its appearance). Here the parallel ends. Nothing can alter the 'appearance' of the sensation. Nothing counts as mistaking its identity. If we assimilate identifying sensations to identifying colours, because in neither instance reasons are relevant, we conceal the philosophically more important difference. To insist that the parallel is perfect, that one identifies colours, is like saying that 'there must also be something boiling in the pictured pot' (*Inv.* 297). Identifying one's own sensation is nothing that is either in error or *not* in error. It is not, in *that* sense, *identifying*. When I identify my sensation, I do not *find out* its identity, not even from 'the sensation itself'. My identification, one could say, *defines* its identity.

We use a man's identification of his sensation as a criterion of what his sensation is. But this is a *dependent* criterion. His verbal reports and identifications would not *be* a criterion unless they were grounded in the primitive sensation-behaviour that is the primary and independent criterion of his sensations. If we cut out human behaviour from the language-game of sensations (which Strawson does in defending the 'private language-game') one result will be that a man's identifying a sensation as the 'same' that he had a moment before will no longer be a criterion of its being the same. Not only the speaker but *no one* will have a criterion of identity. Consequently, for no one will it have any meaning to speak of a man's being 'struck by the *recurrence* of a certain sensation) (p. 29 above, my italics).

PRIVATE LANGUAGE

Let us see something of how Wittgenstein attacks what he calls 'the idea of a private language'. By a 'private' language is meant one that not merely is not but *cannot* be understood by anyone other than the speaker. The reason for this is that the words of this language are supposed to 'refer to what can only be known to the person speaking; to his immediate private sensations' (*Inv.* 243). What is supposed is that I '*associate* words with sensations and use these names in descriptions' (*Inv.* 256). I fix my attention on a sensation and establish a connection between a word and the sensation (*Inv.* 258).

It is worth mentioning that the conception that it is possible and even necessary for one to have a private language is not eccentric. Rather it is the view that comes most naturally to anyone who philosophises on the subject of the relation of words to experiences. The idea of a private language is presupposed by every programme of inferring or constructing the 'external world' and 'other minds'. It is contained in the philosophy of Descartes and in the theory of ideas of classical British empiricism, as well as in recent and contemporary phenomenalism and sense-datum theory. At bottom it is the idea that there is only a contingent and not an *essential* connection between a sensation and its outward expression – an idea that appeals to us all. Such thoughts as these are typical expressions of the idea of a private language: that I know only from my *own* case what the word 'pain' means (*Inv.* 293, 295); that I can only *believe* that another person cannot have *my* pains (*Inv.* 253); that I can undertake to call *this* (pointing inward) 'pain' in the future (*Inv.* 263); that when I say 'I am in pain' I am at any rate justified *before myself* (*Inv.* 289).

In order to appreciate the depth and power of Wittgenstein's assault upon this idea you must partly be its captive. You must feel the strong grip of it. The passionate intensity of Wittgenstein's treatment of it is due to the fact that he lets this idea take possession of him, drawing out of himself the thoughts and imagery by which it is expressed and defended – and then subjecting those thoughts and pictures to the fiercest scrutiny. What is written down represents both a logical investigation and a great philosopher's struggle with his own thoughts. The logical investigation will be understood only by those who duplicate the struggle in themselves.

One consequence to be drawn from the view that I know only from my *own* case what, say, 'tickling' means is that 'I know only what *I* call that, not what anyone else does' (*Inv.* 347). I have not *learned* what 'tickling' means, I have only called something by that name. Perhaps others use the name differently. This is a regrettable difficulty; but, one may think, the word will still work for me as a name, provided that I apply it consistently to a certain sensation. But how about 'sensation'? Don't I know only from my *own* case what *that* word means? Perhaps what I call a 'sensation' others call by another name? It will not help, says Wittgenstein, to say that although it may be that what I have is not what others call a 'sensation', at least I have *something*. For don't I know only from my own case what 'having something' is? Perhaps my use of *those* words is contrary to common use. In trying to explain how I gave 'tickling' its meaning, I discover that I do not have the right to use any of the relevant words of our common language. 'So in the end when one is doing philosophy one gets to the point where one would like just to emit an inarticulate sound' (*Inv.* 261).

Let us suppose that I did fix my attention on a pain as I pronounced the word 'pain' to myself. I think that thereby I established a connection between the word and the sensation. But I did not establish a connection if subsequently I applied that word to sensations other than pain or to things other than sensations, e.g. emotions. My private definition was a success only if it led me to use the word correctly in the future. In the present case, 'correctly' would mean '*consistently* with my own definition'; for the question of whether my use agrees with that of others has been given up as a bad job. Now how is it to be decided whether I have used the word consistently? What will be the difference between my having used it consistently and its *seeming* to me that I have? Or has this distinction vanished? 'Whatever is going to seem right to me is right. And that only means that here we can't talk about "right"' (*Inv.* 258). If the distinction between 'correct' and 'seems correct' has disappeared, then so has the concept *correct*. It follows that the 'rules' of my private language are only *impressions* of rules (*Inv.* 259). My impression that I follow a rule does not confirm that I follow the rule, unless there can be something that will prove my impression correct. And the something cannot be another impression – for this would be 'as if someone were to buy several copies of the morning paper to assure himself that what it said was true' (*Inv.* 265). The proof that I am following a rule must appeal to something *independent* of my impression that I am. If in the nature of the case there cannot be such an appeal, then my private language does not have *rules*, for the concept of a rule requires that there be a difference between 'He is following a rule' and 'He is under the impression that he is following a rule' – just as the concept of understanding a word requires that there be a difference between 'He understands this word' and 'He thinks that he understands this word' (cf. *Inv.* 269).

'Even if I cannot prove and cannot know that I am correctly following the rules of my private language,' it might be said, 'still it *may* be that I am. It has *meaning* to say that I am. The supposition makes sense: you and I *understand* it.' Wittgenstein has a reply to this (*Inv.* 348–53). We are inclined to think that we know what it means to say 'It is five o'clock on the sun' or 'This congenital deaf-mute talks to himself inwardly in a vocal language' or 'The stove is in pain'. These sentences produce pictures in our minds, and it *seems* to us that the pictures tell us how to *apply* them – that is, tell us what we have to look for, what we have to do, in order to determine whether what is pictured is the case. But we make a mistake in thinking that the picture contains in itself the instructions as to how we are to apply it. Think of the picture of blindness as a darkness in the soul or in the head of the blind man (*Inv.* 424). There is nothing wrong with it *as a picture*. 'But *what* is its application?' What shall count for or against its being said that this or that man is blind, that the picture applies to him? The *picture* doesn't say. If you think that you understand the sentence 'I follow the rule that *this* is to be called "pain"' (a rule of your private language), what you have perhaps is a picture of yourself checking off various feelings of yours as either being *this* or not. The picture appears to solve the problem of how you determine whether you have done the 'checking' right. Actually it doesn't give you even a hint in that direction; no more than the picture of blindness provides so much as a hint of *how* it is to be determined that this or that man is blind (*Inv.* 348–53, 422–6, II, p. 184).

One will be inclined to say here that one can simply *remember* this sensation and by remembering it will know that one is making a consistent application of its name. But will it also be possible to have a *false* memory impression? On the private-language hypothesis, what would *show* that your memory impression is false – or true? Another memory impression? Would this imply that memory is a court from which there is no appeal? But, as a matter of fact, that is *not* our concept of memory.

> Imagine that you were supposed to paint a particular colour 'C', which was the colour that appeared when the chemical substances X and Y combined. – Suppose that the colour struck you as brighter on one day than on another; would you not sometimes say: 'I must be wrong, the colour is certainly the same as yesterday'? This shews that we do not always resort to what memory tells us as the verdict of the highest court of appeal (*Inv.* 56).

There is, indeed, such a thing as checking one memory against another, e.g. I check my recollection of the time of departure of a train by calling up a memory image of how a page of the timetable looked – but 'this process has got to produce a memory which is actually *correct*. If the mental image of the time-table could not itself be *tested* for correctness, how could it confirm the correctness of the first memory?' (*Inv.* 265).

If I have a language that is really private (i.e. it is a logical impossibility that anyone else should understand it or should have any basis for knowing whether I am using a particular name consistently), my assertion that my memory tells me so and so will be utterly empty. 'My memory' will not even mean – my memory *impression*. For by a memory impression we understand something that is either accurate or inaccurate; whereas there would not be, in the private language, any *conception* of what would establish a memory impression as correct, any conception of what 'correct' would mean here.

THE SAME

One wants to say, 'Surely there can't be a difficulty in knowing whether a feeling of mine is or isn't the *same* as the feeling I now have. I will call this feeling "pain" and will thereafter call the *same* thing "pain" whenever it occurs. What could be easier than to follow that rule?' To understand Wittgenstein's reply to this attractive proposal we must come closer to his treatment of rules and of what it is to follow a rule. (Here he forges a remarkably illuminating connection between the philosophy of psychology and the philosophy of mathematics.) Consider his example of the pupil who has been taught to write down a cardinal number series of the form '0, n, $2n$, $3n$ ...' at an order of the form '+n', so that at the order '+1' he writes down the series of natural numbers (*Inv.* 185). He has successfully done exercises and tests up to the number 1,000. We then ask him to continue the series '+2' beyond 1,000; and he writes 1,000, 1,004, 1,008, 1,112. We tell him that this is wrong. His instructive reply is, 'But I went on in the same way' (*Inv.* 185). There was nothing in the previous explanations, examples and exercises that made it *impossible* for him to regard that as the continuation of the series. Repeating *those* examples and explanations won't help him. One must say to him, in effect, 'That isn't what we *call* going on in the *same* way.' It is a fact, and a fact of the kind whose importance Wittgenstein constantly stresses, that it is *natural* for human beings to continue the series in the manner 1,002, 1,004, 1,006, given the previous training. But that is merely what it is – a fact of human nature.

One is inclined to retort, 'Of course he can misunderstand the instruction and misunderstand the order '+2'; but if he *understands* it he must go on in the right way.' And here one has the idea that 'The understanding itself is a state which is the *source* of the correct use' (*Inv.* 146) – that the correct continuation of the series, the right application of the rule or formula, springs from one's understanding of the rule. But the question of whether one understands the rule cannot be divorced from the question of whether one will go on in that one particular way that we call 'right'. The correct use is a criterion of understanding. If you say that knowing the formula is a state of the mind and that making this and that application of the formula is merely a *manifestation* of the knowledge, then you are in a difficulty: for you are postulating a mental apparatus that explains the manifestations, and so you ought to have (but do not have) a knowledge of the construction of the apparatus, quite apart from what it does (*Inv.* 149). You would like to think that your understanding of the formula determines in advance the steps to be taken, that when you understood or meant the formula in a certain way 'your mind as it were flew ahead and took all the steps before you physically arrived at this or that one' (*Inv.* 188). But how you meant it is not independent of how in fact you use it. 'We say, for instance, to someone who uses a sign unknown to us: "If by '*x*!2' you mean x^2, then you get *this* value for *y*, if you mean $2x$, *that* one" – Now ask yourself: how does one *mean* the one thing or the other by "*x*!2"?' (*Inv.* 190). The answer is that his putting down *this* value for *y* shows whether he meant the one thing and not the other: '*That* will be how meaning it can determine the steps in advance' (*Inv.* 190). How he meant the formula determines his subsequent use of it, only in the sense that the latter is a criterion of how he meant it.

It is easy to suppose that when you have given a person the order 'Now do the *same* thing', you have pointed out to him the way to go on. But consider the example of the man who obtains the series 1, 3, 5, 7 . . . by working out the formula $2x + 1$ and then asks himself, 'Am I always doing the same thing, or something different every time?' (*Inv.* 226). One answer is as good as the other; it doesn't matter which he says, so long as he continues in the right way. If we could not observe his work, his mere remark 'I am going on in the same way' would not tell us what he was doing. If a child writing down a row of 2's obtained '2, 2, 2,' from the segment '2, 2' by adding '2' once, he might deny that he had gone in the *same* way. He might declare that it would be doing the same thing only if he went from '2, 2' to '2, 2, 2, 2' in *one* jump, i.e. only if he *doubled* the original segment (just as it doubled the original single '2'). That could strike one as a *reasonable* use of 'same'. This connects up with Wittgenstein's remark: 'If you have to have an intuition in order to develop the series 1 2 3 4 . . . you must also have one in order to develop the series 2 2 2 2 . . .' (*Inv.* 214). One is inclined to say of the latter series, 'Why, all that is necessary is that you keep on doing the *same* thing.' But isn't this just as true of the other series? In both cases one has already *decided* what the correct continuation is, and one calls that continuation, and no other, 'doing the same thing'. As Wittgenstein says: 'One might say to the person one was training: "Look, I always do the same thing: I . . ."' (*Inv.* 223). And then one proceeds to show him what 'the same' *is*. If the pupil does not acknowledge that what you have shown him is the *same*, and if he is not persuaded by your examples and explanations to carry on as you wish him to – then you have reached bedrock and will be inclined to say 'This is simply what I do' (*Inv.* 217). You cannot give him more reasons than you yourself have for proceeding in that way. Your reasons will soon give out. And then you will proceed, without reasons (*Inv.* 211).

PRIVATE RULES

All of this argument strikes at the idea that there can be such a thing as my following a rule in my private language – such a thing as naming something of which only I can be aware, 'pain', and then going on to call the same thing, 'pain', whenever it occurs. There is a charm about the expression 'same' which makes one think that there cannot be any difficulty or any chance of going wrong in deciding whether *A* is the same as *B* – as if one did not have to be *shown* what the 'same' is. This may be, as Wittgenstein suggests, because we are inclined to suppose that we can take the identity of a thing *with itself* as 'an infallible paradigm' of the *same* (*Inv.* 215). But he destroys this notion with one blow: 'Then are two things the same when they are what *one* thing is? And how am I to apply what the *one* thing shows me to the case of two things?' (*Inv.* 215).

The point to be made here is that when one has given oneself the private rule 'I will call this same thing "pain" whenever it occurs,' one is then free to do anything or nothing. That 'rule' does not point in any direction. On the private-language hypothesis, no one can teach me what the correct use of 'same' is. I shall be the sole arbiter of whether this is the *same* as that. What I choose to call the 'same' will *be* the same. No restriction whatever will be imposed upon my application of the word. But a sound that I can use *as I please* is not a *word*.

How would you teach someone the meaning of 'same'? By example and practice: you might show him, for instance, collections of the same colours and same shapes and make him find and produce them and perhaps get him to carry on a certain ornamental pattern uniformly (*Inv.* 208). Training him to form collections and produce patterns is teaching him what Wittgenstein calls 'techniques'. Whether he has mastered various techniques determines whether he understands 'same'. The exercise of a technique is what Wittgenstein calls a 'practice'. Whether your pupil has understood any of

the rules that you taught him (e.g. the rule: This is the 'same' colour
as that) will be shown in his practice. But now there cannot be a
'private' practice, i.e. a practice that cannot be exhibited. For there
would then be no distinction between believing that you have that
practice and having it. 'Obeying a rule' is itself a practice. 'And to
think one is obeying a rule is not to obey a rule. Hence it is not
possible to obey a rule "privately"; otherwise thinking one was obeying a rule would be the same thing as obeying it' (*Inv.* 202; cf. 380).

If I recognise that my mental image is the 'same' as one that I
had previously, how am I to know that this public word 'same'
describes what I recognise? 'Only if I can express my recognition
in some other way, and if it is possible for someone else to teach me
that "same" is the correct word here' (*Inv.* 378). The notion of
the private language doesn't admit of there being 'some other way'.
It doesn't allow that my behaviour and circumstances can be so
related to my utterance of the word that another person, by noting
my behaviour and circumstances, can discover that my use of the
word is correct or incorrect. Can I discover this for myself, and how
do I do it? That discovery would presuppose that I have a conception of correct use which comes from outside my private language
and against which I measure the latter. If this were admitted, the
private language would lose its privacy and its point. So it isn't
admitted. But now the notion of 'correct' use that will exist within
the private language will be such that if I *believe* that my use is
correct then it is correct; the rules will be only impressions of rules;
my 'language' will not be a language, but merely the impression of a
language. The most that can be said for it is that I *think* I understand it (cf. *Inv.* 269).

SENSATIONS OF OTHERS

The argument that I have been outlining has the form of *reductio ad
absurdum*: postulate a 'private' language, then deduce that it is not
language. Wittgenstein employs another argument that is an external, not an internal, attack upon private language. What is attacked
is the assumption that once I know from my *own* case what pain,
tickling, or consciousness is, then I can transfer the ideas of these
things to objects outside myself (*Inv.* 283). Wittgenstein says:

If one has to imagine someone else's pain on the model of one's

own, this is none too easy a thing to do: for I have to imagine
pain which I *do not feel* on the model of the pain which I *do feel.*
That is, what I have to do is not simply to make a transition in
imagination from one place of pain to another. As, from pain in
the hand to pain in the arm. For I am not to imagine that I feel
pain in some region of his body. (Which would also be possible.)
(*Inv.* 302).

The argument that is here adumbrated is, I think, the following:
If I were to learn what pain is from perceiving my own pain then I
should, necessarily, have learned that pain is something that exists
only when *I* feel pain. For the pain that serves as my paradigm of
pain (i.e. my own) has the property of existing only when *I* feel it.[4]
That property is essential, not accidental; it is nonsense to suppose
that the pain I feel could exist when I did not feel it. So if I obtain
my *conception* of pain from pain that I experience, then it will be
part of my conception of pain that *I* am the only being that can
experience it. For me it will be a *contradiction* to speak of *another's*
pain. This strict solipsism is the necessary outcome of the notion of
private language. I take the phrase 'this is none too easy' to be a
sarcasm.

One is tempted at this point to appeal to the 'same' again: 'But
if I suppose that someone has a pain, then I am simply supposing
that he has just the same as I have so often had' (*Inv.* 350). I will
quote Wittgenstein's brilliant counterstroke in full:

That gets us no further. It is as if I were to say: 'You surely know
what "It is 5 o'clock here" means; so you also know what "It's
5 o'clock on the sun" means. It means simply that it is just the
same time there as it is here when it is 5 o'clock.' – The explanation by means of *identity* does not work here. For I know well
enough that one can call 5 o'clock here and 5 o'clock there 'the
same time', but what I do not know is in what cases one is to
speak of its being the same time here and there.

In exactly the same way it is no explanation to say: the supposition that he has a pain is simply the supposition that he has the
same as I. For *that* part of the grammar is quite clear to me: that
is, that one will say that the stove has the same experience as I,
if one says: it is in pain and I am in pain (*Inv.* 350).

II Could language be invented by a Robinson Crusoe?

(i) *A. J. Ayer*

In a quite ordinary sense, it is obvious that there can be private languages. There can be, because there are. A language may be said to be private when it is devised to enable a limited number of persons to communicate with one another in a way that is not intelligible to anyone outside the group. By this criterion, thieves' slang and family jargons are private languages. Such languages are not strictly private, in the sense that only one person uses and understands them, but there may very well be languages that are. Men have been known to keep diaries in codes which no one else is meant to understand. A private code is not, indeed, a private language, but rather a private method of transcribing some given language. It is, however, possible that a very secretive diarist may not be satisfied with putting familiar words into an unfamiliar notation, but may prefer to invent new words: the two processes are in any case not sharply distinct. If he carries his invention far enough he can properly be said to be employing a private language. For all I know, this has actually been done.

From this point of view, what makes a language private is simply the fact that it satisfies the purpose of being intelligible only to a single person, or to a restricted set of people. It is necessary here to bring in a reference to purpose, since a language may come to be intelligible only to a few people, or even only to a single person, merely by falling into general disuse: but such 'dead' languages are not considered to be private, if the limitation of their use was not originally intended. One may characterise a private language by saying that it is not in this sense meant to be alive. There is, however, no reason, in principle, why it should not come alive. The fact that only one person, or only a few people, are able to understand it is purely contingent. Just as it is possible, in theory, that any code should be broken, so can a private language come to be more widely understood. Such private languages are in general derived from public languages, and even if there are any which are not so derived, they will still be translatable into public languages. Their ceasing to be private is then just a matter of enough people becoming able to translate them or, what is more difficult but still theoretically possible, not to translate but even so to understand them.

If I am right, then, there is a use for the expression 'private language' which clearly allows it to have application. But this is not the use which philosophers have commonly given it. What philosophers usually seem to have in mind when they speak of a private language is one that is, in their view, necessarily private, inasmuch as it is used by some particular person to refer only to his own private experiences. For it is often held that for a language to be public it must refer to what is publicly observable: if a person could limit himself to describing his own sensations or feelings, then, strictly speaking, only he would understand what he was saying; his utterance might indirectly convey some information to others, but it could not mean to them exactly what it meant to him. Thus Carnap, who gives the name of 'protocol language' to any set of sentences which are used to give 'a direct record' of one's own experience, argues, in his booklet on *The Unity of Science* (pp. 76 ff.), that if an utterance like 'thirst now', belonging to the protocol language of a subject S_1, is construed as expressing 'only what is immediately given' to S_1, it cannot be understood by anyone else. Another subject S_2 may claim to be able to recognise and so to refer to S_1's thirst, but 'strictly speaking' all that he ever recognises is some physical state of S_1's body. 'If by "the thirst of S_1" we understand not the physical state of his body, but his sensations of thirst, i.e. something non-material, then S's thirst is fundamentally beyond the reach of S_2's recognition' (*The Unity of Science*, p. 79). S_2 cannot possibly verify any statement which refers to S_1's thirst, in this sense, and consequently cannot understand it. 'In general,' Carnap continues, 'every statement in any person's protocol language would have sense for that person alone. . . . Even when the same words and sentences occur in various protocol languages, their sense would be different, they could not even be compared. Every protocol language could therefore be applied only solipsistically: there would be no intersubjective protocol language. This is the consequence obtained by consistent adherence to the usual view and terminology (rejected by the author) (*The Unity of Science*, p. 80).

Since Carnap wishes to maintain that people can understand one another's protocol statements, if only on the ground that this is a necessary condition for statements made in what he calls the physical

language to be intersubjectively verifiable, he draws the inference
that 'protocol language is a part of physical language'. That is, he
concludes that sentences which on the face of it refer to private
experiences must be logically equivalent to sentences which describe
some physical state of the subject. Other philosophers have followed
him in giving a physicalist interpretation to the statements that one
makes about the experiences of others, but have stopped short of
extending it to all the statements that one may make about one's
own. They prefer to hold that certain sentences do serve only to
describe the speaker's private experiences, and that, this being so,
they have a different meaning for him from any that they can possibly have for anybody else.

In his *Philosophical Investigations* Wittgenstein appears to go
much further than this. He seems to take the view that someone who
attempted to use language in this private way would not merely be
unable to communicate his meaning to others, but would have no
meaning to communicate even to himself; he would not succeed in
saying anything at all. 'Let us', says Wittgenstein (*Inv.* 258),
'imagine the following case: I want to keep a diary about the recurrence of a certain sensation. To this end I associate it with the
sign "E" and write this sign in a calendar for every day on which I
have the sensation. – I will remark first of all that a definition of the
sign cannot be formulated. – But still I can give myself a kind of
ostensive definition. – How? Can I point to the sensation? Not in the
ordinary sense. But I speak or write the sign down, and at the same
time I concentrate my attention on the sensation – and so, as it
were, point to it inwardly. – But what is this ceremony for? for that
is all it seems to be! A definition surely serves to establish the meaning of a sign. – Well, that is done precisely by the concentration of
my attention; for in this way I impress on myself the connection
between the sign and the sensation. But "I impress it on myself"
can only mean: this process brings it about that I remember the connection *right* in the future. But in the present case I have no
criterion of correctness. One would like to say: whatever is going to
seem right to me is right. And that only means that here one can't
talk about "right".'

Again, 'What reason have we for calling "E" the sign for a *sensation*? For "sensation" is a word of our common language, not of
one intelligible to me alone. So the use of this word stands in need
of a justification which everybody understands' (*Inv.* 261).

This point is then developed further: 'Let us imagine a table
(something like a dictionary) that exists only in our imagination. A

dictionary can be used to justify the translation of a word X into a word Y. But are we also to call it a justification if such a table is to be looked up only in the imagination? – "Well, yes; then it is a subjective justification." – But justification consists in appealing to something independent. – "But surely I can appeal from one memory to another. For example, I don't know if I have remembered the time of departure of a train right, and to check it I call to mind how a page of the time-table looked. Isn't it the same here?" – No; for this process has got to produce a memory which is actually *correct*. If the mental image of the time-table could not itself be *tested* for correctness, how could it confirm the correctness of the first memory? (As if someone were to buy several copies of the morning paper to assure himself that what it said was true.)

'Looking up a table in the imagination is no more looking up a table than the image of the result of an imagined experiment is the result of an experiment' (*Inv.* 265).

The case is quite different, Wittgenstein thinks, when the sensation can be coupled with some outward manifestation. Thus he maintains that the language which we ordinarily use to describe our 'inner experiences' is not private because the words which one uses to refer to one's sensations are 'tied up with [one's] natural expressions of sensation' (*Inv.* 256), with the result that other people are in a position to understand them. Similarly he grants that the person who tries to describe his private sensation by writing down the sign 'E' in his diary might find a use for this sign if he discovered that whenever he had the sensation in question it could be shown by means of some measuring instrument that his blood pressure rose. For this would give him a way of telling that his blood pressure was rising without bothering to consult the instrument. But then, argues Wittgenstein, it will make no difference whether his recognition of the sensation is right or not. Provided that whenever he thinks he recognises it, there is independent evidence that his blood pressure rises, it will not matter if he is invariably mistaken, if the sensation which he takes to be the same on each occasion is really not the same at all. 'And that alone shows that the hypothesis that [he] makes a mistake is mere show' (*Inv.* 270).

Let us examine this argument. A point to which Wittgenstein constantly recurs is that the ascription of meaning to a sign is something that needs to be justified: the justification consists in there being some independent test for determining that the sign is being used correctly; independent, that is, of the subject's recognition, or supposed recognition, of the object which he intends the sign to signify. His claim to recognise the object, his belief that it really is the same, is not to be accepted unless it can be backed by further evidence. Apparently, too, this evidence must be public: it must, at least in theory, be accessible to everyone. Merely to check one private sensation by another would not be enough. For if one cannot be trusted to recognise one of them, neither can one be trusted to recognise the other.

But unless there is something that one is allowed to recognise, no test can ever be completed: there will be no justification for the use of any sign at all. I check my memory of the time at which the train is due to leave by visualising a page of the time-table; and I am required to check this in its turn by looking up the page. But unless I can trust my eyesight at this point, unless I can recognise the figures that I see written down, I am still no better off. It is true that if I distrust my eyesight I have the resource of consulting other people; but then I have to understand their testimony, I have correctly to identify the signs that they make. Let the object to which I am attempting to refer be as public as you please, let the word which I use for this purpose belong to some common language, my assurance that I am using the word correctly, that I am using it to refer to the 'right' object, must in the end rest on the testimony of my senses. It is through hearing what other people say, or through seeing what they write, or observing their movements, that I am enabled to conclude that their use of the word agrees with mine.[1] But if without further ado I can recognise such noises or shapes or movements, why can I not also recognise a private sensation? It is all very well for Wittgenstein to say that writing down the sign 'E', at the same time as I attend to the sensation, is an idle ceremony. How is it any more idle than writing down a sign, whether it be the conventionally correct sign or not, at the same time as I observe some 'public' object? There is, indeed, a problem about what is involved in endowing any sign with meaning, but it is no less of a problem in the case where the object for which the sign is supposed to stand is public than in the case where it is private. Whatever it is about my behaviour that transforms the making of a sound, or the inscription of a shape, into the employment of a sign can equally well occur in either case.

But, it may be said, in the one case I can point to the object I am trying to name, I can give an ostensive definition of it; in the other I cannot. For merely attending to an object is not pointing to it. But what difference does this make? I can indeed extend my finger in the direction of a physical object, while I pronounce what I intend to be the object's name; and I cannot extend my finger in the direction of a private sensation. But how is this extending of my finger itself anything more than an idle ceremony? If it is to play its part in the giving of an ostensive definition, the gesture has to be endowed with meaning. But if I can endow such a gesture with meaning, I can endow a word with meaning, without the gesture.

I suppose that the reason why the gesture is thought to be important is that it enables me to make my meaning clear to others. Of course they have to interpret me correctly. If they are not intelligent, or I am not careful, they may think that I am pointing to one thing when I really intend to point to another. But successful communication by this method is at least possible. The object to which I mean to point is one that they can observe. On the other hand, no amount of gesturing on my part can direct their attention to a private sensation of mine, which *ex hypothesi* they cannot observe, assuming further that this sensation has no 'natural expression'. So I cannot give an ostensive definition of the word which I wish to stand for the sensation. Nor can I define it in terms of other words, for how are they to be defined? Consequently I cannot succeed in giving it any meaning.

This argument is based on two assumptions, both of which I believe to be false. One is that in a case of this sort it is impossible, logically impossible, to understand a sign unless one can either observe the object which it signifies, or at least observe something with which this object is naturally associated. And the other is that for a person to be able to attach meaning to a sign it is necessary that other people should be capable of understanding it too. It will be convenient to begin by examining the second of these assumptions which leads on to the first.

Imagine a Robinson Crusoe left alone on his island while still an infant, having not yet learned to speak. Let him, like Romulus and Remus, be nurtured by a wolf, or some other animal, until he can fend for himself; and so let him grow to manhood. He will certainly be able to recognise many things upon the island, in the sense that he adapts his behaviour to them. Is it inconceivable that he should also name them? There may be psychological grounds for doubting whether such a solitary being would in fact invent a language. The development of language, it may be argued, is a social phenomenon. But surely it is not self-contradictory to suppose that someone, uninstructed in the use of any existing language, makes up a language for himself. After all, some human being must have been the first to use a symbol. And even if he did so as a member of a group, in order to communicate with other members, even if his choice of symbols was socially conditioned, it is at least conceivable that it should originally have been a purely private enterprise. The hypothesis of G. K. Chesterton's dancing professor about the origin of language, that it came 'from the formulated secret language of some individual creature', is very probably false, but it is certainly not unintelligible.

But if we allow that our Robinson Crusoe could invent words to describe the flora and fauna of his island, why not allow that he could also invent words to describe his sensations? In neither case will he be able to justify his use of words by drawing on the evidence provided by a fellow creature: but while this is a useful check, it is not indispensable. It would be difficult to argue that the power of communication, the ability even to keep a private diary, could come to him only with the arrival of Man Friday. His justification for describing his environment in the way that he does will be that he perceives it to have just those features which his words are intended to describe. His knowing how to use these words will be a matter of his remembering what objects they are meant to stand for, and so of his being able to recognise these objects. But why should he not succeed in recognising them? And why then should he not equally succeed in recognising his sensations? Undoubtedly, he may make mistakes. He may think that a bird which he sees flying past is a bird of the same type as one which he had previously named, when in fact it is of a different type, sufficiently different for him to have given it a different name if he had observed it more closely. Similarly, he may think that a sensation is the same as others which he has identified, when in fact, in the relevant aspects, it is not the same. In neither case may the mistake make any practical difference to him, but to say that nothing turns upon a mistake is not to say that it is not a mistake at all. In the case of the bird, there is a slightly greater chance of his detecting his mistake, since the identical bird may reappear: but even so he has to rely upon his memory for the assurance that it is the identical bird. In the case of the sensation, he has only his memory as a means of deciding whether his identification is correct or not. In this respect he is indeed like Wittgenstein's man who buys several copies of the morning paper to assure himself that what it says is true. But the reason why this seems to us so absurd is that we take it for granted that one copy of a morning paper will duplicate another; there is no absurdity in buying a second newspaper, of a different type, and using it to check the first. And in a place where there was only one morning newspaper, but it was so produced that misprints might occur in one copy without occurring in all, it would be perfectly sensible to buy several copies and check them against each other. Of course there remains the important difference that the facts which the newspaper reports are independently verifiable, in theory if not always in practice. But verification must stop somewhere. As I have already argued, unless something is recognised, without being referred to a further test, nothing can be tested. In the case of Crusoe's sensation, we are supposing that beyond his memory there is no further test. It does not follow that he has no means of identifying it, or that it does not make sense to say that he identifies it right or wrong.

So long as Crusoe remains alone on the island, so long, that is, as he communicates only with himself, the principal distinction which he is likely to draw between 'external' objects and his 'inner' experiences is that his experiences are transient in a way that external objects are not. He will not be bound to draw even this distinction; his criteria for identity may be different from our own; but it is reasonable to suppose that they will be the same. Assuming, then, that his language admits the distinction, he will find on the arrival of Man Friday that it acquires a new importance. For whereas he will be able to teach Man Friday the use of the words which he has devised to stand for external objects by showing him the objects for which they stand, he will not, in this way, be able to teach him the use of the words which he has devised to stand for his sensations. And in the cases where these sensations are entirely private, in the sense that they have no 'natural expressions' which Man Friday can identify, it may well be that Crusoe fails to find any way of teaching him the use of the words which he employs to stand for them. But from the fact that he cannot teach this part of his language to Man Friday it by no means follows that he has no use for it himself. In a context of this sort, one can teach only what one already understands. The ability to teach, or rather the ability of someone else to learn, cannot therefore be a prerequisite for understanding.

Neither does it necessarily follow, in these circumstances, that Man Friday will be incapable of learning the meaning of the words which Crusoe uses to describe his private sensations. It is surely a contingent fact that we depend upon ostensive definitions, to the extent that we do, for learning what words mean. As it is, a child is not taught how to describe his feelings in the way he is taught to describe the objects in his nursery. His mother cannot point to his pain in the way that she can point to his cup and spoon. But she knows that he has a pain because he cries and because she sees that something has happened to him which is likely to cause him pain; and knowing that he is in pain she is able to teach him what to call it. If there were no external signs of his sensations she would have no means of detecting when he had them, and therefore could not teach him how to describe them. This is indeed the case, but it might easily be otherwise. We can imagine two persons being so attuned to one another that whenever either has a private sensation of a certain sort, the other has it too. In that case, when one of them described what he was feeling the other might very well follow the description, even though he had not 'external' evidence to guide him. But how could either of them ever know that he had identified the other's feeling correctly? Well, how can two people ever know that they mean the same by a word which they use to refer to some 'public' object? Only because each finds the other's reactions appropriate. Similarly one may suppose that Man Friday sympathises when Crusoe's private sensation is painful, and congratulates him when it is pleasant, that he is able to say when it begins and when it stops, that he correctly describes it as being rather like such and such another sensation, and very different from a third, thereby affording proof that he also understands the words that stand for these sensations. Admittedly, such tests are not conclusive. But the tests which we ordinarily take as showing that we mean the same by the words which we apply to public objects are not conclusive either: they leave it at least theoretically open that we do not after all mean quite the same. But from the fact that the tests are not conclusive it does not, in either case, follow that they have no force at all. It is true also that such tests as the expressed agreement about the duration of the experience require that the two men already share a common language, which they have no doubt built up on the basis of common observations. It would indeed be difficult, though still, I think, not necessarily impossible,[2] for them to establish communication if all their experiences were private, in Wittgenstein's sense. But even if their understanding each other's use of words could come about only if some of the objects which these words described were public, it would not follow that they all must be so.

It is not even necessary to make the assumption that Man Friday comes to know what Crusoe's sensations are, and so to understand the words which signify them, through having similar sensations of his own. It is conceivable that he should satisfy all the tests which go to show that he has this knowledge, and indeed that he should actually have it, even though the experience which he rightly ascribes to Crusoe is unlike any that he has, or ever has had, himself. It would indeed be very strange if someone had this power of seeing, as it were, directly into another's soul. But it is strange only in the sense that it is something which, on causal grounds, we should not expect to happen. The idea of its happening breaks no logical rule. An analogous case would be that of someone's imagining, or seeming to remember, an experience which was unlike any that he had ever actually had. To allow that such things are possible is, indeed, to admit innate ideas, in the Lockean sense, but that is not a serious objection. The admission is not even inconsistent with the prevalent varieties of empiricism. It can still be made a rule that in order to understand a word which signifies a sensation one must know what it would be like to have the sensation in question: that is, one must be able to identify the sensation when one has it, and so to verify the statement which describes it. The peculiarity of the cases which we are envisaging is just that people are credited with the ability to identify experiences which they have not previously had. There may indeed be causal objections to the hypothesis that this can ever happen. The point which concerns us now is that these objections are no more than causal. The ways in which languages are actually learned do not logically circumscribe the possibilities of their being understood.

If the sort of insight which we have been attributing to Man Friday were commonly possessed, we might well be led to revise our concepts of publicity and privacy. The mistake which is made by philosophers like Carnap is that of supposing that being public or being private, in the senses which are relevant to this discussion, are properties which are somehow attached to different sorts of objects, independently of our linguistic usage. But the reason why one object is publicly and another only privately accessible is that in the one case it makes sense to say that the object is observed by more than one person and in the other it does not.[3] Tables are public; it makes sense to say that several people are perceiving the same table. Headaches are private: it does not make sense to say that several people are feeling the same headache. But just as we can assimilate tables to headaches by introducing a notation in which two different persons' perceiving the same table becomes a matter of their each sensing their own private 'tabular' sense-data, so we could assimilate headaches to tables by introducig a notation in which it was correct to speak of a common headache, which certain people only were in a condition to perceive. As things are, this notation would not be convenient. But if people were so constituted that they were communally exposed to headaches in the way that they are communally exposed to the weather, we might cease to think of headaches as being necessarily private. A London particular might come to be a local headache as well as, or instead of, a local fog. Certain persons might escape it, just as certain persons, for one reason or another, may fail to perceive the fog. But the fog exists for all that, and so, given this new way of speaking, would public headache. The conditions which would make this way of speaking useful do not, indeed, obtain; but that they do not is, once again, a purely contingent fact.

The facts being what they are, we do not have a use for such expressions as 'S_2's feeling S_1's thirst' or 'S_2's observing the sensation of thirst which S_1 feels'. On the other hand, we do attach a meaning to saying that the same physical object, or process, or event, for instance a state of S_1's body, is observed by S_2 as well as by S_1. Does it follow, as Carnap thinks, that for this reason S_2 cannot understand a statement which refers to S_1's feeling of thirst, whereas he can understand a statement which refers to the condition of S_1's body? Suppose that we modified our rules for identity, in a way that many philosophers have proposed, and allowed ourselves to say that what was ordinarily described as S_1 and S_2's observing the same physical event was 'really' a case of each of them sensing his own sense-data which, while they might be qualitatively similar, could not be literally the same. Should we thereby be committed to denying that either could understand what the other said about this physical event? Surely not. And equally the fact that S_2 cannot feel, or inspect, S_1's feelings in no way entails that he cannot understand what S_1 says about them. The criteria for deciding whether two people understand each other are logically independent of the fact that we do, or do not, have a use for saying that literally the same objects are perceived by both.

I conclude, first, that for a person to use descriptive language meaningfully it is not necessary that any other person should understand him, and, secondly, that for anyone to understand a descriptive statement it is not necessary that he should himself be able to observe what it describes. It is not even necessary that he should be able to observe something which is naturally associated with what it describes, in the way that feelings are associated with their 'natural expressions'. If we insist on making it a necessary condition for our understanding a descriptive statement that we are able to observe what it describes, we shall find ourselves disclaiming the possibility of understanding not merely statements about other people's private sensations, but also statements about the past; either that, or reinterpreting them in such a way that they change their reference, as when philosophers substitute bodily states for feelings, and the future for the past. Both courses, I now think, are mistaken. No doubt it is a necessary condition for my understanding a descriptive statement that it should be, in some way, verifiable. But it need not be directly verifiable, and even if it is directly verifiable, it need not be directly verifiable by me.

(ii) *Rush Rhees*

The problem about private languages is the problem of how words mean. This is much the same as the question of what a rule of language is.

When we talk about something, our language does not point to it, nor mirror it. Pointing or mirroring could refer to things only within a convention, anyway: only when there is a way in which pointing is understood and a way in which mirroring is understood. I point for the sake of someone who understands it. Apart from that it were an idle ceremony; as idle as making sounds in front of things.

Our words refer to things by the way they enter in discourse; by their connections with what people are saying and doing, for instance, and by the way they affect what is said and done. What we say makes a difference. What expressions we use makes a difference. And the notion of a rule goes with that. If it made no difference what sound you made or when, you could not be understood and you would have said nothing. If you have said something, your utterance will be taken in one way and not in another. In many cases you will have committed yourself to saying other things, to answering in certain ways if you are asked, or to doing certain things. That belongs to the regular use of your words, and that is why it would not have been just the same if you had used others instead. That is also why it is possible to learn the language.

When we speak of "use" we may think of general practice and we may think of rules. Sometimes these can be left together, but sometimes there are differences we ought to notice. When I learn the use of an expression, or learn what it means – that is how other people speak. Yet I do not say I have learned what other people do; I have learned what it means. I may learn what it means *by* observing what other people do, and of course if I know what it means I know that others who speak the language will use it in that way. But I have not learned what generally happens. I have learned a rule.

That is in some ways like learning the rules of a game, although in some ways it is very different. It is different from learning the rules of a calculus, too. In fact in some ways it is misleading to talk of rules at all here. But it does make some things clearer – that it is possible to use an expression wrongly, for instance.

A rule is something that is *kept*. That is why we can know what we are talking about. When you have learned how the expression is used, then you can not merely behave as other people do, you can also *say* something. That is not a matter of behaving in a particular way. 'This is red' does not mean 'Everyone calls this red'. If that were all there were to it nothing would mean anything.

And yet, that there should be rules at all does depend on what people do, and on an agreement in what they do. If you teach someone the meaning of a colour word by showing him samples of the colour, then he will probably understand; and if he understands he will go on to use the word in new situations just as you would. If he remembered your instruction all right but differed wildly from you in what he called 'the same as' the samples you had shown him, and if this went on no matter how often you repeated your explanation, then he could never learn what that colour word means. And this holds generally, not just with colours. It is a point to which Wittgenstein is referring in *Inv*. 242. Of course that situation practically never arises. And if it were at all general we could not speak.

I am not saying, 'People see that their reactions tally, and this makes communication possible'. That would assume considerable understanding and language already. The agreement of which I am speaking is something without which it would not be possible for people to 'see' that their reactions tallied or that anything else tallied. We see that we understand one another, without noticing whether our reactions tally or not. *Because* we agree in our reactions, it is possible for me to tell you something, and it is possible for you to teach me something.

The consensus of reactions is in this sense prior to language, but the reactions themselves are not languages, nor are they language. Neither does the agreement in reactions come first or anticipate languages. It appears as the language does, it is a common way of taking the expressions of the language. They are common reactions within the course of language – not to anything there might have been before language or apart from it.

Because there is this agreement we can understand one another. And since we understand one another we have rules. We might perhaps speak of being 'trusted' to go on in the way that is for us the only natural one. But if you have learned the language you take it for granted. If any one did not, we could never understand him.

Because there is this agreement it is possible to say something. When I tell you that the patch on a patient's skin is red, I am not saying that it is called red, but that it *is* red. But I could mean nothing definite by that, and you could not understand me, unless people who have learned the words as we have would agree in calling this red. If people could not be brought to use the word in any regular way, if one man who had been taught as we have should go on to give the name to what we should call the complementary colour, if another used it as we do on Monday but in a different way on Tuesday, and if others did not show even these degrees of regularity – then it would not mean anything to say that someone had used the word mistakenly. There would be no distinction between mistakenly and correctly. And there would be no distinction between saying that it is red and saying anything else.

It is not a statement about what I do or about what people generally do. But unless the words had a regular use I should not know it was red, and I should not know what colour it was, because there would be nothing to know. I know what colour it is because I know red when I see it; I know what red is. A bull may charge at a red flag, and rats may be trained to react in one way to red lights and in another way to blue lights, but neither the bull nor the rat knows what red is, and neither knows that this is red. We might put this by saying that neither of them has the concept 'red' and neither of them has the concept 'colour'. No one can get the concept of colour just by looking at colours, or of red just by looking at red things. If I have the concept, I know how the word 'red' is used. There must *be* a use, though; there must be what I have been calling common reactions. The phrase 'the same colour' must mean something and be generally understood, and also 'a different colour'. I must know when it makes sense to talk about different shades of the same colour; and so on. Unless I did know what it makes sense to say, unless I were used to talking about colours and to understanding people when they did, then I should not know what red is and I should not know red when I see it.

Of course the colour red is not the word 'red'. And I suppose if
a man cannot see he will never know what it is. But the colour red
is not *this*, either. This is red. But if I say 'This is the *colour* red',
that is a definition – I am giving you a definition by showing you a
sample. And the point of that depends upon the definition's being
taken in a particular way; and also on its connection with other
uses of language: If I had just shown you that sample without saying anything, and without your asking – what would you have
learned from this? Not what the colour red is, anyway.

Someone might say, 'I know what *I* mean by "red". It is what I
experience when I look at this. Whether I have this experience
under the same circumstances as lead you to use the word – that is
a further question, which may be important in deciding the description of physical objects. But I know what colour *I* see in these circumstances.' (It would be hard to keep from asking, 'Well, what
colour *do* you see?') I suppose the point would be that I know this
independently of having learned the (public) language. If I know
what I mean, in this way – if I know what colour *I* am referring to
– then apparently I have done something like giving myself a definition and following a definition. It is this which allows me to evade
the difficulty of what I am going to *call* 'following the definition'.
Which is a real difficulty: what could it mean to say that I had followed the definition – 'my' definition – incorrectly? But if that has
no sense, then what on earth is the point of the definition? And what
does the definition *establish*?

Suppose someone asked 'What colour is red?' and thought it was
like asking 'What colour is blood?' This, he might think, is something which I can learn only by my own experience, my immediate
experience. And although I can tell you what colour blood is, I
cannot tell you what colour red is. I can only suggest things that
may enable you to find out for yourself. Well, but in this case what
is the sense of 'what colour red *is*'? If it is something nobody can
say, then nobody can ask it either. Suppose I ask it only of myself
– but whatever is it I am asking? Something I should like to know?
But if that has no sense, then there is nothing I tell myself either.
Perhaps I say 'What a colour!', but that is all.

I cannot learn the colour unless I can see it; but I cannot learn it
without language either. I know it because I know the language.
And it is similar with sensations. I know a headache when I feel it,
and I know I felt giddy yesterday afternoon, because I know what
giddiness is. I can remember the sensation I had, just as I can
remember the colour I saw. I feel the same sensation, and that is

the same colour. But the identity – the sameness – comes from the language.

A rule is something that is kept. The meaning of a word is something that is kept. It is for this reason that I can say this is the same colour I saw a moment ago. I can see the same colour just because I know red when I see it. And even with shades for which we have no special names, the same thing holds: I know the same colour when I see it.

It is similar, I have said, with sensations. I can say what I felt and I can say what I feel, and I can say it is the same sensation this time – because I know what sensations I am speaking of. It might be said that I can know it is the same only if it *feels* the same; and that is something no language can tell me. Nor can I know whether you are feeling the same as you have felt before. Only you can tell me that, because you are the only one who knows what it feels like. Well I agree that no language can tell me whether this feels the same. No language can tell me whether those two are the same colour, either. And my familiarity with methods of measurement will not tell me whether those two plots have the same area before I have measured them. But without language I could not have told whether this feels the same, either; if only because I could not have asked.

Of course recognising a sensation is a different sort of thing from recognising a colour. This holds whether I am speaking of my own or another's. It is different from recognising what anything looks like or what is going on. When I say the dog is in pain I am not describing what the dog is doing, any more than I describe what I am doing when I give expression to pain. It is more like an expression of pity. At any rate, feeling pity, trying to ease him and so on – or perhaps turning away from the sight – is all part of believing that he is in pain. And to say that I was obviously justified in that – or maybe that I was mistaken – is a different sort of thing from saying that I was justified or mistaken in believing that he had a fracture. 'Mistake' means something different here, although it is just as definite. If I made a mistake in thinking the boy was in pain, well he was shamming and my pity was misplaced. The mistake was not that I supposed something was going on in him when nothing was. I may have supposed that too, perhaps that he had a cramp, but this is a different mistake. The dog's pain is not something going on. It is just his *being* in pain. I know for certain that he is in pain, and I know this because I know what pain is and what suffering is. There is an important difference between seeing

that he is in pain and being in pain myself, because I do not see that
I am in pain, and while it is conceivable that I am mistaken about
him, that makes no sense in my own case. But this does not mean
that I know something about myself which I cannot know about
him.

We do not speak of sensations in the same way as we speak of
processes or of colours. The name of a sensation is a different sort of
name from the name of a colour. But if it means anything to say
I am in pain again or that he is in pain again, this is because the
word 'pain' has a regular use and because we know this we know
what pain is. If it were something I knew only in myself, then I
might say 'This is something different now' or 'This is the same
again' or I might say neither, and in any case it would not make
any difference. This is not a question of whether I can trust my
memory. It is a question of when it makes sense to speak of remembering; either of a good memory or a faulty one. If I thought I
could not trust my memory, then of course I might look for confirmation. But there cannot be any question of confirmation here,
nor any question of doubting either. There is just no rule for what
is the same and what is not the same; there is no distinction between
correct and incorrect; and it is for that reason that it does not make
any difference what I say. Which means, of course, that I say
nothing.

I cannot say anything unless I know the language. But I cannot
know the language – any language – privately. I may have a secret
code, but that is not the point here. It is a question of whether I
can have a private understanding; whether I can understand something which *could* not be said in a language anyone else could
understand. ('He may understand the language I speak, but he
will not understand what I understand.') I say I cannot know a
language privately, for what would there be to *know*? In language
it makes a difference what you say. But how can it make any difference what you say privately? (I do not mean talking to yourself.) It
seems that in a private language everything would have to be at
once a statement and a definition. I suppose I may define a mark in
any way I wish. And if every use of the mark is also a definition –
if there is no way of discovering that I am wrong, in fact no sense in
suggesting that I might be wrong – then it does not matter what
mark I use or when I use it.

One might ask, 'Why can I not give myself a definition and
decide for myself what following the definition is going to be?' But
when? Each time? If I decide once and for all, that only renews the

problem: what is 'according to my decision'? But what would the decision be anyway? In ordinary language I may decide to use an expression in a particular way, and I know how to keep to this. I do this in connection with established usages and rules. That is why 'in a particular way' means something. That is also why I can decide to use the expressions of a secret language or the signs of a code in a particular way. For I am dealing with expressions that can be understood, and I know how the matter could be said in ordinary language. I know whether I am saying the same as I said before, and I know what I am deciding. But not when it is something which *could* not be said in ordinary language. Here there would be no point in saying, for instance, 'I am going to use S to mean that', because I do not know what 'meaning that' could be.

The reason is not that others must see what my words refer to. It is just that if my words are to refer to anything they must be understood. They cannot refer at all except in connection with a use, a use which you learn when you learn what the word means. They cannot refer to anything unless there is a way in which the language is spoken. That is why there cannot be a private understanding. If it makes no difference what is said, nothing is understood.

There is of course no reason why I should not give an account of something which only I can see. Or of something which only I can feel: as when I tell a doctor what I feel in my abdomen. He does not feel my sensations (if that means anything), but he knows what I am talking about; he knows what sensations they are.

Ayer asks why Crusoe should not invent names for his sensations. (He actually says 'names to *describe* his sensations', but I do not understand this.) *I* can invent names for my sensations. But that is because I speak a language in which there are names for sensations. I know what the name of a sensation is. Inventing a name or giving it a name is something that belongs to the language as we speak it.

It is possible, certainly, to invent new expressions, and even in one sense new languages. But it is a different question whether anyone could have invented language. If language were a device or a method which people might adopt, then perhaps he could. But it is not that. And you could as easily speak of someone's inventing commerce; more easily, in fact. For he would have to invent what we call use and meaning. And I do not say so much that this would be beyond anyone's powers as rather that it is unintelligible.

The expressions of a language get their significance and their force from their application, from their extensive uses. Many of them enter in almost everything we do. And this gives them the force and obviousness they have in new contexts. So even if someone dreamed of a language before there was any, how could he put that forward as 'a practical proposition'? Or *what* would he put forward? Marks and sounds would be so much gibberish. To invent a vocabulary he would have at least to invent ways of using these sounds in various circumstances – in circumstances of a social life which has in fact grown up *with* language and could no more be invented than language could. And people would have to understand them. They would have to see not just that this sign occurs here and that there; they would have to see the difference it makes if you use the one or the other. And once again the difficulty is that there would be nothing to understand; because there would be no established use, and nothing we should call 'the difference it makes'.

Wittgenstein did not say that the ascription of meaning to a sign is something that needs justification. That would generally be as meaningless as it would if you said that language needs justification. What Wittgenstein did hold was that if a sign has meaning it can be used wrongly. On the other hand, if anyone had tried to invent language and teach it to others, then you might say the language and the use of expressions did stand in need of justification.

But why could not a dominant individual have brought people to behave as the people in one of Wittgenstein's primitive language-games do? Why could he not force them to that as we train animals? Why could he not train them to respond in regular ways when ordered, and perhaps to answer?

Well, no animals have been trained to do even the primitive things that are done in those language-games. Those people are not just going through a complicated trick; what they say depends upon what they need and what they find. They are not just carrying out orders. They use the expressions they do because they have something to say, and because that use is understood by all parties. Whereas, although you may train animals to make the 'correct' responses to different words or signs, the animals themselves do not *use* different words. A dog may respond in one way to 'Slippers!' and in another way to 'Basket!', but he does not himself have one sound for the one and a different sound for the other; neither does he do anything like always giving two barks when he wants food and one bark when he wants a drink. No training has brought an animal to speak, even in a primitive way. This is not a question of the capacities of animals. If any animals do learn to speak, they will not learn it just as they learn tricks. A dog 'knows what you want him to do' when you utter the word, but he does not know what it means.

If people merely carried out orders and made certain utterances when they were ordered – if this were 'making the signs they were supposed to make when they were supposed to make them' – they would not be speaking. I suppose people might be trained to do that with Greek sentences without knowing Greek. And the people in our example would not understand what they were saying. They could not do that unless they used the expressions themselves, and using them is not just doing what you are told with them. What we call following a rule in language is not following orders. That is why we talk about 'taking part in' a language – the language is not any one man's doing more than another's, and the rules, if they are rules of language, are not one man's rules. This is essential for understanding.

It might be that when people had been trained as we imagined they would eventually begin to speak. But that would not be what was invented, and it would not have come about by invention. It would have grown up through the initiative and spontaneous re-actions of various people, none of whom was inventing language.

We might ask for *whom* would anyone invent language? Or for what? For animals, for instance? Or for people who have a social life as we have? If it is the latter, he need not trouble, for we have it. But unless it is for those who have the kind of social life people with languages do have – then what is the point and what is he inventing? What would a 'language' for a flock of parrots be, for instance? Can you get anywhere except by absurdly imagining them to live as human beings do, as in children's stories?

The point is that no one could invent just *language*. Language goes with a way of living. An invented language would be a wall-paper pattern; nothing more.

A man might invent marks to go with various objects. That is not language. And when Ayer's Crusoe invents *names* to *describe* flora and fauna, he is taking over more than he has invented. He is sup-posed to keep a diary, too. Ayer thinks that if he could do that when Friday was present he could surely have done it when he was still alone. But what would that be – keeping a diary? Not just making marks on paper, I suppose (or on a stone or what it might be). You might ask, 'Well what is it when *I* do it? And why should it not be the same for him, only a bit more primitive?' But it cannot be that. My marks are either marks I use in communication with other people, or they stand for expressions I use with other people. 'What difference does that make? He can *use* them just as I do.' No, because I use them in their various meanings. He cannot do that.

What is it he cannot do? What is it that I can do and he cannot? There seems to be nothing logically absurd in supposing that he behaves just as I do. To a large extent I agree. But it is absurd to suppose that the marks he uses mean anything; even if we might want to say that he goes through all the motions of meaning something by them.

I should agree that if 'meaning something' were something psychological, he might conceivably do that. If it were a question of what is put into my mind by my association with other people, then there is nothing logically absurd in supposing this to come into someone's mind without that association.

'What is it that I can do . . . ?' To say that meaning something must be something *I* do is rather like saying it is something that happens at the moment. The point is that I speak a language that is spoken. What I say has significance in that language, not otherwise. Or in other words, if I *say* anything I must say it in some language. If there were no more than my behaviour, the marks I make and so on, then I should not mean anything either.

If I say there is 'more' than that – it is that I use the expression in the meanings they have. If Crusoe used the same expressions he would not do that. Nor can he use different expressions but in these meanings. He does not use expressions in any meanings at all.

Using them in their meanings is what we call following a rule. For language there must be 'the way the expressions are used', and this goes with the way people live. I need not live that way myself when I use them. Defoe's Crusoe could have kept a diary, but Ayer's could not. Defoe's Crusoe's diary need never be read by anyone, and the meaning of what he writes does not depend on that. What he writes down may never play a part in the lives of other people. But the language in which he has written it does. And for that reason he can understand what he writes, he knows what he is saying. He knows the use or application of the expressions he uses, and it is from that they get the significance they have for him. He knows what he is talking about. Ayer's Crusoe does not and cannot.

Ayer's Crusoe may use marks for particular purposes – to show where he has hidden something, perhaps – and with as great regularity as we care to think. This is not what we mean by the regular use of an expression in a language. If he should suddenly do something which *we* should call using these marks entirely differently, it would have no sense to say that he had done anything wrong or anything inconsistent with what he had done before. We could not speak of his using them in the same meaning or in a different meaning. If he always uses them for the same purpose – as he might always gather wood for the same purpose – this is not what we mean by using an expression in the same way. *Using an expression in the same way does not mean using it for the same purpose.* (What I said about identity is connected with this.) And if there is any sort of discrepancy between what I said at one time and what I say at another – this does not mean that what I do with a mark or sound at one time is different from what I did with it before. If I have always done this with the mark, there is nothing of a rule of language in that.

'But if he uses them just *as* they would be used by someone who spoke the language, so that they *could* be understood, what is the trouble with saying that he uses them in their meanings?' The first trouble is that he does not understand them. And this really means that he does *not* use them just as someone who spoke the language would. For he cannot be guided by his signs in just the way in which you and I may be guided by words.

This is not a question of something beyond his powers. If we ask whether a machine could follow words, or whether a machine might speak, we are not asking what a machine might be designed to do. It is not a question of capacity or performance at all.

If you say something to me I understand you. If a tape recorder plays back what you have said, I understand what I hear but I do not understand the tape recorder. Which is a grammatical statement: I do not fail to understand either. If I say that you have said something but the tape recorder has not, I am not saying that something has happened in your case which did not happen in the other. But I do have an entirely different attitude towards you and towards what I hear from you, and I behave towards you in a host of ways as I should never behave towards a machine – for instance I may answer you, and I should never answer the recorder. I should not try to answer you either, nor should I suppose you had said anything, unless I assumed you knew the language; or unless I thought you said something in a language I did not understand. And I take it for granted you are speaking the language as it is spoken.

I am hardly ever in doubt whether you said something, if I have heard you. But I should begin to doubt if I found that you did not follow my answer, and that you did not seem to know anything about the matters to which your words referred. What I should be doubtful about, in that case, would not be whether something went on in you. I should be doubtful whether you knew what you were saying. But for all I know you may have 'done' all that you would have done if you had. The trouble is that your utterance was not a move you were making in the conversation or in the language at all.

If I doubt whether you know the language, or if I doubt whether you ever know what you are saying, then in many ways I must regard you more as I should regard the tape recorder. This is not because you do not do anything that other people do. It is because you do not take part in what they do. You do not speak the language they speak. And *speaking* the language they speak is not just uttering the words; any more than understanding the language is just 'recognising' the words. It is carrying on a conversation, for instance; or it may be writing reports, or listening to a play in a theatre. It is being someone to whom the rest of us can speak and get an answer; to whom we can tell something and with whom we can make a joke and whom we can deceive. All this, and of course immeasurably more, belongs to speaking the language. And it belongs to being able to follow words. You can follow words because you know how to speak. And for the same reason a machine cannot follow words. This has nothing to do with any question of what physics and engineering may achieve. It is just that it makes no sense to say that a machine might follow words.

One can say that absolutely of a machine, but not of Crusoe, because Crusoe might learn a language. But so long as he never has learned a language, in the sense of taking part in a language, it is as meaningless to say of him that he follows words as it would be to say this of an electronic computer.

I cannot ask whether a machine has made a mistake or whether it meant what it said. A machine may be out of order, and then you cannot rely on it. But it is not making a mistake. (And when I make a mistake myself there is nothing out of order.) A machine may 'correct mistakes' in connection with the operation of negative feedback. But there is nothing there like a mistake in understanding; nor like a mistake in calculation either. This is one reason why a machine cannot follow words – why that makes no sense. I can follow words only where a mistake or a misunderstanding is at least conceivable. ('Yes, of *course* that's what it means.') Otherwise there would be nothing like what we call understanding them.

I may react to words, rightly or wrongly, when I do not understand them. They may be words in a language I do not know, but

I may have been taught to obey the orders of someone who shouts them. Maybe no one else would use them in these orders as he does, and that is of no consequence to me. It would have been exactly the same if he had used sounds of his own instead of words. I may react wrongly, as an animal might. But if I call this making a mistake, it is not like mistaking the meaning of the words he uses; any more than I have shown I understand the words if I make no mistake. I know what he wants, that is all. (I know enough to get out of the way of a barking dog, too.) If I had understood the words I should probably know what they would mean in other situations; and at any rate I should know what they would mean if somebody else used them too. The latter is the important point. It is connected with the fact that if I understand the words I should be able to use them, at least in some measure, myself. That is essential if I am guided by the words or if I follow them. But if that is necessary for understanding the words, it is also necessary for misunderstanding them; by which I mean again that it makes no sense to talk about misunderstanding apart from that. Misunderstanding or mistaking the meaning belongs to taking part in the language. You cannot speak of it otherwise.

Ayer's Crusoe may make the kind of mistakes animals do. He may mistake a bird which he does not like to eat for one which he likes. This is not like a mistake in understanding the meaning of an expression, or a mistake in following what was said.

'Why not? He calls the edible bird *ba*, and when he sees the inedible one he says "ba" and kills it.'

That is not a mistake in following the meanings of words. He could have made the same mistake without using words at all. (Perhaps it is roughly the kind of mistake that is corrected through negative feed-back.) You cannot ask whether he made the other kind of mistake; any more than you could ask this of a machine.[4]

I can mistake the meanings of the words you use, because I might use those words myself. If different people can use the same words, then the meanings are independent. I may also take your words in the wrong way. That is rather different, but it is connected with this. He said, 'I wonder how long it can last', and she thought he was finding the affair intolerable, whereas he meant the opposite. She knew the meanings of the words he was using, and she could not have misunderstood him in that way unless she had. He might have used the same words to mean what she thought he meant. But he could not have meant either the one or the other unless his words had meant what they do independently; unless they had been the words of a language. I call their meanings 'independent', partly because they have to be learned. That is characteristic of language.

Unless the meanings of words were independent – unless they had to be learned – they could not be misunderstood. You do not misunderstand just a sound. You might mistake the cry of an animal for the cry of a bird. You may mistake the call of an enemy for the call of a friend. That is not misunderstanding, not in the present sense. If one spoke of learning the meaning of a sound, that would not be like learning the meaning of a word. Perhaps it would not be nonsense to say that he 'knew instinctively' that it was the cry of an animal. But it is nonsense to say that he knew instinctively the meaning of a word.

You can misunderstand what you can learn. And you are misunderstanding a rule – not a matter of fact. Mistaking the cry of a bird for an animal cry is not misunderstanding a rule.

If one spoke of the independent existence of a tree, this might mean partly that I could think there was no tree there and be wrong. But the meanings of words are not quite comparable with that, and by their independence I do not mean quite the same. If I am wrong about the tree, I may run into it. If I am wrong about the meaning of a word, it is not like that. It is just that I use the word incorrectly, or understand it incorrectly. And that seems almost like saying that if I am wrong I am wrong. Which in a sense is just what I do mean. That is why it is better in this case to say that 'the meanings are independent' means just that they have to be learned; as a rule has to be learned. And that is why it is natural to speak of *misunderstanding* here; as it is not, so much, when you you are speaking of a mistake in fact.

If anyone did not understand what kind of mistake it is, he would not understand the difference between correct and incorrect; and vice versa. But then he would not understand what words are.

Now since you have learned the meanings of the expressions you use, it may happen that you do not mean what you say. At least it makes sense to ask of anyone who has spoken whether he meant it. If he does not mean what he says, this is familiar and definite enough, but you cannot describe it by describing what he is doing. You can describe it only by taking into account his relation to other people. In this case it is not simply that various people use the same words, although that is a large part of it. What is important is the special role or part played by the person in saying them. That is what his 'not meaning them' is. And it is as characteristic and essential for language as independent meanings are. I have said it is essential that different people may use the same words. But if those people were all doing the same thing, it would not be language. There must be something more like an organisation, in which different people are, as we may put it, playing different roles. (The simile limps, but it has something important too. It must serve here.) That belongs to the use of language. Without it there would not be words and there would not be meaning.

Language is something that is spoken.

III Private language and private sensations

(i) *Helen Hervey*

The cautious framing of the title of this paper is deliberate. I might have given it the title 'Can there be a Private Language?', under which heading originally Professor Ayer argued that there could be a private language, while Mr R. Rhees maintained, following Wittgenstein, that a private language was impossible (Chapter II above). I doubt if I shall be able to give quite such a clear-cut answer as was given by Ayer or Rhees. I do not think it is at all easy to formulate the problem in the first place, and it is likely that different answers are possible depending on the way the problem is interpreted. It may even be that framed in a certain way it has no answer; and even if it has an answer it still has to be considered whether anything significant has been said, or whether anything of importance hangs on it.

Before considering the character of a *private* language it would seem relevant to consider briefly the nature of a public language; in other words, to attempt to specify some of the criteria we have in mind when we speak of a 'language'. It should be noted first that when we speak of a language, we at once think of something that is spoken or written down in the form of words. When we speak of 'our language' we mean the system of verbal signs by means of which we are enabled to communicate with one another. It seems trivially obvious that the main function of language is the function of communication – language just is a social affair.

We have just described a language as a 'system of verbal signs', and the systematic character of a language is one which we should also wish to emphasise. A language just is not a haphazard collection of sounds any more than a building is a haphazard collection of differently shaped bricks, sticks and stones. It is also trivially obvious therefore, that a language has rules, rules governing the use of words, the construction of sentences, and so on. If somebody made a pile of miscellaneous rubbish and then said 'How do you like my new house?' we should simply stare at him and think him crazy. Similarly, if someone told us that he had made a language without any rules we should also stare at him and think him extremely peculiar. We should say to him, 'What a ridiculous idea – how can you possibly have a language without any rules? Don't talk such nonsense!' But we should not feel in saying this that we had said anything of profound significance, nor have we, any more than if we pointed out to someone who said that he had invented a game of cards without any rules, that he might as well assert that he could draw a square circle. The notion of a language without rules can therefore be said to be a contradiction in terms.

So much for a very brief, and no doubt inadequate, account of a language as we all understand it to be. We now come to the notion of a private language, a concept which seems to have been given currency mainly by Wittgenstein because of his discussion of the problem in the *Philosophical Investigations*.[1] As Ayer has pointed out, however, the notion has a forerunner in the protocol language postulated by Carnap, and it might be helpful to sketch part of the background briefly in order to gain some understanding of why Wittgenstein attached such significance to the problem. This protocol or basic language was to consist of bare sensation-utterances, for example of utterances such as 'blue now' or 'cold now', referring to the sense experiences of a particular individual. To quote a passage from Carnap's *The Unity of Science*, p. 80 (quoted by Ayer): 'In general every statement in any person's protocol language would have sense for that person alone. . . . Even when the same words and sentences occur in various protocol languages, their sense would be different, they could not even be compared. Every protocol language could therefore be applied only solipsistically: there would be no intersubjunctive protocol language. This is the consequence obtained by consistent adherence to the usual view and terminology (rejected by the author).' We should note that Carnap allows that individuals may use the same words and sentences to refer to their experiences, words like 'red', 'blue', 'hot', 'cold', etc. He wishes to deny, however, that there is no way of overcoming the solipsistic conclusion of the argument he has sketched, that is, that every individual is talking about his experiences entirely within his own little world of experience, which because it is entirely private to him means that any statement about it has meaning for him only, and for no one else. Carnap believes that common understanding is possible at this level of basic sensation-utterances, and that because of this 'intersubjectivity' solipsism can be avoided and common scientific knowledge built up. From the positivist standpoint all knowledge must be based on experience, and fundamentally on primary sensory experiences; clearly, then, the languages in which these experiences are expressed must convey meaning to other individuals if higher levels of knowledge are to be erected on their foundation. The protocol languages are not therefore entirely private to the individuals speaking them, Carnap believes, although they refer to experiences which are private. Corresponding to subjective feelings are bodily states, and it is these to which the sensation-terms of the languages are also taken to refer; and these physical or bodily states are taken to be the same in everybody. The so-called protocol language is regarded as a sub-language of the (intersubjective) 'physical language' which is supposed to function as the 'basic language of science' (*The Unity of Science*, pp. 88, 95). Carnap thus reassures himself that the foundations of science as he conceives them reveal no breach in the unity of its structure.

It should be noted that Carnap takes for granted that sensation terms *do* refer to something private. Indeed, so strong does he seem to consider the claim of their private significance to the individual that he puts himself to considerable trouble to counteract the possibility that this private meaning is their full content. Carnap thus appears to believe that the language of sensations has a double aspect – a public aspect related to bodily or physical states and a private aspect related to the private sensations of the individual.

This is the sort of thesis which Wittgenstein, in the *Philosophical Investigations*, opposes strongly. Before considering his criticisms of what we might term the notion of 'private' or 'subjective' meaning, however, it is important to try to understand why Wittgenstein attaches such significance to this problem. Why should he trouble to attack the view that words referring to sensations, feelings, etc., have private meanings to the individuals using them? The chief reason seems to be that Wittgenstein wishes to deny the validity of the notion of a private or 'hidden' experience, and to this end aims at showing that it is logically impossible for language to refer to such private experiences. If we *cannot* speak of our private experiences, then (he maintains) it is very doubtful if they exist.

To support the view that Wittgenstein is 'hostile to the doctrine of privacy', as Professor Strawson phrases it in his review of the *Investigations*, many contexts might be cited. For example, Wittgenstein raises the question 'How do words *refer* to sensations?' and in answer describes how the child comes to learn the use of a name for a sensation (*Inv.* 244). So we are led to the very crucial question: 'In what sense', asks Wittgenstein, 'are my sensations *private*?' He at once gives a meaning to this question by drawing the implication that (if sensations are 'private') 'only I can know whether I am really in pain; another person can only surmise it', and proceeds to elaborate his claim that in one way this statement is false, and in another way 'nonsense' (*Inv.* 246). (This shows that Wittgenstein is opposed to the idea that a sensation is a 'private experience'.) The argument is continued at considerable length and subsidiary arguments are introduced. He considers, for example, whether it would be possible to teach names of sensations 'if human beings showed no outward signs' of them and takes the case of toothache. While a child, in such circumstances, *might* invent a name for the sensation of toothache, he would not be able to make himself understood when he used the word; in this case, queries Wittgenstein, 'does he understand the name' himself? (*Inv.* 257). This question, which is intended to plant in our minds the doubt that the child would himself be able to understand the word he had invented, can be related directly to Wittgenstein's general claim that 'An "inner process" stands in need of outward criteria' (*Inv.* 257). By 'outward criteria' he means the characteristic outward expressions of pains, feelings and sensations generally. It is because of what we might term 'sensation-behaviour' that a common sensation-language comes to be built up. If sensations were private experiences without 'outward signs' it would be impossible, according to Wittgenstein, to name them meaningfully, or indeed to name them at all. The 'act of naming' sensations 'makes sense' only if we remember that 'a great deal of stage-setting in the language is presupposed'; in other words, it is presupposed that the names of sensations have their 'grammars' (*Inv.* 257).

Thus, to refer again to Wittgenstein's analysis of the way in which the name of a sensation is learnt, the child learns the name in a certain setting, which we might call the 'objective' or 'public' situation. He learns to apply the word 'pain', for example, to his primitive 'pain-behaviour' (which is public) in this setting, and his verbal expressions of pain, as he is taught them, themselves become a part of his pain-behaviour (*Inv.* 244). The verbal expression of pain does not 'mean' or 'describe' crying, for example, but 'replaces' it. This means that one sort of pain-behaviour, i.e. verbal, may be substituted for another sort, i.e. the primitive, natural expression of pain, such as crying. Wittgenstein perhaps hopes to dissolve the problem by interpreting linguistic expressions of sensations as part (or whole) of sensation-*behaviour* manifested in a particular setting or situation, and not as *describing* anything. It might be asked, however, whether he has not simply shifted the problem. However successful might be the attempt to interpret verbal expression of pain as pain-behaviour, this pain-behaviour is still a manifestation of – pain. Or, speaking generally, however much we include in sensation-behaviour there still seems to be a puzzling 'remainder', if this behaviour is still considered an expression *of* the sensation (and not the sensation itself). There seems to remain 'something' unanalysed. Does a difficulty, for Wittgenstein, lurk in the phrase 'expression *of* . . .'? Perhaps it is this difficulty which bothers him later when he discusses the challenge to his thesis that, nevertheless, there is a difference between pain-behaviour accompanied by pain and pain-behaviour without the presence of pain (*Inv.* 304). He first admits the difference and then attempts to whittle it down by some rather strange arguments. He enquires whether, for example, if someone says to me 'It's not so bad' when I tell him I am in pain, this means that he '*believes* in something behind the outward expression of pain'. To this Wittgenstein replies enigmatically 'His attitude is a proof of his attitude', and then invites us to imagine not merely the words 'I am in pain' but also the remark 'It's not so bad' replaced by 'instinctive noises and gestures' (*Inv.* 310). One is not convinced by this argument that next time one sympathises with someone who is in pain one will not at the same time *believe* or *assume* that he is in fact in pain. In another place Wittgenstein tries to meet this objection by arguing that a presupposition implies a doubt, and that 'doubt may be entirely lacking' (*Inv.* ii, p. 180). Perhaps he switches to the notion of a 'presupposition' because he can hardly argue that a belief implies doubt, for beliefs are not usually doubted. In any case it does not seem clear that doubt always attaches to a presupposition, which we may also characterise as an assumption, which may or may not be doubted. A belief itself can be presupposed, in the sense that one belief can presuppose another. We might say, for example, that belief in the omnipotence of God presupposes belief in His existence. About 'doubt being lacking', it is true that we often believe without any doubt that someone is in pain; but is it not also true that we do have doubts sometimes whether people in fact have the pains they say they have, or whether the pain is as bad as it is asserted to be, as when we say 'It's not so bad', for example? Such doubts may be based on some special knowledge of the person concerned. Can we deny that there are hypochondriacs, who create their pains and their illnesses out of their imagination, but who might, nevertheless, quite well *behave* as if they were in pain or as if they were ill? Perhaps Wittgenstein has such facts in mind when he urges us to 'Just try – in a real case – to doubt someone else's fear or pain' (*Inv.* 303); but this very remark suggests that there *are* cases which are not real, hence that doubt is sometimes justified. Thus it seems perfectly legitimate to argue, which Wittgenstein wishes to deny, that one can believe or disbelieve that someone is in pain.

However, let us look at one or two more of Wittgenstein's arguments to see if they are any more convincing. He enquires what our position is if we try to give ourselves a 'private exhibition' of pain, that is, if we try to imagine it (*Inv.* 311). Perhaps in the attempt we screw up our face, but in this case would we not be giving ourselves a 'private exhibition' of merely a facial expression? With this one can agree entirely, but refuse to draw the conclusion Wittgenstein is encouraging us to draw, namely, that because we cannot imagine pain apart from some form of its expression, therefore pain may be nothing apart from such expression. We cannot imagine wind apart from moving trees and other of its effects, but is wind therefore nothing apart from the effects we can imagine? Or we might ask about the unobservable entities modern physics postulates. Can we imagine an electron, a positron, or a neutron? If not, does this mean that they are merely mythical entities? We seem in such cases to be prepared to base belief in their existence on the observability of certain effects, e.g. tracks of light on photographic plates, and if asked to imagine an electron this is the sort of thing which might come into our minds. Nevertheless, we do not confuse the track of light with the electron itself.

In another argument Wittgenstein asks us to imagine that the surfaces of some things round us have 'patches and regions' which produce 'pain in our skin when we touched them'. In this case, he argues, we should speak of 'pain-patches' on such objects just as we at present speak of 'red patches' (*Inv.* 312). Perhaps Wittgenstein by means of this argument wishes us to think when we sting our hand on a stinging-nettle or bruise our knee against a rock, for example, that the sting or the pain is at least partly in the nettle or the rock. I doubt, however, if any of us are going to say when we bruise ourselves in future, 'There's a patch of pain on that rock'. This might lead us to rub the rock to make our bruise better.

With such arguments Wittgenstein attempts to cast doubts on the notion of a 'private experience'. Although he speaks of 'inner processes' (but we should note that in the statement 'an "inner process" stands in need of outward criteria', the expression 'inner process' is

enclosed in quotation marks, which indicate that the notion has
some doubt attached to it), these processes, whatever they are, are
not to be regarded as 'hidden' or 'private'. On the statement 'What
is *internal* is hidden from us' he cryptically comments: 'The future
is hidden from us. But does the astronomer think like this when he
calculates an eclipse of the sun?' Again, 'If I see someone writhing
in pain with evident cause, I do not think: All the same, his feelings
are hidden from me' (*Inv.* II, p. 223).

Not only does Wittgenstein attempt to deny that sensations are
private, but he argues also that even if there should be a private
element it can have no significance in the language of sensation.
Here he makes use of an analogy, the 'beetle in the box' analogy.
If everyone has a beetle in a box, and no one has access to another's
box, then, even though all those with boxes believe them to contain
beetles, and the word 'beetle' has a use in their language, there is no
reason to suppose that everybody refers to the same thing when
using the word: each person might have 'something different in his
box, or it might be constantly changing'. Therefore, argues Wittgenstein, 'The thing in the box has no place in the language-game
at all; not even as a *something*: for the box might even be empty'
(*Inv.* 293). Thus, if sensations are conceived as 'private', while we
may have names for them, there is no guarantee that they mean the
'same' to the persons using them – they may not refer to anything
at all. This argument Wittgenstein develops in order to counter the
view that a person knows what the word 'pain' means 'only from
his own case', and he concluded by stating that 'if we construe the
grammar of the expression of sensation on the model of "object and
name" the object drops out of consideration as irrelevant' (i.e. because it is considered to be private, and therefore *cannot* be named).
Sensations, whatever they are (but Wittgenstein gives us no positive
thesis on this point), can be named only if there exist 'outward
criteria' by means of which they can be recognised and identified.
In their absence they can be neither recognised nor identified, even
by the individual who has the sensation experience.

There can be no doubt that Wittgenstein's opposition to the 'doctrine of privacy', as Strawson has phrased it, is of fundamental importance in many of his arguments, and if it is kept in mind much
is made clearer and more coherent. We are able to see what Wittgenstein is 'getting at', what he wants to destroy. He is aiming at
the destruction of the notion of an inner world of private experience,
a notion which he seems to think has its origin simply in language
itself. We have been deceived into thinking that such a world exists

because of our 'grammar' which has forced itself on us. To the questions 'Are you not really a behaviourist in disguise?' and 'Aren't you at bottom really saying that everything except human behaviour is a fiction?' he replies, 'If I do speak of a fiction, then it is of a *grammatical* fiction' (*Inv.* 307). Thus, while there once might have been a Loch Ness monster (and still is according to some people), there never *has* been a world of private experiences. This self-deception is mirrored in language. While not forbidding the use of words and phrases which mirror this deception (he could hardly succeed in this) Wittgenstein hopes to make us think very differently about the way we *use* them.

We are now perhaps in a position to assess Wittgenstein's reasons for introducing the notion of a purely private language into his argument. His fundamental purpose is to undermine the belief that our language as we use it *can* and *does* have reference to a private unobservable world of human experiences – to suggest, that is, that all terms by which we refer to sensations, emotions, states of mind, etc., have no meaning, strictly speaking, to each one of us alone purely on the basis of 'observing' our own inner states and processes, for this we cannot do. Our language has no private element or aspect in that certain words have a private meaning to us as individuals, as well as their public meaning. As a means to the end of showing this he takes the extreme case of a *purely* private language; in other words, he asks the question, 'Is it possible to have, or imagine the possibility of a language in which names of sensations, feelings, etc., occur when these are postulated to be entirely private in character?' Such a language must, by definition, be understandable *only* by the individual using it, otherwise it would not be private to him alone (*Inv.* 256). It is necessary, therefore, to ensure that there are *no* means by which it could be understood by anyone else. Hence, the 'inner experiences' to which the language is supposed to refer must have no 'natural expressions', because if the words used are 'tied up' with such expressions someone else might understand them. 'Suppose', writes Wittgenstein, 'I didn't have my natural expression of sensation, but only had the sensation': then the problem would be simply to '*associate* names with sensations and use these names in descriptions' (*Inv.* 256). To this end a diary might be kept and every time a certain sensation was experienced the letter 'E'[2] might be entered in the diary. But how, asks Wittgenstein, can this be done? How can I 'point to the sensation'? By concentrating my attention on it and so, as it were, pointing to it 'inwardly'? But this would mean that I knew I was concentrating on the right thing, whereas in this case I have no 'criterion of correctness' (*Inv.* 258). Wittgenstein is thus arguing that in the absence of the 'natural expressions' of the sensation an individual could have no criteria by which he could judge whether he was having the 'same' sensation or not. This means that if the sensation he is trying to record is an itch, for example, then if he is not permitted to scratch himself (or behave in some other appropriate fashion) then he cannot know whether he has an itch or not. Wittgenstein denies, therefore, that private rules governing the use of sensation-words are possible. If we say, 'Whatever is going to seem right to me is right', this means that 'here we can't talk about "right"' (*Inv.* 258).

This argument is followed by the assertion that it is useless just to '*believe*' that the same sensation has recurred – for the entry in the diary may mean 'nothing whatever' (*Inv.* 260). Further, as the word 'sensation' is a word of our 'common language', there would be no reason for calling 'S' the 'sign for a *sensation*'; nor would it do to say that 'S' stands for '*something*', for the word 'something' also belongs to the common language. So, in the end, the attempt to use a private language to refer to inner experiences would mean that the individual would be reduced to uttering merely inarticulate sounds. (This is a paraphrase of what I take Wittgenstein to mean when he writes that 'in the end when one is doing philosophy one gets to the point where one would like just to emit an inarticulate sound' (*Inv.* 261), a remark made in the context of the argument we have just analysed.) This argument brings us to the second main point about the private language as Wittgenstein appears to characterise it, namely that *no knowledge of the common language must be presupposed*. We who have this knowledge *could* not construct a private language because we would be forced to use in some way the words of our common language. With this conclusion, which Wittgenstein's argument seems to imply, we are left with a rather helpless feeling, for he seems in effect to be telling us that to be really private a private language must not be based in any way on the common language: but then, how could *we*, who have words of our common language in mind, construct a private language? We would be bound to devise words which would be based, at some level, on words of the ordinary language. Thus, it appears, as Ayer has pointed out, that the private language is not in any sense to be a code. Not only are words of the common language not permitted, but also words which are transcriptions of them. Ayer makes the point also that a private language constructed in such a way would be translatable into the public language, and so could quite well cease to be 'private'. Are we to conclude, therefore, that the Wittgensteinian private language is not to be translatable, either in principle or in practice, into the public language? This would seem odd, for it would appear to amount to the demand that the private language is not to have rules, and as we have seen, a ruleless language is a contradiction in terms.

Now, Wittgenstein is certainly not explicitly making such an absurd demand, but it seems that when his argument is pressed further this is where it *may* lead. Take the demand, for example, that the private language must not be understandable by anyone else. Does this mean that it must not in *principle* be understandable, that is to say, that it is logically impossible for someone else to understand it, or does it simply mean that he could not understand it in practice? If the former is meant, then this would appear to amount to the demand that the 'language' shall be ruleless or have no regularities whatsoever, either of usages or constructions. This demand clearly could not be taken seriously, for if it were fulfilled what we would obtain would not be a language. If it is not fulfilled (i.e. if there are rules) then it would appear that the language could not be said to be absolutely private, because in principle understandable by others.

The only sensible interpretation of the demand, then, is to interpret it as meaning that the language could in *principle* be understood by someone else, but that it could not in practice be understood unless its inventor were in a position to explain it or provide clues for understanding it and he chose to do so. Whether he could in fact do this, on the basis of the conditions laid down by Wittgenstein, we shall consider later. The real problem is not, therefore, to construct a language which could not in principle be understood by others (for this seems impossible if what is constructed is a language) but whether an individual is able to recognise and classify his inner experiences, and know when his different sensations repeat themselves, apart from his outward expressions of them and apart from any knowledge of a common language.

Because it appears that Wittgenstein denies that any words of the common language are to be available to the individual, either directly or indirectly, it seems that Ayer is on the right lines in considering the case of a Robinson Crusoe left alone on an island while still an infant unable to speak. Ayer maintains that it is not 'self-contradictory' to suppose that he might conceivably develop names for the objects he sees around him, because there is no doubt of his ability to recognise them and to remember what he sees, although of course he may sometimes make mistakes – he may think, for example, that a bird he sees is the same as one he had seen previously when in fact it was a different bird. The question is whether he is in any a worse position when it comes to recognising and identifying his own sensations. Ayer points out quite rightly that he has only his memory to rely on whether he is trying to identify objective things or subjective sensations. Is his position any worse when it comes to remembering his sensations? We must remember that Crusoe is not allowed to scratch himself, to wipe his perspiring brow, to rub his bruised shin, to groan, or to weep when he feels sad and lonely. For such actions might become objective criteria to him of his sensations and feelings, and on Wittgenstein's thesis these are ruled out. So let us imagine a Crusoe who never betrays by any kind of expression or action the feelings he experiences. Even Wittgenstein could not deny that such a stoical figure would *have* feelings – the poor fellow would be a mass of repressions, and we would hope that Man Friday when he came would be a psychiatrist! But Wittgenstein would deny that he would be able to remember or recognise any of his feelings; it thus appears that his world of inner experiences would seem to him chaotic and unordered because he would have no means of reducing it to order. We now have to enquire whether this would be likely to be the case, as Wittgenstein's argument implies.

Although Wittgenstein can deny to Crusoe external actions or other ways of expressing his sensations, he can hardly deny that many of his sensations will be localised. Crusoe may not be permitted to rub his shin but he still has the pain in his *shin*. He can hardly help, too, differentiating between the pain from a bruise and an itch, because in the former case he knocks some part of himself against an external object (assuming for the moment that 'inner criteria' are impossible). However, perhaps Wittgenstein would not permit us to consider pains arising from bruises because of the presence of an external object to help in identification. Perhaps we are permitted to consider only sensations which arise in us somehow spontaneously, without any apparent external cause. Unfortunately, Wittgenstein does not sort out sensations in this way. However, to try to put his case in a strong light let us take the case of the headache. When Crusoe has a headache would it seem to him a new experience on each occasion it occurred? We can say at once of course that he would not mistake it for a toe-ache, because presumably he does not confuse his toes with his head; and if he does distinguish between his toes and his head, would he not be able to dis-

tinguish (and recognise) sensations in his toes and head respectively?
Wittgenstein does not appear to have considered the factor of
localisation as one of the means by which we are able to differentiate and order sensations. However, assuming that Crusoe will
know where his sensations are, in the case of those which can be
localised, and that this fact may help him to sort some of them out,
we are still left with the question whether he can distinguish, for
example, a spontaneously arising ache in his elbow from a spontaneously arising itch on his elbow. But this example won't do
either, for he might be able to tell that the itch seems on the surface
of his skin while the ache seems inside his elbow. Well, then, would
he be able to differentiate between an itch and a pain felt at different times somewhere on the surface of his skin, assuming that the
itch is a well-defined itch and the pain a well-defined pain? Even
if he is not allowed to scratch in the one case or rub in the other,
can we deny him the right to *want* to scratch or rub, and why should
not such impulses be to him criteria of his sensations? And might he
not be able to remember that he had wanted to scratch or rub on
previous occasions? Someone might reply that to want to do something is simply another feeling, and no more capable of being remembered than the itch or the pain. However, it seems legitimate
to distinguish between thoughts and feelings, although they may
accompany each other. If Crusoe could remember that he had on
previous occasions wanted to scratch or rub himself (without actually doing so) then this may help him to order his inner experiences.
If he wanted to weep then he would know that he was sad, if he
wanted to laugh then he would know that he was happy. The question seems to be whether there are *any* sort of internal criteria which
Crusoe could apply, that is, if we try to argue on the basis of Wittgenstein's assumption of the necessity of criteria.

This assumption could, of course, be questioned. Strawson states
bluntly that it is untrue that one cannot recognise and identify sensations 'unless one uses criteria', and considers sensations where 'the
rival pull of "expression" or "manifestation" is weaker or non-
existent', as in the case of tastes. Here, he argues, if one pushes the
question 'What is the criterion of identity?', one can only reply,
'Well, the taste itself' (p. 30 above). However, it is a fact that when
we taste, we taste *something*, and this external object may help us
to identify the taste. When we taste something we have not tasted
before we try to remember if it tastes like anything else – we might
say 'It tastes like onions', for example, but without directly comparing the new taste with the taste of an onion by obtaining an

onion and tasting it. Strawson thinks apparently that the external
object plays no part in identifying tastes, for he states that 'we do
not identify the taste by means of the associated substance by allusion to which we name it'. While this may be true in some cases, it
seems doubtful in the case of tastes which may not be well defined or
which may be easily confused.

To leave Wittgenstein's demand for criteria for the moment, one
might be tempted to discuss the physiological aspects to which he
pays little attention. Thus one might argue that because sensory
experiences do in some way modify the nervous system, there may
be something like a physiological 'memory' (or familiarity) which
plays a part in our conscious remembering; that because our nervous
apparatus is affected, or modified, in a similar way by similar sensory experiences, we are assisted to recognise and to classify these
experiences mentally. Perhaps 'bells can be rung' at the physiological
level which is in some way responsible (in some cases at least) for
bells being run in our conscious remembering. Such a thing might
happen even in the case of emotional states (as distinct from sensations), for it cannot be denied that emotional states affect the
nervous system. However, one would need to be a competent physio-
logist to put all this in the proper language, and to show its ten-
ability clearly, if it is tenable. If it were, then it would seem that
Wittgenstein's stress on external criteria, or what we have termed
'sensation-behaviour', might be gravely misplaced from some points
of view. It would not need to be held that these criteria are of such
importance in the individual's recognition and identification of his
own sensations. Hence it would make little difference to Crusoe's
ability to recognise and identify his sensations if he were denied the
external 'natural expressions' of them.

Another, and related, physiological argument, which may suggest
that some sort of internal private criteria are possible, rests on the
fact that we are conscious of recurring bodily states and it is to these
states that sensation names are often attached. When our body is in
a certain condition, of which we are aware, we say we feel cold;
when in another condition, that we feel hot, and so on. It is hard
to conceive that a person might be very hot or very cold without
showing any outward sign of his condition, but his behaviour and
appearance might be the same when he felt cool and when he felt
moderately warm; and yet there would be differences in his internal
physiological condition which certain tests might reveal, and which
would be revealed in the reports he gave on the two occasions. Wittgenstein does not seem to stress the fact that we can be aware of

certain of our bodily states, and that this is an important factor in the sensation-language that we have built up. His concentration on the external manifestations of sensations seems to have led him to attach far less significance to physiological factors than perhaps he ought to have done. The expression 'feeling hot' may be regarded as related to a set of physiological statements, some of which will refer to external factors, but others of which will refer to internal bodily conditions. Why should not the internal physiological correlatives of sensations in some cases at least be regarded as private criteria to the individual? – that is, if we still wish to talk in terms of criteria.

If it is agreed that Crusoe, in the absence of outward criteria, would nevertheless be able to recognise and identify his sensations (especially in the case of those related to specific bodily conditions, such as heat, cold, thirst, etc., of which he would be aware), then it is not impossible that he should develop names for them. It might be objected, however, that although he might develop certain signs for his sensations (as well as for external objects), these signs would not constitute a language. This is one objection brought by Rhees against Ayer's argument. Rhees writes: 'Ayer's Crusoe may use marks for particular purposes – to show where he has hidden something perhaps – and with as great regularity as we care to think', but this 'is not what we mean by the regular use of an expression in a language'. He then argues that Crusoe, even though he might use his signs regularly, still 'does not understand them' because 'he cannot be guided by his signs in just the way in which you and I may be guided by words' (p. 71 above). Perhaps Crusoe *would* be guided by his signs in a different way from the way in which we are guided by our words, but what is important is the possibility that Crusoe *might* come to use certain signs consistently. If this much is admitted, and Rhees does appear to admit it, then it would seem to become very difficult to argue that Crusoe's world of inner experiences would seem to him chaotic and unordered because he would have no way of telling whether he was remembering his sensations correctly or not; or if he did remember that he would only *think* that he remembered. It is on these grounds that Wittgenstein denies that the individual using a private language could understand the words he uses although he might '*appear to understand*' them (*Inv.* 269). It is difficult to know if Wittgenstein is conceding anything by this remark, but if one admits that regular usage might be involved in this 'appearance of understanding', then it would seem hardly possible to argue on the same grounds as Wittgenstein that he does not *really* understand the words he uses. For it seems a chief point in Wittgenstein's argument that he *could* not use his words consistently. Perhaps this is why Rhees shifts the level of argument, contrasting Crusoe's use of his signs with the use of words in a public language, asserting that even though Crusoe might use his signs 'for the same purpose', this is not the same as 'using an expression in the same way'; and so, that there would be 'nothing of a rule of language in that'. We must recall, however, that when Wittgenstein sets out to show the impossibility of a private language, he imagines that the individual constructing the language writes down the letter 'S' every time he experiences a certain sensation. This he cannot do meaningfully, maintains Wittgenstein; hence he is quite unable to construct a private language, because there is no means of knowing whether he has used 'S' consistently and he certainly cannot know himself. From this we may conclude that, if it could be reasonably maintained that the individual was capable of using 'S' consistently, this *would* be a rule of his language, i.e. that the sign 'S' stood for or named such-and-such a sensation. So it seems that Rhees's argument amounts to the denial of the possibility of a private rule of language on the grounds that languages *are* public and that we can therefore speak only of public rules. Such an argument leaves us at a loss what to call a private regular use of an expression or sign if it is admitted that such regular usage is possible. However, perhaps it does not matter much if one does not wish to call private regular uses of signs 'rules', for, as emphasised already, the crucial point is whether or not such private regular uses are possible (rather than what we call them); and if preferred we can simply call them 'regularities of private usage'.

It now remains to consider whether our Crusoe, if he could develop signs as names for his sensations and use them consistently, would be able to explain their meaning to anyone else. It was asserted earlier that for a private set of signs to be a language it must *in principle* be understandable by someone else, for the signs must be regularly and consistently used – in this sense it must have rules. Wittgenstein denies that a private language could be understood by anyone else in the absence of 'outward criteria' of sensations. Ayer, again disagreeing with Wittgenstein, imagines that Man Friday comes along, and considers the possibility that he might be so mentally and emotionally attuned to Crusoe (we might even go as far as to imagine that Man Friday is Crusoe's long-lost Siamese twin, separated from him shortly after birth) that whenever one of them experienced a certain sensation, the other experienced it also.

'In that case,' maintains Ayer, 'when one of them described what he was feeling the other might very well follow the description, even though he had no external evidence to guide him' (p. 58 above). Ayer, of course, admits the extreme difficulty of mutual understanding if all their experience were private, but goes so far as to assert that it is conceivable that Man Friday might 'see into Crusoe's soul' and understand his language even if his (i.e. Man Friday's) experiences were unlike Crusoe's (p. 58 above). One wonders, however, whether it is necessary to press the argument to such extremes as this. Wittgenstein's thesis does not bar us from assuming that Man Friday's experiences are in fact similar to Crusoe's. Nor is it necessary to assume that Man Friday's experiences are private in the sense that Crusoe's are. He, we may assume, will express his sensations in the usual way and will speak the language of the people among whom he was brought up. Under these conditions, would he be able to understand Crusoe's sensation-language? Now it seems that Crusoe is in a better position to understand Man Friday's language, and let us imagine that Man Friday laboriously sets about teaching Crusoe, by means of his (i.e. Man Friday's) sensation-behaviour, what the words of his (public) sensation-language stand for. Crusoe, of course, has only his private sensations and feelings to match against Man Friday's behaviour, and the question is whether he could match correctly the words of his language with those of Man Friday's. It has to be admitted that if Crusoe were totally unable to understand the significance of Man Friday's sensation-behaviour, except to observe that different sounds (or words) accompanied various types of behaviour, he would not be able to match his own signs correctly with those used by Man Friday. But if, as was suggested before, he had impulses to perform certain actions when he experienced his sensations, and if these actions that he wanted to carry out, but did not, corresponded to Man Friday's actions, then he could work out a correct correspondence between his words and Man Friday's. When he had done this he would be able to teach Man Friday the meanings of the words in his language, at least of those which referred to the sort of sensations which Man Friday had also. If Crusoe's sensations were entirely different from Man Friday's, then the latter could not come to understand the former's language, except on the basis of a hypothesis such as that introduced by Ayer – that is, that Man Friday might be able to see into Crusoe's soul.

All this, of course, may sound implausible, but then so does the claim that our Crusoe might develop a private language in the first instance. All that we can speak of, it seems, are conceivabilities and logical possibilities. With Ayer, I am not convinced that Wittgenstein or Rhees has shown that a private language in the sense defined by Wittgenstein is a logical impossibility, and I hold therefore that it is not self-contradictory to suppose that Crusoe *might* develop such a language. I have tried to adduce some further grounds for this belief – but I do not believe that *in practice* an individual isolated on an island from infancy would ever come to develop a language. It can hardly be denied that language is first and foremost a social affair which developed as a means of communication *between* individuals and not as a means whereby a man communicated with himself, although we can agree with Ayer that some particular individual must have been the first to use a particular symbol (or symbols) (p. 55 above).

Finally, it remains to discuss just how much significance is to be attached to the problem we have considered, and whether the possibility or otherwise of a Wittgenstein private language is crucial for deciding whether or not we are entitled to assert that our sensations (feelings, etc.) are, in part at least, private. I am inclined to think that it is not as crucial as one might think at first, or as crucial as Wittgenstein seemed to think it was, and I shall try to show this briefly. In the first place, as we have seen, it does not seem at all easy to meet the conditions laid down by Wittgenstein, and if we do try to meet them they seem so extreme that we are inclined to say at once that it would be impossible for an individual in those circumstances to develop any language whatsoever, whether referring to public objects or to his private sensations. It seems reasonably clear that any of us could invent new words for our sensations to replace the familiar ones, and it might be impossible for our new words to be understood, unless we chose to explain them, or give their meanings in terms of the familiar words. But this, it seems, is not what Wittgenstein means by a private language, for such a language would be based directly on the public language. This is why it seems necessary to consider the case of someone not in a position to be taught a common language. If we are convinced that it is not logically impossible or self-contradictory that such an individual might develop a set of signs by means of which he named some at least of his sensations, let us say those of which he would be most acutely aware, then it would seem more likely that our public sensation-language, besides having reference to publicly observable manifestations of sensations, also has reference to inner private experiences themselves. This need not lead us to say that we know what 'pain' means, for example, *only* from our own case, but it suggests that our own inner experience of pain plays a part, even a considerable part, in our understanding of the word. The problem might be put in this way: Could a person who had never experienced a pain be said to have as full an understanding of the word as a person who had had such an experience, even though the former might learn to apply the word correctly to cases of pain in other people? Is this all there is to the understanding of words standing for sensations, feelings, etc.?

If the possibility of a private language strengthens the case for arguing that a public language may have private reference, does it follow that the public language has no such private reference if we are convinced that it is logically impossible for an individual in isolation to develop a private language? I would suggest that it does not follow. Even if an individual, entirely locked up in his world of private experiences, without any means of giving expression to his sensations, were totally unable to order his sensations or detect in them any regularity, so that any names he attempted to give them would be so ambiguous as to be meaningless, this would not imply that he would have no sensations or feelings at all. There seems little objection to saying that our public language is a means whereby we are enabled to order and classify our sensations, but it does not seem to follow that, if we were in a position in which we could not name our sensations, we might as well say that they do not exist apart from our ability to order and name them (or apart from our natural expressions of them). Thus, even those who accept Wittgenstein's argument that a private language is impossible because in the absence of external 'criteria' there are no means of recognising and identifying sensations, cannot thereby argue that the notion of a 'private experience' is for this reason satisfactorily dispensed with. In any case, when it *can* be recognised and identified a sensation is still presumably a 'something' and the question still remains what this 'something' is.

Whatever this 'something' is, on Wittgenstein's terms it cannot of course be private. In an interesting passage Wittgenstein considers the statement 'Another person can't have my pains' (*Inv.* 253). He asks 'What are *my* pains?' and claims that 'In so far as it makes *sense* to say that my pain is the same as his, it is also possible for us both to have the same pain'. He adds that Siamese twins might even feel pain in the same, not merely a corresponding, place. One feels that only in this case, however, might it make sense to say that two individuals had the same pain; but even here it might be doubtful, for one individual (although connected to another) might feel pain more acutely than the other. In the case of separate individuals I doubt very much if one would ever want to claim that two people could have the *same* pain, if 'same' is taken to mean 'one and the same'. We might say that they both had pains in the same places, or that their pains were similar if they seemed to have a similar cause (e.g. pains caused by the prick of a needle), but this is not asserting that their pains are exactly the same in intensity, duration, etc., and still less that they have one and the same pain. We might say that one person is wearing a hat the same as that of another person, but this does not mean that they are wearing one and the same hat, or that it is possible for them to do so.

I do not take such a public view of sensations as Wittgenstein takes. I consider that it makes sense for me to speak of *my* pains, not only as implying that it is *I* who have them, but as also suggesting that they are my personal private experiences which it is unlikely that anyone else can fully comprehend, no matter how carefully he may observe my external manifestations of them. I do not believe, therefore, that anyone else can have *my* pains, although he might well have pains *like* mine. But why do I believe that someone else's pains might be similar to mine? Partly of course because it is true, as Wittgenstein points out, that pains, and other inner experiences, often do have characteristic outward expressions. If someone puts his hand to his head and says, 'My head is simply *splitting!*' then I believe that his pain is something like the pain I have when I have a headache. I think, however, that this is only part of the story. To try to fill it out (I will not say *complete* it) one might refer again to physiological aspects of the matter, and raise the question what part our knowledge that other people have similar physiological constitutions as ourselves plays in our belief that they do in fact have similar sorts of sensory experiences as we do. Would it not seem odd if this were not so? I think it is because of his lack of physiological considerations that Wittgenstein's beetle in the box analogy goes astray. The beetle is not part of the box, nor connected in any way with it. Are sensations *in* us in the same way as beetles are in boxes? If they are not, and if there is some sort of connection between sensations and the 'boxes' (i.e. the bodies) they are 'in', then if these 'boxes' (or bodies) are alike, are we not justified in believing that inner experiences, such as pain, may be felt in a similar way by different people? This does not mean that we can know *exactly* how another's pain feels to him, but we might often feel justified in saying that we have a fairly good idea, especially if we have ourselves a pain in the corresponding place and/or arising from a similar cause. And we can say this without ruling out individual differences – there are differences in the physiological structures of different individuals and why should there not be differences, corresponding differences perhaps, in the sensations they feel? Thus, given normal physiological conditions, I do not think we have said everything, as Wittgenstein seems to think we have, when we emphasise the part played by the external manifestations of sensations in our use and understanding of our sensation-language. I do not think that this is *all* that is involved in our understanding. Certainly sensation-behaviour plays an important part in our learning of the language, for that can be pointed to by someone else when teaching us the words, whereas *our* experiences cannot be pointed to.

(ii) *Newton Garver*

Wittgenstein poses a problem by asking: 'Could we also imagine a language in which a person could write down or give vocal expression to his inner experiences – his feelings, moods, and the rest – for his private use? (*Inv.* 243). The doctrine contained in the following sections is one of the central results of Wittgenstein's later work, and our aim in this paper will be to set it out in clear form.

It is crucial for understanding what follows not to confuse this problem about the possibility of private language with either (*a*) the question whether I can, for my private use, keep a diary in ordinary English to record my pains, moods, and so on; or (*b*) the question whether there could be a language *in fact* used by only one person but *capable* of being understood by any explorer clever enough to see the connection between certain sounds (or marks) and certain circumstances. The answer to question (*a*) is clearly affirmative, and no one will mistake it for the question Wittgenstein raised. But the discussion between Professor A. J. Ayer and Mr. R. Rhees (Chapter II above) indicates that question (*b*) is more difficult and that it may become confused with Wittgenstein's problem. Both Ayer and Rhees show a correct verbal understanding of the problem: Ayer formulates the thesis he is attacking as 'that for a person to be able to attach meaning to a sign it is necessary that other people should

be capable of understanding it too' (p. 55 above); and Rhees
says that the main question 'is a question of whether I can have a
private understanding; whether I can understand something which
could not be said in a language which anyone else could understand'
(p. 66 above). Appearances notwithstanding, however, the point of
contention between them is question (*b*). Ayer's argument shows that
there might be a Robinson Crusoe with a language which no one
else understands, but which could be understood by another person
(say by a Man Friday). Rhees's main concern is to reject this argument, on the grounds that a language must consist of rules, and
there could be nothing to show that a Crusoe was following rules
rather than simply behaving (as ants do) with regularity. It appears
to me that Rhees is wrong in this contention against Ayer; but at
any rate this controversy should be distinguished from the question
they formulated – viz. the question raised by Wittgenstein about
private language.

Wittgenstein's direct discussion of the problem he has posed continues through *Inv.* 280; it forms the initial part of an investigation
of the grammar of 'pain' and other sensation-words, which extends
through *Inv.* 317. The two sections of this paper will be devoted to
an exegesis of the first two steps in this presentation: (*a*) the exposé
of certain considerations which lend plausibility to the notion of a
private language (*Inv.* 244–54), and (*b*) a *reductio ad absurdum* of
the notion of private language or private understanding[3] (*Inv.* 256–
270).

I

Inv. 244–54 can best be understood against the background of the
following argument (P):

(1) Sensations are private; no one else can have my pains.
(2) I commonly use words to refer to my sensations.
(3) In any category the meanings of at least some of the words I
use to refer to things are the things to which these words refer.
Therefore, (4) the meanings which I have for the words which
I use to refer to my sensations *cannot* be grasped by another
person; I have a private understanding of these words, and so
(by analogy) does every other person when he uses such words.

Each of the steps in P has a great deal of plausibility, and the
argument itself, although not strictly deductive, has a great deal of

force. Even without (3), which is the only premise that can be flatly rejected,[4] one is strongly tempted to agree to the conclusion on the basis of (1) and (2). And yet the conclusion is unacceptable, because all the evidence (apart from this philosophical argument) supports the proposition that other people *do* understand me when I refer to my pains, itches, etc. The first problem for Wittgenstein is to remove this puzzle by bringing out the real import of (1) and (2).

When Wittgenstein asks the question at the begining of *Inv.* 244 'How do words *refer* to sensations?' he is not asking a question about private language but about our ordinary everyday language. And of course there is no problem about that: we all know how to use words to refer to and talk about our sensations. If we then ask how the connection between the name and the thing named (the sensation) is established, what kind of answer do we expect? Wittgenstein reminds us that the only way to answer such a question is to see how a human being learns the meaning of names of sensations – of the word 'pain', for example. A child might be taught verbal expressions of pain (exclamations or sentences) in circumstances when adults see from his behaviour, from his natural expressions of pain, that he is hurt. A foreigner might learn by our pricking him with a pin and saying, 'See, that's pain!' or by our pretending to be in pain. What is common to these and other learning situations is certain circumstances, which always include a particular sort of action or expression on the part of some living being viz. pain-behaviour); and what is learned is the regular connection between the word 'pain' and such circumstances. Therefore the meaning of 'pain' is logically dependent upon there being natural expressions of pain. Wittgenstein generalises this point in *Inv.* 281: 'It comes to this: only of a living human being and what resembles (behaves like) a living human being can one say: it has sensations; it sees; is blind; hears; is deaf; is conscious or unconscious.'

The point of these remarks is to show that our use of words for sensations is tied up with the natural expressions of sensation (which are publicly observable): 'pain' depends upon pain-behaviour rather than on any inner private experience for its meaning. Hence when we explain how it is that words refer to sensations we do not have to fall back on mysterious private experiences. If we understand this much about premise (2) of P we shall be less tempted to use it as a justification for asserting (4).

The examination of premise (1) extends through *Inv.* 246–54. Wittgenstein's main point is that both parts of (1) are grammatical statements; that is to say, they might be used to teach a person how to use the words 'pain' or 'sensation', but could not be used for ordinary communication between persons already fully conversant with the language. In this respect these propositions differ sharply (in spite of a resemblance in the pattern of words) from 'My head-aches are severe' and 'No one else can look at my diary'. They are – like 'You play solitaire by yourself' (cf. *Inv.* 248) and 'Every rod has a length' (cf. *Inv.* 251) – propositions which are misleading because their form makes them look empirical, whereas they are really grammatical.

Three points should be noted about the logic of grammatical propositions: (i) The absurdity which results from the denial of a grammatical proposition is not a formal contradiction,[5] and in this respect a grammatical proposition differs from what has ordinarily been called an analytic one.[6] (ii) There is no sharp boundary be-tween grammatical and empirical propositions. Wittgenstein is aware of this when he takes note of 'the fluctuation of scientific definitions: what today counts as an observed concomitant of a phenomenon will tomorrow be used to define it (*Inv.* 79). (iii) Some propositions may be used as either grammatical or empirical – e.g. 'Pure water freezes at 0° Centigrade' may either be used to teach someone what we mean by '0° Centigrade' or to teach him a physical fact.

The fact that the propositions in (1) are grammatical bears on the issue in hand in two ways: First, the natural employment for a grammatical proposition is to teach someone about the use of a word, and *not* to support a metaphysical thesis. This fact gives us a good reason for maintaining that (1) is misused in P. In particular, 'No one else can have my pains' cannot be used to support the con-tention that your pains must be different from mine; for if there is no criterion for my pain being identical with yours, it makes no sense to say that our pains are different ones. Second, to say that a proposition is grammatical is to say that it expresses some feature of the language – in the case of 'No one else can have my pains' that it ordinarily *makes no sense* to say of two people that they both have one and the same pain. This tells us something about the *use* of 'pain', about the common practice with the word. If there were no common practice with the word, there could be no grammatical propositions about it. If, therefore, the warrant for saying 'No one else can have my pains' is the grammar of the word 'pain' (and it is), 'pain' must have a use, must have an ordinary meaning rather than a private and incommunicable one. Understood in this way (1) not only does not support (4) but is incompatible with it.

II

P is only one of a number of arguments which have led people to accept (4) or some similar doctrine. Probably the most influential of the views which lead to an acceptance of such a doctrine is Cartesian dualism, which maintains that Mind has nothing to do with Matter – i.e. that there can be no causal or conceptual connections between 'mental phenomena' (such as sensations) and material or physical phenomena (such as bodily movements or other behaviour). An obvious consequence of this view is that the meaning of 'pain' and other sensation-words *cannot* be tied up with natural expressions of pain and certain physical circumstances. It would seem that on this view we must be able to learn these words only by associating them (each one of us privately) with appropriate sensations.

In *Inv.* 256 Wittgenstein proposes a thoroughly Cartesian account of the matter: 'But suppose I didn't have my natural expression of sensation, but had only the sensation? And now I simply *associate* names with sensations and use these names in descriptions.' In the following section, speaking for himself now, he makes two observations on this account: first, a person could not make himself understood when he used these words, since no one else could know with what he associated them; second, we cannot say that these words are names of sensations, since to name sensations presupposes the *grammar* of sensation-words, and this grammar, as we have seen, depends on the natural expression of sensations which is by hypothesis ruled out.

These comments are apparently accepted by Wittgenstein's Cartesian interlocutor, and the problem that then remains is the one which Rhees rightly regards as central (p. 66 above): Can't there be a *private* understanding of such words, even though they could not be understood by other people? In order to proceed with his *reductio ad absurdum* argument against this proposal, Wittgenstein allows his interlocutor to propose the following case for consideration at the beginning of *Inv.* 258: 'Let us imagine the following case. I want to keep a diary about the recurrence of a certain sensation. To this end I associate the sign "E" and write this sign in a calendar for every day on which I have the sensation.' Wittgenstein's examination of this case and its absurdity extends through *Inv.* 270.

In order to understand the case which is being examined it is important to realise that it is being proposed by the Cartesian interlocutor and not by either Wittgenstein or an ordinary man. It could not be seriously put forward by Wittgenstein because on his view the case is unintelligible (though not logically self-contradictory); for to say that 'E' is used to record the recurrence of some sensation implies that 'E' is in some sense a sign for a sensation, and this in turn presupposes that 'E' shares the ordinary grammar of sensation-words, which is precisely what the proposed case attempts to rule out. It also could not be an ordinary man who proposes the case; for I can write 'E' in a diary to keep track of the recurrence of a certain sensation (say an ache in my left shoulder) and, because the grammar of the sensation-words is presupposed, many of the difficulties which Wittgenstein urges against the proposed case will not arise. It is only when the case is proposed by a Cartesian, who rules out any conceptual connection between sensation-words and natural expressions of pain, that the case is philosophically interesting.

The only avenue open to the Cartesian is to suggest that the connection is established by a kind of ostensive definition – not the ordinary sort, to be sure, since no one can point to a sensation, but a *private* ostensive definition: I concentrate inwardly on the sensation when I write the sign down. The whole idea of giving oneself a private definition is suspect from the start, because it is pointless: like my right hand's giving money to my left hand, no one would be any the richer for it (*Inv.* 268). But pointless or not, let us see if the idea might work. Wittgenstein presents three telling objections which show that it cannot.

(i) If this private ostensive definition is to achieve anything it must enable you to get the connection *right* each time, but in the present case there is no criterion of correctness: because there could be no distinction between thinking you were right and being right we cannot speak of rightness here at all (*Inv.* 258). You cannot even *believe* you get the connection right (that that sensation is the same one again); for you can only believe what can be true or false, and that that sensation is the same one again could not be determined to be true or false; at best you may believe that you believe it (*Inv.* 260). Since there is no criterion for saying that a sensation is that certain one again, you could not promise yourself, or privately undertake, always to use 'E' for that certain sensation: the undertaking would be empty because you could never know whether you had fulfilled it or not (*Inv.* 263). In all of these ways Wittgenstein shows us that the lack of any criterion of identity for the sensation makes a 'private' definition impossible. Therefore there is no possible way, on the Cartesian view, that a connection could be established between a word and a sensation, and the mere fact that we do use words to refer to sensations is a refutation of dualism.

(ii) We naturally assume that when you write down 'E' in your diary you must be making a note of something, but Wittgenstein reminds us that the assumption is unjustified. 'E' is an idle mark; it has no use, no function, no connection with anything. How *could* we make a record of anything with such an idle mark?[7]

(iii) Even assuming, *per impossibile*, that a connection between 'E' and a certain sensation were to be established by means of a private ostensive definition, where would that get us? There would be a certain sign 'E' which you privately understand. Could we call it the name of a sensation? We would have no justification for doing so, for by calling some mark the name of a sensation we make it intelligible in the common language (or perhaps better: in calling it the name of a sensation we presuppose it to be intelligible in the common language), whereas 'E' is intelligible to you alone (*Inv.* 261). Names of sensations have a certain grammar, and 'E' as yet has none.

These points constitute an effective *reductio ad absurdum* of the Cartesian's proposal: writing 'E' in the diary is a pointless act, a record of nothing whatever; 'E' itself is a meaningless mark, having no established connection with anything and no possible use.

We have now left to consider only the perplexing section in which Wittgenstein appears to make an about-face (*Inv.* 270). He says: 'Let us now imagine a use for the entry of the sign "E" in my diary. I discover that whenever I have a particular sensation a manometer shows that my blood-pressure rises. So I shall be able to say that my blood-pressure is rising without using any apparatus. This is a useful result.' After what Wittgenstein has said about 'E', this turn strikes us as a bit surprising. A moment ago the entry of 'E' in the diary was 'a note of nothing whatever', and now it leads to a useful result! There is a weird twist here; all of a sudden the whole case changes.

Note first that we can give a sort of definition of 'E' now: 'E' is the sign for the sensation you have when your blood-pressure rises.[8] From this it follows (*a*) that when you write 'E' in your diary, you are really making a note of something, viz. of a sensation, and (*b*) that the sign 'E' can be explained to other people; it is no longer intelligible only to you. 'E' is presented to us in *Inv.* 270 as a sign for a sensation, and since it is no longer supposed that the whole significance of the sign comes from being 'associated' with 'something about which nothing can be said' (*Inv.* 304), we no longer have any ground for doubting that it really is just what it is presented as; and we have a further justification in calling 'E' the name of a sensation in the fact that 'E' has the grammar of a sensation-word: only you can know when to write down 'E', and so on. Note second that the problem about the identity of the sensation which you record by the entry of 'E' in your diary has completely disappeared. If your blood-pressure has risen, it makes no difference at all whether, in the sense required by the Cartesian, the sensation was 'really' the same or not. As Wittgenstein says: 'Now it seems quite indifferent whether I have recognised the sensation *right* or not. Let us suppose that I regularly identify it wrong, it does not matter in the least. And that alone shows that the hypothesis that I made a mistake is mere show' (*Inv.* 270; see also 271, 293).

Thus we see that in *Inv.* 270 the entry of 'E' in your diary can no longer be supposed to get its significance in the Cartesian manner outlined in *Inv.* 256; in order to give it a use we have to jettison all of the restrictions of the Cartesian proposal. In *Inv.* 256–69 Wittgenstein's purpose is to show that a sign which is supposed to be simply 'associated' with a sensation cannot have a use; in *Inv.* 270 he wants to show the converse, viz. that any sign which has a use cannot be supposed to be simply 'associated' with a sensation. The utility of a sign and its intelligibility in the common language go hand in hand, and it is this point which Wittgenstein brings out in *Inv.* 270 – another nail, as it were, in the coffin of the idea that there might be a private language.

IV Behaviourism and the private language argument

(i) C. W. K. Mundle

Though Wittgenstein professed to eschew philosophical theories, he seems to have accepted a theory which could not be confirmed simply by observing how people talk when not doing philosophy, namely a form of Behaviourism. Consider his suggestion (*Inv.* 244) that a word like 'pain' is used in place of the natural expressions of pain such as crying, that 'the verbal expression of pain replaces crying and does not describe it'; in other words, that 'I am in pain' is a sophisticated way of groaning, and is no more a statement than is a groan.[1] This account could of course apply only to utterances in the first person: ascriptions of pain to other people would presumably be treated as statements referring to their actual or potential behaviour. If Wittgenstein had formulated this view explicitly, it would presumably have run something like this: that words which are ostensibly used to name or refer to private experiences can have meaning only by referring to overt behaviour (as in 'he is in pain') or by deputising for other, and 'natural', forms of behaviour (as in 'I am in pain'). Wittgenstein's main reason for putting forward this account seems to have been his acceptance of a questionable theory of meaning, namely that statements can be meaningful only if they are *publicly* verifiable.

Wittgenstein did not adopt the crudest kind of Behaviourism – denying the occurrence of private experiences (see *Inv.* 308). Such a denial would be vacuous according to his theory of meaning. He does, however, make statements which it is difficult to interpret otherwise than as asserting that *nothing can be said* about private experiences, for example: 'if we construe the grammar of the expression of sensation on the model of "object and name" the object drops out of consideration as irrelevant' (*Inv.* 293); and 'it [the sensation itself] is not a something, but not a nothing either! The conclusion was only that a nothing would serve just as well as a something about which nothing could be said' (*Inv.* 304).

The thesis that nothing can be said about private experiences can fairly be labelled Linguistic Behaviourism. I shall not survey all of Wittgenstein's pronouncements which might be cited for or against interpreting him as holding this thesis. My purpose is to examine two arguments which he used, apparently in order to establish this kind of behaviourism, and which have been used by others for the same purpose; for if one wishes to reject this thesis, as I do, these arguments must be met. I refer to (1) his Diary argument (as I shall call it), concerning the man who set out to record the recurrence of a certain sensation by writing 'the sign "E"' in his diary each day he has the sensation (*Inv.* 258–65); and (2) his Beetles argument, in which he invites us to suppose that everyone has a box with something in it which we call 'a beetle', but 'no one can look into anyone else's box, and everyone says he knows what a beetle is only by looking at *his* beetle' (*Inv.* 293).

Wittgenstein seems to have thought that each of these arguments establishes the same conclusion – that private experiences can have no place in the language-game, i.e. that we cannot (logically) talk about private experiences. (Notice that my last sentence is an appropriate way of formulating Wittgenstein's conclusion only if 'talking about *x*' is used, as I shall use it, literally, i.e. as involving *referring* to *x*. A behaviourist could of course formulate his thesis by saying, not 'we cannot talk about private experiences', but 'people do of course "talk about" e.g. their pains, but what they are then doing is not referring to anything private, but referring to, or exhibiting, pain-behaviour'.) In fact Wittgenstein's above-mentioned arguments would, if valid, establish different conclusions. His Beetles argument would establish that you can never know what, if anything, another person is referring to when he talks about his private experiences; but this argument would not establish the more extreme conclusion of the Diary argument: that you cannot significantly talk even to yourself about your own private experiences. If the Diary argument were valid, it would be superfluous to use or to discuss the Beetles argument. There is no point in asking whether your utterances can enable another person to understand your reference to your private experiences, if *you* cannot use them to *make* such a reference! So whether the Diary argument is valid is crucial and is the logically prior question.

Unfortunately Wittgenstein's extreme thesis – that a person cannot talk even to himself about his own private experiences – has been confused with other questions. This has resulted from Wittgenstein's problem being worded: 'can there be a private language?' This wording is unfortunate because it blurs the difference between the following questions:

1. Can a person meaningfully talk to himself about (use words or other symbols to refer to) his own private experiences?
2. Can a person tell others anything about his private experiences?
3. Can there be a language whose rules are kept secret by their inventor (irrespective of what this language is used to talk about)?

If 'can there be a private language?' is equated with questions 1 or 2, the meaning of saying that a symbol is private is (A) *that what it is used to refer to is a private experience*. (I shall later explain my use of 'private' in 'private experience'.) If 'can there be a private language?' is equated with question 3, the meaning of saying that a symbol is private is (B) *that the rules for its use are known only by its inventor*.

Regarding question 2, if a person can tell others something about his private experiences, the language he uses for this purpose cannot be private in sense B, but at least one of the symbols he uses must be private in sense A. Note that the anti-behaviourist need not answer question 2 by saying that it is possible to tell others *everything* about one's private experiences; it will suffice if we can tell others *something* about what goes on inside ourselves.

Regarding question 1, if a person can talk to himself about his own private experiences, he must use for this purpose symbols which are private in sense A, but these might be either private or public in sense B; for the sensation which Wittgenstein's diarist uses 'E' to (try to) refer to might be one which he would describe as, e.g., 'that pain in my left eye', and in that case the diarist can divulge his use of 'E' by explaining this in English. Alternatively, the diarist might reveal (something about) his use of 'E' by his behaviour, by groaning and clutching his left eye whenever he wrote 'E'. But Wittgenstein, when leading up to the Diary argument, says things which imply that if the diarist *could* reveal his use of 'E' in either of these ways, his signs, 'E' etc., would not count as a private language (*Inv.* 243 and 256). Thus Wittgenstein seems to have been *defining* 'private language' as a language in which communication is impossible. But there was no need for Wittgenstein to restrict 'private language' to signs whose use cannot be explained in English. That the diarist's 'E' might have the same function as 'that pain in my left eye' ought not to have worried Wittgenstein, since he denies that 'pain' or any other word in a natural language is used to refer to a private experience, and has offered an alternative account of the function of such words. If the diarist uses 'E' to refer to a sensation, or to a certain quality of a sensation, for which no natural language known to him provides a name, and which has no 'natural expression' (and no known cause), then he cannot divulge his use of 'E', and 'E' is then private in Wittgenstein's rigorous sense.

Wittgenstein seems to have confused the two senses of 'private' which I distinguished above, with the result that his own account of what he means by 'a private language' begs important questions. His account is given in *Inv.* 243 and 256.

> But could we also imagine a language in which a person could write down or give vocal expression to his inner experiences – his feelings, moods, and the rest, for his private use? – Well, can't we do this in our ordinary language? – But that it not what I mean. *The individual words of this language are to refer to what can only be known to the person speaking; to his immediate private sensations. So another person cannot understand the language.* (*Inv.* 243. My italics.)

Notice the force of 'so' in the italicised passage. Wittgenstein here takes it for granted that if a person uses words which are private in sense A (i.e. used to refer to his private experiences), these words must be private in sense B (i.e. incomprehensible to others).

> Now what about the language which describes my inner experience and which only I can understand? How do I use words to stand for my sensations? – As we ordinarily do? Then *are my words for sensations tied up with my natural expressions of sensation? In that case my language is not a 'private' one. Someone else might understand it as well as I.* (*Inv.* 256. My italics.)

Wittgenstein here lays it down that if a person's use of 'words for sensations' can be inferred by others from his behaviour, these words are not to be called 'private'. This is to *define* 'a private language' as one in which communication is impossible. But one important question which may be intended by a person who asks 'Can there be a private language'? is my question 2: Can we communicate about our private experiences? To guarantee a negative answer to this question by giving an arbitrary definition of 'private language' seems frivolous.

I want to reconsider the symposium, 'Can there be a Private Language?', by Ayer and R. Rhees (see Chapter II above). Ayer, in the opening paper, argued that my questions 1 and 2 must be answered in the affirmative. He opened his discussion by distinguishing my questions 3 and 1, and by pointing out that the answer to question 3 is obviously affirmative, but that this is not the main question which preoccupied Wittgenstein. Ayer then made some penetrating criticisms of the Diary argument, criticisms which should, I think, have finally disposed of it – but which seem to have had no effect upon Wittgenstein's followers. Perhaps this was because, in developing these criticisms, Ayer unfortunately made much use of an example – of a Robinson Crusoe alone on a desert island since early infancy – which introduced yet another interpretation of 'can there be a private language?', namely:

4. Could a person who had been completely isolated from other people since early infancy invent a language?

It was not, I think, Ayer's intention to discuss this question for its own sake. He introduced his Crusoe in order to challenge Wittgenstein's assumption that for a person to be able to attach meaning to a sign, it is necessary that other people should be capable of understanding it. Still, Ayer did, in the course of his argument, maintain that the answer to question 4 is affirmative. This was unfortunate in that it permitted Rhees to devote much of his paper to challenging Ayer on this issue by arguing that language is essentially a social institution, thus diverting attention from Ayer's arguments for answering question 1 in the affirmative.

I wish to challenge Wittgenstein's apologists to defend his negative answer to question 1. This question concerns what *we* do, or can do, so we may ignore Ayer's Robinson Crusoe. In order to try to forestall replies which change the subject, I concede that language is primarily a public institution (public in sense B), and that our learning to talk about publicly observable objects is logically and temporarily prior to our learning to talk, assuming that we do so talk, about our private experiences. As Wittgenstein points out (*Inv.* 257), if people showed no outward signs of pain, it would be impossible to teach a child the use of a word like 'toothache'. I am not going to dispute a claim which Rhees makes several times – that we could not talk about sensations unless we had already learned a language; for example, when he says that 'without language' I could not have told that one sensation feels the same as another 'if only because I could not have asked' (p. 65 above). My question is whether a person who has already learned to talk in the way that

we all have – by means of ostensive definitions, explicit or implicit
– can proceed to talk about his private experiences. An affirmative
answer to this question is all that we need to refute Linguistic Behaviourism.

Wittgenstein's Diary argument runs as follows:

> I want to keep a diary about the recurrence of a certain sensation.
> To this end I associate it with the sign 'E' and write this sign in
> the diary for every day on which I have the sensation ... I can
> give myself a kind of ostensive definition [of 'E'] ... I speak, or
> write this sign down, and at the same time I concentrate my
> attention between the sign and the sensation. – But 'I impress it
> on myself' can only mean: this process brings it about that I
> remember the connection *right* in the future. But *in the present
> case I have no criterion of correctness*. One would like to say:
> whatever is going to seem right to me is right. And that only
> means that we can't talk about 'right' (*Inv*. 258).

The sentence which I have italicised is the crux of the argument.
It is not strengthened by the assertion in *Inv*. 261 that the diarist's
use of 'E' 'stands in need of a justification which everybody understands'; for this is simply an assertion of Wittgenstein's theory of
meaning, whose adequacy is at issue. Wittgenstein's reasoning is,
however, made more explicit in *Inv*. 265, where he says that 'justification consists in appealing to something independent', and that
you cannot 'justify' one memory by appealing to another memory,
for this would be like buying several copies of the [same] morning
paper to assure yourself that what it says is true. It is clear from
this that Wittgenstein's thesis is that the diarist cannot have any
use for 'E', that 'E' cannot have any meaning for him, because the
diarist would not be in a position to verify the correctness of his
application of 'E' on any occasion.

The short answer to this argument is to say: 'Presumably the
diarist has a memory, has the capacity to recognise what he feels as
well as what he sees or hears; and what grounds are there for em-
bracing scepticism concerning people's capacities to recognise their
sensations, and to remember some of their earlier sensations and
compare these with their present ones?' This is one of the main
points made by Ayer, but Ayer goes further. His further point could
be put like this: 'Wittgenstein requires that for a word to have
meaning for me, independent confirmation of the correctness of my
use of it must be obtainable. Well, suppose I say: "That is an apple,

isn't it?" What constitutes independent confirmation of the correctness of my use of 'apple'? It is my hearing a sound *which I have to recognise as* a token of the sentence "Yes, it's an apple"; so I have to rely on my own capacity to recognise my experiences in order to get such confirmation.' This is a well-taken point, but it would, I think, have been even more telling if Ayer had been prepared to go a stage further, by continuing thus: 'My recognising the sound I hear as the sentence "Yes, it's an apple" confirms the correctness of my own use of "apple" only because this sound (so interpreted) is evidence that another person (*a*) is having private experiences of seeing, touching, tasting or smelling the object in question, and (*b*) has performed a private act of ostensible recognition, i.e. an act of the kind that I had performed before saying "That is an apple, isn't it?" '

My talking here of '*acts*' of recognition may cause qualms. I do not wish to discuss whether recognising an apple is active rather than passive (though, as a matter of grammar, recognising is something we *do*, not something we *suffer* or *undergo*). In speaking of 'private acts' of recognition, all I wish to insist on is that as we normally use the sentence-form 'A recognised *x*', the verb refers *primarily* to an occurrence which is datable and private. It is private in the following sense (and this is how I am using 'private' when I talk about 'private experiences') – that when I recognise what I see as an apple, there need be no changes in my body from which another person could detect what I've done; and that even if there happen to be concurrent behavioural or physiological changes in my body, it is not by observing and interpreting these changes that *I* discover that I have recognised an apple.

Suppose that a follower of Wittgenstein challenges my argument by saying that 'recognise' is a word in our public language, and cannot therefore refer to a private occurrence. My reply would be (1) that to say this is blatantly to confuse the two senses, which I distinguished earlier, in which a word may be said to be private; (2) that we could not indeed have learned to use 'recognise' if it were *simply* the name of a private occurrence. Recognising a thing is often accompanied by characteristic behaviour-patterns, and it must have been by reference to the latter that we first learned to ascribe acts of recognition to others (and that others ascribe such acts to us). When learning to use 'recognise', this word presumably became associated for each of us with both the characteristic behaviour patterns and the kind of private occurrence which we have usually experienced when an act of recognition is ascribed to ourselves. We have each learned that in our own case such private occurrences are not always accompanied by corresponding behaviour; and what other people say confirms that they are like us in this respect. (E.g. I hear John say 'I recognised Jack as soon as he entered the room, but I concealed this fact', and I had been watching John and he had indeed shown no sign of recognising Jack.) We thus learn to distinguish between recognising, in the experiential sense, and the corresponding behaviour-patterns. And surely we do use 'recognise' to refer solely or primarily to private occurrences. 'Recognise' is one of the words like 'pain' in whose meaning the experiential content has become dominant and the behavioural content peripheral. When the poacher turns and runs, we regard this not as *constituting* his recognition of the keeper, but as *evidence* that he has (consciously) recognised the keeper.

But surely there is a simpler way of persuading the followers of Wittgenstein that a person can talk to himself about his private experiences. 'What is this ceremony for?', Wittgenstein asked, referring to the diarist's decision to use 'E' to refer to a certain type of sensation. If 'meaning' = 'use', can the diarist's 'E' have a use? Well, it is easy to think of possible uses.

Suppose our diarist is liable to suffer from spells of tummy trouble which his doctor cannot diagnose. The onset of such attacks has been preceded by distinctive shooting sensations in his midriff, and has involved several days of different but equally unpleasant sensations, during which time, unless he sticks to a light and simple diet, he vomits and has to retire to bed. Our diarist starts writing 'E' in his diary ('E' being short for 'those damned twinges') in order to verify whether E's are *regularly* followed by the other symptoms, because this information might help the doctor's diagnosis. Having confirmed this, he continues to record E's in his diary to remind himself to cancel all engagements to eat out for the next few days.

It is surely unwarranted dogmatism to say that in such cases 'E' has no meaning for the diarist. Does not everyone experience some types of sensation which are so distinctive and so frequent that he has no more difficulty in recognising them than he has in recognising apples or 'apples'?

Let us now consider whether Rhees's paper contains any arguments which would, after all, oblige us to give a negative answer to question 1. One of Rhees's reasons for his conclusion seems to be that he would so define 'language' that the diarist's 'E' cannot count as part of a language. Rhees argues that words 'cannot refer at all except in connection with a use, a use which you have to learn when you learn what the word means' (p. 67 above), and that 'the words of a language ... have to be learned. This is characteristic of language' (p. 74 above). Well, admittedly the diarist did not initially *learn* the use of 'E' – he *gave* it a use. (I waive the point that the diarist could be said to be learning his rule when he is committing it to memory.) But if this were the only reason for saying that 'E' is not a *word* in the *language* of the diarist, it need not worry us, for we can still say that 'E' is a symbol and that our diarist has a use for (attaches meaning to) such symbols. Moreover, when Rhees says that words 'cannot refer at all except in connection with a use', one may retort that referring *is* a use, and that it is *the* use for which our diarist employs 'E'.

Regarding Rhees's other arguments, it is often not clear to me to which of the four questions that I have distinguished they are addressed. I shall examine what seem to be his main arguments for answering question 1 in the negative. These seem to be his only arguments designed to answer Ayer's claim that we can recognise our sensations. Rhees wrote:

> I cannot learn the colour unless I can see it; but I cannot learn it without language, either. I know it because I know the language. And it is similar with sensations. I know a headache when I feel it, and I know I felt giddy yesterday afternoon, because I know what giddiness is. I can remember the sensation I had, just as I can remember the colour I saw. I feel the same sensation, and that is the same colour. But the identity – the sameness – comes from the language.
>
> A rule is something that is kept. The meaning of a word is something that is kept. It is for this reason that I can say that this is the same colour I saw a moment ago. I can see the same colour just because I know red when I see it. And even with shades for which we have no special names the same thing holds: I know the same colour when I see it (pp. 64–5 above).

My chief difficulty here is in understanding what Rhees meant by saying: 'the identity – the sameness – comes from the language'. The obvious interpretation would be that our recognising things as similar in some respect(s) depends upon our having a word to mark this similarity. But Rhees presumably did not mean this, for his statement would then be obviously false –

(*a*) because we do not *make* a similarity in learning to use the

relevant word, e.g. 'red', for unless we recognised the similarity between the shades in question independently of learning to call them 'red', we should not know what red is (what
'red' means);

(*b*) because, as Rhees acknowledges, we can recognise shades of
colour for which we have no special (specific) names, and this
fact contradicts the above interpretation of 'sameness comes
from the language'.

Perhaps Rhees's statement 'the sameness comes from the language' is simply asserting the truism that without language one
could not *say* that two things are the same. This interpretation is
indeed suggested by Rhees's statement: 'no language can tell me
whether this feels the same [as that]. . . . But without language I
could not have told whether this feels the same' (p. 65 above). If
'told' means either *told someone else* or *said*, then this statement is
tautological, and provides no reason for answering question 1 (or
question 2) in the negative. If 'told' means *recognised*, Rhees's
statement is false; for I may say 'this is the same as that', referring
to the nameless specific shade of two things that I now see, and
here it is obvious that the sameness (exact similarity) is in (between)
the things ostensively referred to by 'this' and 'that' and does not
'come from language'; for otherwise there would be nothing to
prevent us saying of *any* two ostensively identified entities 'this is
the same as that'.[2]

Unless or until we are given some explanation of 'the sameness
comes from the language' different from those mentioned above, it
seems sufficient to point out that just as a person can invent his own
names to distinguish specific shades of colour for which English
provides no names, so he can invent his own names for, e.g., different species of the many very different sensations which he has learnt
to call 'pains' – the sensations which we indiscriminately lump together because, presumably, their behavioural symptoms are much
the same. If this is granted, Rhees's analogy between colours and
somatic sensations tells against the Wittgenstein thesis he seeks to
defend.

Rhees also wrote:

But if it means anything to say I am in pain again or that he is
in pain again, this is because the word 'pain' has a regular use
and because we know this when we know what pain is. . . . This
is not a question of whether I can trust my memory. It is a question of when it makes sense to speak of remembering; either of a

good memory or a faulty one. If I thought I could not trust my memory, then of course I might look for confirmation. But there cannot be any question of confirmation here, nor any question of doubting either. There is just no rule for what is the same and what is not the same; there is no distinction between correct and incorrect; and it is for this reason that it does not make any difference what I say. Which means, of course, that I say nothing (p. 66 above).

There are several points here which need attention. (i) The appeal to 'regular use' in the first sentence settles nothing. 'Regular use' is not equivalent to 'public use' in either sense of the latter phrase. Our diarist may use 'E' *regularly* to refer to the same kind of sensation, yet his use may be private in sense B as well as in sense A. (ii) Rhees claims (or certainly seems to be claiming) that *it does not make sense* to speak of 'remembering that' or of 'doubting whether' I have previously had a sensation of the same kind as this one. There are, however, contexts in which we do use 'remember' and 'doubt' in the ways proscribed by Rhees. The doctor asks me: 'Is it the same kind of pain that you had before your last tummy upset?' It is perfectly correct to answer *either* 'I am sure it is the same for I remember the earlier pains clearly', *or* 'I doubt if it is the same for I don't remember clearly'. Rhees is denying facts about English usage because these are inconsistent with Wittgenstein's theory of meaning! (Remember Wittgenstein's maxim: 'don't think, look'.) (iii) Rhees ends: 'It doesn't make any difference what I say. Which means of course that I say nothing.' But what the diarist says may well make a difference to the doctor who is trying to diagnose the cause of his tummy upset; and to the diarist since he may have to cancel a dinner-date for tomorrow.

In reformulating Wittgenstein's Diary argument, Rhees has weakened it. Indeed he seems to have denied what gave this argument such force as it has, by saying that it is 'not a question of whether I can trust my memory'. For surely the point of Wittgenstein's argument was just this: that a person cannot trust his memory in any case where there is no way of testing it by appealing to something other than his own memories. But to this we may reply:

(i) Unless we trust *some* of our memories, we are committed to total scepticism. Rhees keeps appealing to established usage and the rules of language. But he could never know that other people's (or his own) use of any word is *regular* – that they (or he) follow a *rule* – except by trusting his own memory.

(ii) Admittedly there are many cases in which I do, or may, doubt
whether a past sensation is of the same kind as a present one;
but there are *some* cases in which I know this as surely as I
know anything, especially in cases in which little time has
elapsed, e.g. if a severe pain keeps recurring every few
minutes. Wittgenstein's thesis implies that I cannot talk to
myself about my private experiences even in a case like this;
which is surely a *reductio ad absurdum*.

If question 1 had to be answered in the negative there would be
no point in asking question 2. Since, however, we can talk to ourselves about our own private experiences, it is in order to ask
whether a person can communicate to others any information about
his private experiences. Here I acknowledge Wittgenstein's beetles-
in-the-boxes model as an apt analogy for the situation in which we
find ourselves, in that we cannot observe other people's beetles, their
private data. We have each learned to call 'red' the shades we each
see when we look at human blood, ripe tomatoes, etc.; and no one
can verify that the shade he sees when he looks at a ripe tomato is
the same as, or similar to, the shade seen by another when he looks
at the same tomato. But Wittgenstein went too far when he said
'the box might even be empty', i.e. that for all I know the box of
any other person might be empty, i.e. that for all I know other
people may have no private experiences. I have adequate evidence
that other people see things as coloured, for they will, on request,
describe and draw things which we are both looking at, and their
descriptions and drawings tally closely with what I see; and they
could not *discriminate* the different things which I and they are looking at *unless they saw them, as I see them, as differently coloured.*
Similarly with pains, etc. – I have no way of verifying that what
you feel when you have a dental abscess is the same as what I feel
when I have one. But your behaviour and your description of your
pain may leave me no room for doubting that you are feeling
localised sensations for which you feel strong aversion, and this is all
I need to be sure about to have a reason for, e.g., giving you my
last aspirin; and I'd have no reason for acting thus unless I believed
that you were feeling sensations in *some* degree similar to *some*
species of the sensations which I call 'pains' when I have them.

If we have to choose between accepting some version of the Verification Principle and denying *meaning* to the statement that similar physiological conditions give rise to more or less similar sensations in different people, surely we must reject the former principle,

for the latter statement *is* meaningful, and nearly all of us believe it; and it forms the basis for the arguments from analogy on which we have to depend, if we are to defend against philosophical scepticism our conviction that other people have private experiences which are more or less like our own.

What we may infer – what we, more commonly, just take for granted – about the private experiences of others may of course be false. The results of Francis Galton's questionnaires concerning mental imagery illustrate this. 'To my astonishment,' he wrote, 'I found that the great majority of men of science to whom I first applied protested that mental imagery was unknown to them, and they looked upon me as fanciful and fantastic in supposing that the words "mental imagery" really expressed what I believed everybody supposed them to mean. . . . They had a mental deficiency of which they were unaware, and naturally enough supposed that those who affirmed that they possessed it, were romancing' (*Inquiries into Human Faculty*, Everyman's Library, pp. 58–9). People who have clear and vivid imagery are equally astonished when they first discover what Galton's men of science reported. We are all disposed to take it for granted that the 'inner lives' of others are like our own.

The very fact that one can sometimes do what Galton did – discover that one's beliefs about other people's private experiences had been mistaken – is sufficient to establish an affirmative answer to my question 2. Obviously we can tell each other *something* about what (if anything) we 'see in the mind's eye' when we try to visualise our breakfast tables. When a person answers the questions Galton asked, concerning the brightness, definition, colouring, apparent distance, etc., of his visual images, we interpret his utterances as *referring* to his private data. How else could we interpret them? We cannot apply to his utterances the account Wittgenstein gave of 'I am in pain', for what could be the 'natural', non-verbal, expression of imaging, for which 'I "see" *x*' is a substitute?

Wittgenstein's version of Behaviourism is incoherent, in that he uses the phrase 'natural expressions of pain/sensations' (cf. *Inv.* 244), for this presupposes that we can (as indeed we do) distinguish between and refer separately to a sensation and to its expression, which is just what Wittgenstein wants to deny. This sort of inconsistency is to be found more obviously in the writings of some behaviourist psychologists. Where 'M' is some word or phrase which is used to refer to a private experience, e.g. 'seeing an after-image', and where *x y z* are behavioural or physiological, processes, they argue that 'M' means – or that M really consists of – *x y z*, because

M and *x y z* are invariably correlated. The psychologists who argue thus *either* (*a*) ignore the fact that the correlation in question was, and could only have been, established by accepting the reports of their experimental subjects, who had been asked to *describe* their private experiences, *or* (*b*) to camouflage this inconsistency, they say that they are treating their subjects' reports 'merely as verbal behaviour'. But this dodge cannot be allowed. When these psychologists publish their experimental reports, they do not wish *their* words to be taken merely as records of their verbal behaviour, i.e. of the movements which a spectator could have observed them performing when they wrote or dictated their papers – they wish us to take their writings as *statements about* (inter alia) their private experiences, about what they saw, heard, thought, etc., while conducting their experiments. Why then should the psychologist deny that their subjects' reports are to be taken in the way that they must wish their own reports to be taken?

I wish to anticipate a possible reply to my arguments. It may be claimed that I have misunderstood the purpose of Wittgenstein's remarks in *Inv.* 243 to 315; that when he asked whether there can be a private language, the question he really intended to ask is:

5. Could we have learned to use such words of our common language as 'pain', if people who felt pain did not commonly show 'outward signs of pain'?

It may be claimed that it was not Wittgenstein's intention to show that my questions 1 and 2 must be answered in the negative, only that question 5 must be answered in the negative.

My reply would then be that when discussing the work of an important philosopher whom one admires, it is tempting to assume that if he says things which are indefensible, he cannot really have meant them; and that admittedly Wittgenstein's presentation of his thoughts leaves much scope for differing interpretations – much scope but not limitless scope. Anyone who adopted the interpretation I have just described would have to admit that Wittgenstein's actual discussion is quite astonishingly devious and misleading. How could one then explain the facts that Wittgenstein devoted only a few lines to answering question 5 (the opening of *Inv.* 257), and that most of his remarks are addressed to different questions; that he used the Diary argument, which would, if valid, have proved that a negative answer must be given to question 1; that he used the Beetles argument, concluding that: 'The thing in the box has no place in the language-game at all ..., for the box might even be empty', for this argument, if valid, would show that a negative answer must be given to question 2?

Wittgenstein deserves credit for getting us to see that the answer to question 5 must be negative. He evidently believed that this fact entails that we cannot use words of our common language like 'pain' to talk about, to refer to, our private experiences. In this he was surely mistaken. Admittedly I could only have been taught the use of 'pain' via ostensive definitions, e.g. 'He is in pain' when the person ostensibly identified was evincing pain-*behaviour*, and 'You are in pain' when the person addressing me had recognised my pain-*behaviour* as such. But having gone through this stage of associating the word 'pain' with *both* pain-behaviour which I have observed *and* painful sensations which I have felt, I could and did go on to learn our familiar distinctions between '*being in* pain' and '*evincing or expressing* pain' and '*behaving as if in, or simulating,* pain'. I learned to use 'pain' (as all of us do except behaviourists) to refer *primarily* to sensations of certain kinds; and to describe pain-behaviour not as 'pain' (as 'being in pain'), but as '*symptoms* or *expressions* of pain'. And this is how we all talk when not doing philosophy or psychology.

(ii) *L. C. Holborow*

While reluctant to be branded as a 'follower of Wittgenstein' without qualification, I would like to take up some of the challenges issued by Professor C. W. K. Mundle.[3] I shall in the process try to outline a more coherent interpretation than Mundle manages to derive from the admittedly difficult sections of the *Philosophical Investigations* which he considers. Mundle claims that Wittgenstein gives a negative answer to both of the following questions:

(1) Can a person meaningfully talk to himself about (use words or other symbols to refer to) his own private experiences?

(2) Can a person tell others anything about his private experiences?

These negative answers are held to commit him to a thesis which 'can fairly be labelled Linguistic Behaviourism' (p. 104 above). Much depends on the force of the term 'private experience' as used in (1) and (2), and Mundle accordingly explains the sense in which he intends it (p. 109 above). Any experience of mine is 'private' if there need be no changes in my body from which another person could detect its occurrence. Even if there happen to be current behavioural or psychological changes in my body, the experience is still 'private' provided that it is not by observing and interpreting these changes that I discover its occurrence. My recognition of an apple when I see one is accordingly given as an example of a private experience in the sense intended. It is a clear consequence of this definition that giving negative answers to (1) and (2) involves, *inter alia*, denying that we can be in pain without expressing pain, and denying that there is a distinction between simulating and really being in pain. Mundle thinks that Wittgenstein is in fact committed to both of these consequences, but that his position is 'incoherent' in that he uses a vocabulary which presupposes that these distinctions can be made (pp. 116–17 above).

But was this the way in which Wittggenstein used the word 'private'? It seems obvious from many passages in the *Investigations* that he has no intention of denying that we can talk meaningfully about experiences which are 'private' in Mundle's sense (e.g. *Inv.* 154, 246, 304, 308). But the central question raised by Mundle is whether the diary argument and the beetles argument are consistent with these other passages. If we can show that these two arguments are consistent with an affirmative answer to Mundle's questions (1) and (2), *given that the crucial word 'private' is taken in the sense explained*, we shall be able to rescue Wittgenstein from the charge of incoherence.

Mundle correctly remarks (p. 105 above) that the diary argument is stated in a way which implies that if the diarist can divulge his use of the controversial term 'E' by giving a description, or by behaving in a way which reveals the nature of his sensation, then 'E' does not stand for a private experience. This restriction of the term 'private' to signs whose use cannot be explained in English seems quite unjustified to Mundle, for he sees no reason for Wittgenstein to object if 'E' is being used in just the way that our normal words for sensations are, given that Wittgenstein holds that these are not used to refer to private experiences. But it is clearly not the possibility of 'E' being used in this allowable way that worries Wittgenstein, but the diarist's claim that it is being used to refer to a private experience in the prohibited sense when it is so used. There is no confusion here, for it is a consequence of Wittgenstein's account of the way in which we can teach the pain-vocabulary, if and only if there are overt expressions of pain, that any word which stands for an expressible experience can be taught and understood and is thus not part of a private language. Wittgenstein's conclusion that there cannot be a private language in which communication of any type is possible is secured by argument, and not by question-begging definition as Mundle alleges.

The argument begins at *Inv.* 243–4 with an account of how we could learn the names of sensations. It is vital to realise that this is an account of how we can learn, and *not* of all that we can do with the words once we have learnt them, as Mundle (p. 103 above) and many others assume. The account in *Inv.* 244 begins with the words 'Here is one possibility', and it is clear from other passages that Wittgenstein holds that there are other ways in which these words can be used (see esp. *Inv.* ii, ix; an unjustly ignored passage which I attempt to interpret below). But they get their meaning by being 'tied up with my natural expressions of sensations' (*Inv.* 256). The 'immediate private sensations' considered in *Inv.* 243, and contrasted with the inner experiences that can be referred to in language, are obviously intended to be 'private' in the sense that they lack a 'natural expression'; by which is meant not just that I do not, e.g., wince on this occasion because the pain is not severe enough, but that this is a feeling of a type that has no natural expression in terms of which the appropriate language could be taught. It is the possibility of a language referring to private feelings of this type that Wittgenstein is concerned to deny, and it is only because of his failure to appreciate this that Mundle regards *Inv.* 243 and 256 as 'frivolous' attempts to guarantee a negative answer to the question whether we can communicate about our private experiences by giving an arbitrary definition of 'private language' (p. 106 above). Mundle's definition of 'private experience' includes in the one category what Wittgenstein regards as two utterly different types. He is quite happy with those experiences that are not on this occasion expressed in language or other behaviour, but wishes to deny that there could be a language which referred to experiences which were *radically private*, i.e. completely without 'natural expressions'.

We can now see how the diary argument fits into Wittgenstein's over-all strategy. It is directed towards establishing not only that it is impossible for there to be a public language for them, i.e. a language that is private in Mundle's sense B (see p. 105: '... the rules for its use are known only to its inventor'). This thesis is still a controversial one, and it seems clear to me that both Mundle and Ayer

would still wish to challenge it, even given that they accepted the
further restriction on the concept of privacy that I have marked by
the term 'radical privacy'. But once it is understood that it is
radically private experiences which are in question, we can see more
clearly how the diary argument operates.

I agree with Mundle that the crucial sentence is the following:
'But in the present case I have no criterion of correctness' (*Inv.* 258).
But the point of this sentence is not to cast doubt on the accuracy or
reliability of the diarist's memory. Wittgenstein is claiming not that
he might misremember the criterion that he has, just for this
instance, fixed; but that he has not by this ceremony fixed any
criterion at all. This point is further elaborated in *Inv.* 259, where
Wittgenstein asks how a ceremony of this sort could give rise to a
rule, and in *Inv.* 260, by pointing out that the sign 'E' *so far* has no
function. The point is that nothing in the ceremony defined the
limits within which the sign was to be used, and that unless there
is a rule for the use of the sign which determines when it is correctly
applied, there is no criterion for its use. Section 261 now follows on
from this quite naturally by reminding us that such a rule cannot be
derived from the fact that 'E' was called 'a sensation', for 'sensation is a word of our common language and thus must have a justification which everybody understands – a justification of a type
which the diarist can give only if he abandons the claim that his
language is radically private.

But it might appear that Wittgenstein attacks the diarist's memory
in *Inv.* 265, where he asserts that a justification must appeal to
something independent. He then raises the objection that I can
appeal from one memory to another, as when I call to mind how
the relevant page of a time-table looked in order to check the time
of departure of a train. But the reply is that this is not like looking
up the table in the imagination because the mental image of the
time-table can itself be tested for correctness. The point is not that
this procedure is of no use unless one has an infallible memory, but
that the possibility of testing it makes it possible to speak of its being
correct or mistaken. By contrast, the connection between sign and
sensation in *Inv.* 258 is such that it makes no sense to speak of
correct or incorrect memory because the procedure of 'inner ostensive definition' did not give us anything corresponding to the table
to appeal to.[4] Hence Wittgenstein's comparison with buying several
copies of the morning paper, as if what was written there determined what was true quite regardless of what had in fact happened.
The following sections 266–9 are clearly consistent with this inter-

pretation in providing further examples of the way in which genuine checking-procedures are well founded.

We can now see how Wittgenstein would rebut Ayer's charge (p. 54 above; cf. Mundle, pp. 108–9 above), that the diarist's recognition of the private object is in principle no different from the recognition that is required if we are to justify the use of a sign that stands for a public object. For Ayer holds that in this latter case there must be some point at which I just correctly recognise without further ado certain shapes, noises or movements. Every process of justification must stop somewhere, and there can therefore be nothing vicious in the notion of an uncheckable identification.

But surely we need to distinguish between what is uncheckable in principle and what is unchecked, in fact? The claim that the private object was correctly called 'E' could not be checked at all, for the occurrence of 'E' is not tied in any way to the occurrence of anything else. The lack of connection with a standard cause or stimulus means that there is no way in which I can produce something that is now undoubtedly 'E' to compare with my present experience. (Cf. *Inv.* 56 on checking my memory of a colour.) And, although Ayer suggests that this is a possibility (p. 54 above and p. 277 below, note 1), I cannot see how acts of recognition of a private sensation could be held to corroborate each other. For what could such 'corroboration' be? Unless we have given sense to the notion of being right here, we cannot say that I know that my memory has been reliable in general in this field, and thus that the correctness of past acts of recognition makes it reasonable to assume that this recognition of 'E' now is correct. We cannot rely on any connections between past private sensations, for we are not yet in a position to say that we recognised them correctly, and thus not in a position to claim that there were reliable correlations. By contrast, in the case where the recognition is of a public object it is clear that there are in principle further tests available, though they may not be needed or used in any particular case. But the possibility of such further tests is what gives sense to the claim that I am now getting it *right*. The recognition is not in this case uncheckable in principle, though it might be in fact uncheckable – for there might not have been anyone else there at the time to check that I was in fact correct in thinking that I saw a chamois deer through the trees when I was out stalking on my own. But we know what it would be for this to be correct, for this sort of recognition can be checked. Thus Ayer's attempt to show that these two types of identification are analagous does not succeed.

But our earlier consideration of Wittgenstein's argument demonstrated that there is also another respect in which the claim to have recognised a private object differs from that to have recognised a public one. This lies in the ways in which the criteria for the application of the relevant terms have been fixed. For even if it could be established that our diarist had correctly remembered the process of inner ostensive definition, it is argued that he did not in this process fix a criterion for the application of the term 'E'. It is clear that Ayer wishes to take issue with this part of the argument also. For he holds that here also the private language is in no worse a position than a public one. 'Whatever it is about my behaviour that transforms the making of a sound, or the inscription of a shape, into the employment of a sign can equally well occur in either case' (p. 54 above). That we can in the one case give an ostensive definition does not provide any distinction between the two cases in this respect, for if the gesture is to play its part it has to be endowed with meaning – and if I can endow the gesture with meaning, I can endow a word with meaning, without the gesture.

In reply to this, it should first be noted that Wittgenstein nowhere says that the giving of an ostensive definition of this type is sufficient for the explanation of a sign. He himself stresses the point that an ostensive definition can be misunderstood, and is certainly not sufficient to guarantee that the word in question will be understood. The early sections of the *Investigations* stress how misleading it is to think that words are correlated with elements of the world in such a way as to make ostensive definition a universally applicable method of teaching. It is clearly unjustified to suggest that Wittgenstein wished to argue that because I cannot give an ostensive definition of the word which I wish to stand for the sensation, I cannot succeed in giving it any meaning (p. 54 above). Wittgenstein in *Inv.* 288 gives a brief account of how we might explain the meaning of the English word 'pain' to a man who did not know it – and this is not a matter of ostensively referring to an object. Ayer concedes on p. 57 above that 'as it is, a child is not taught how to describe his feelings in the way he is taught to describe the objects in his nursery'. But he does not appear to notice that Wittgenstein also made this point, and that for this reason the argument about the impossibility of giving a purely ostensive definition played no part in his reasoning.

It is clear, however, that Wittgenstein does want to hold to what Ayer calls the 'second assumption' of the argument that he imputes, namely that for a person to be able to attach meaning to a sign it is necessary that other people should be capable of understanding it also. This is connected with the crucial requirement that there be a criterion of correct use. As an illustration, let us consider how we might try to teach the meaning of the word 'chair'. Pointing to a chair and saying the word has hope of succeeding only if the person who is being taught has a conception of what it is for something to be the same material object. If he thinks that I am referring only to the momentary appearance, and that when he looks away it makes no sense to speak of its being the same chair on any future occasion, he has to this extent not understood how this word is used and to this extent does not know the meaning of the word. And there is much else that he must be able to do, such as counting how many chairs there are in a room (provided that he can count), applying the term to kitchen chairs as well as armchairs, etc. It is to facts such as this that Wittgenstein refers when in *Inv.* 257 he speaks of the great deal of 'stage setting in the language' that is presupposed if the mere act of naming is to make sense. I take advantage of this 'stage setting' if I invent a private code for my sensations, for although I use different words they have the same 'grammar' as the words of the common language, and could be taught to someone else. There is consequently no problem about what is to count as a correct use of these terms. But, by contrast, in the private case there is no such established use by reference to which we can speak of correctness, and it is claimed that the 'inner ostensive definition' could not provide a criterion in the absence of any established 'grammar'. For how could my concentrating on an inner object now determine how similar to this, and in what respects similar to this, a future inner object must be before I can correctly call it 'E'? This is not a problem in the case of naming a new physical object or a new person, for our established language provides us with the general criteria that we need. Similarly if we name a new sensation in terms of its standard cause, location in the body, or expression, we know what it is for another sensation to be 'the same as this' in any or all of the possible respects.

I hope that it is now clear why Mundle's example of the diarist who suffers from tummy trouble which his doctor cannot diagnose (pp. 110 and 113 above) is not a simple counter-example to Wittgenstein's thesis. This diarist makes claims which are not 'private' in various vital respects. Terms such as 'tummy trouble', 'stomach ache' and 'damned twinges' are not radically private, for we could teach their use in the same way as we teach the use of the word 'pain'. These are all words of our public language, and it is not

Wittgenstein's intention to deny the obvious fact that they are meaningfully used. But this does not completely deal with cases of this type. For the term 'E' was supposed to stand not just for any twinges in the stomach at all, but for a distinctive type of twinge which the sufferer recognises as unusual and unlike any other, but is unable to describe in our public language. The claim is that the term 'E' refers to the radically private internal character of a sensation whose general species can be given in the normal way. What are we to say about this as a counter-example to Wittgenstein's thesis?

The first comment must be that if this is our paradigm of a private experience, the language in which we refer to such experiences is only partially private. To show that we can make sense of such a language is not to show that Wittgenstein's diary argument is without force. His concern is with a more full-blooded claim than this, for *Inv.* 257 and 261 make it clear that the private language which he was attacking was independent of our established language in the crucial respect that it did not depend on presupposing the 'great deal of stage setting in the language' to 'show the post where the new word is stationed'. These sections also make it clear that Wittgenstein thought that one of the ways in which we might be tempted to think that a radically private language was possible involved illegitimately and unconsciously assuming that the sensation in question had already been identified in one of the normal ways. This is the mistake that he singles out as the crucial one in *Inv.* 308: 'The first step is the one that altogether escapes notice. We talk of processes and states and leave their nature undecided.'

But even if Mundle's example does not compel Wittgenstein to allow a thoroughgoing private language, it might still be thought that he is committed to an unsupportable denial of even a 'dependent' private language. If this is not utterly clear from the passages already considered, it surely becomes so in *Inv.* 270, where Wittgenstein himself considers the sign's being given a use – whenever I report the sensation in question a manometer shows that my blood-pressure rises. The passage then continues:

> So I shall be able to say that my blood-pressure is rising without using any apparatus. This is a useful result. And now it seems quite indifferent whether I have recognised the sensation *right* or not. Let us suppose I regularly identify it wrong, it does not matter in the least. And that alone shows that the hypothesis that I make a mistake is mere show.

But this is not quite the same type of case as Mundle's. For we do not in this case have any general description of the sensation corresponding to Mundle's 'damned twinge in the stomach'. It is important to see that the connection with the rise in blood-pressure in this case is not like the tie with the natural expressions of sensation that was singled out as the feature enabling us to communicate about the sensations referred to in our normal language. For the rise in blood-pressure is not connected with the sensation in the way that the expressions of pain are to this sensation. It is just a contingent fact that happened to be discovered that there was the correlation with the blood-pressure, but it is not a contingent fact in this way that I cry out and writhe when I am in severe pain. If 'E' were a feeling of constriction around the heart which increased as my blood-pressure did, it would be connected with the rise in blood-pressure in the required way. But it is then no longer radically private. The point which Wittgenstein is concerned to make with this example is that a contingent connection of the type described with a public phenomenon does not corroborate my claim to have identified a private sensation. The inner 'recognition' is still logically independent of the overt 'corroboration'.

There is, then, a difference between the manometer example and Mundle's, but the latter does still have the feature that we are claiming to make a finer discrimination than we can publicly express or convey, and it does therefore seem that the diarist's claim that this is the same sensation as the one which preceded his last gastric attack rests on an identification which is uncheckable in principle as well as in fact. Here, too, it seems to be open to Wittgenstein to argue that there is no justification for talk of correctness or mistake. In a case of this type, as in the manometer case, our only reason for accepting that the person was having the same sensation was that he used the same sign on two occasions. But this way of stating the matter brings to light a crucial ambiguity. For the mere lack of independent justification in a particular case does not necessarily rule out a sensation-statement. It is central to Wittgenstein's account that when I say 'I am in pain' I normally (that is, in standard circumstances) have no need of justification. 'To use a word without a justification does not mean to use it without a right' (*Inv.* 289). There is consequently no doubt in these cases that the words are appropriately used. By contrast, it is possible for a claim that two sensations are the same to lack justification in the sense that there is as much to be said for the denial of the claim as for the claim itself. As an example, we could imagine two people arguing whether an electric shock was or was not like a severe attack of pins and needles. They might agree that both were tingles, but still dispute as to how different they were, and we might eventually be convinced that their difference was merely that they were inclined to say different things. The diarist's claim to recognise the same stomach-pain is clearly not of this second type. Could Wittgenstein therefore justify treating it as analogous to the sensation-statements in the first category, which require no justification?

It is important to note that Wittgenstein holds that in these cases also, there is no room for doubt: 'it means nothing to doubt whether I am in pain' (*Inv.* 288). This I regard as a mistake, if it is intended to rule out the possibility of these words ever being given a sense. It is true that in many situations it is in fact impossible to doubt whether one is in pain. But in many cases of mild internal sensations there is often at least an initial uncertainty about the precise details of the sensation, and where there is room for uncertainty there is room, at least in principle, for mistake. Patients often have to give the matter some thought before they are in a position to answer some of the doctor's questions about even their present feelings. This is obviously not true of those clear-cut cases of severe pain in which much of the behaviour that comprises the 'expression' of the sensation is involuntary. We noticed above the suggestion in *Inv.* 243 that the use of sensation-words as 'expressions' is not their only use. Is it possible that Wittgenstein includes reports of this apparently fallible type in yet another category?

I think that Wittgenstein does define another category in *Inv.* II, pp. 187–9, where he labels as a 'result of observation' the statement that today I feel the pain only when I think about it. He holds that we say that a person is observing:

Roughly: when he puts himself in a favourable position to receive certain impressions in order (for example) to describe what they tell him (p. 187).

Is there anything analagous to this in the case of having sensations? In a sense, I think that there is, for one can be prevented from giving an accurate description of the nature of a sensation by being distracted, in at least two ways. First, when something else is at the centre of one's attention. The sensation can continue as if out of focus in the background. In this case one puts oneself in a better position to describe the sensation by concentrating on it, i.e. bringing it into the focus of one's attention. The second possibility is more controversial. It seems to me that one can take a sensation for what it is not on the basis of a mistaken expectation. An extreme example of this is that of an initiation ceremony where the initiate is shown a red-hot poker, and ordered to bare his breast. He doesn't really believe at this stage that he will be branded, but when he is blind-folded and a block of ice is thrust against his chest he cries out as if in pain. It is possible that he takes some time to realise the decep-tion, and until he does it seems clear to me that he is appropriately described as mistakenly believing that he is in pain.

Against this, it could be argued that the man is mistaken not about the sensation, but about what is happening to him. I agree that he is *also* mistaken in this second way, but cannot see how the man can believe that he is being branded without believing that the sensation is painful, given that he believes it on having the sensa-tion, and reacts as if in pain. I am not maintaining that there is a mistake in *feeling* here, for this would commit me to the objection-able thesis that what was felt could be separated, in the manner of an independent object of perception, from the feeling of it. The thesis is rather that in cases of the type discussed we can be misled into thinking that a sensation is what it is not. Philosophers often appear to assume that sensations always come to us already labelled, so that nothing could intervene between the feeling and the realiza-tion that this is a sensation of a certain sort. It is true that very often nothing does intervene, but I hope that I have shown that there is nevertheless an epistemological distinction between having a sensa-tion and knowing what it is.[5]

Wittgenstein's description of some sensation-statements as 'results of observation' therefore provides some justification for interpreting him as allowing that there can be meaningful descriptions over and above the linguistic 'expressions' of sensation. But once this view is developed as above it is difficult to reconcile with what he says in *Inv.* 288. We can still agree that in the type of case that he there envisages it is hardly intelligible that there should be a genuine doubt, unless of course the sensation is a borderline one, in which case our hesitation expresses that fact. Even where we have wanted to say that one might take a sensation for something other than what it is, which he denies, we have agreed with the premiss of his argument, that we do not need a private criterion of identity for the sensation. The extent of our disagreement lies in our having found a small set of cases where what he says does not hold.[6] These cases do not require any retraction of our earlier objections to the doctrine of the radical privacy of sensations.

We must now return to Mundle's diarist and his stomach pains. It is now clear that his claim that this pain is just like the others that have troubled him all morning is a 'result of observation' in Wittgenstein's sense. But the claim rests on the contention that this is a specific type of pain which can be discriminated, but not publicly described. Others can be told that it is a sharp type of stomach pain, but this does not give its *infima species*. We must now attempt to determine whether this claim can be accommodated in our account.

Wittgenstein does allow in the case of various other psychological statements (i.e. thoughts, dreams and intentions) that my truthful report is decisive. The truth of my confession is 'guaranteed by the special criteria of *truthfulness*' (*Inv.* II, p. 222; cf. also *Inv.* 666–84). As Malcolm has pointed out (p. 34 above) Wittgenstein also acknowledges a use of 'recognise' with mental images in *Inv.* 377–8. But it is important to note that although I have no criterion for sameness of image when it is my image (*Inv.* 377), I can only know that the word 'same' describes what I recognise if I can express my recognition in some other way, and if it is possible for someone else to teach me that 'same' is the correct word here. 'For if I need a justification for using a word, it must also be one for someone else.' It is clear from this passage that Mundle was mistaken in assuming (p. 115 above) that Wittgenstein held that we could never communicate about our mental images. This mistake is yet another consequence of Mundle's failure to distinguish 'radically' private experiences from those which are private in a less problematic sense.

But it is also clear that *Inv.* 378 still requires that the recognition of mental images be subject to a type of check that we do not have in the case described above, and the sense of 'recognise' that Malcolm proceeds to allow for sensations also has this feature. For the example that he gives is that of a man who on arising complains of an unusual sensation, and then claims to identify it as the same as he has when he goes down in an elevator. If the man employs the rest of the sensation-language as we all do, and 'if his behaviour in this case was approximately what it was when he was affected by the downward motion of an elevator', Malcolm allows that his declaration that it was this sensation would be decisive. But what is the characteristic behaviour of a person affected by the downward motion of an elevator? It seems that even here Malcolm has, albeit implausibly, tried to keep a strong connection between observable behaviour and the precise type of sensation in question.

I think that we can see why Wittgenstein requires this justification of my claim to recognise mental images as the same by considering Rhees's contention (p. 65 above), that when we recognise two things as the same in some respect 'the identity – the sameness – comes from the language', and again 'no language can tell me whether this feels the same.... But without language I could not have told whether this feels the same.' Mundle objects that if this last sentence means that without language we could not recognise whether this is the same as that, it is false:

> for I may say 'this is the same as that', referring to the nameless specific shade of the two things that I now see, and here it is obvious that the sameness (exact similarity) is in (between) the things ostensively referred to by 'this' and 'that' and does not 'come from language'; for otherwise there would be nothing to prevent us saying of *any* two ostensively identified entities 'this is the same as that' (p. 112 above).

This is surely misleading as it stands, for it is most unlikely that the two things will be exactly similar in all respects; they are exactly similar *in the respect that* they are of the same shade. This reference to a *respect in which* is required to give content to the judgment that they are the same. The sameness does not 'come from language' in the sense that any two things can just be said to be the same without further specification, but it does require language in the sense that the notion of a 'respect' needs to be explained in terms of the ways in which our language classifies the world. With sufficient ingenuity we might be able to think of 'respects' which are not utilised by our present language. But to do this would be to formulate rules which could be used to amend or supplement our present language.[7] But once we know that the speaker's concern is with the precise shade of colour, we just recognise that the two objects are the same in this respect, for our language cannot do this job for us. The importance of this point for the private language argument is that the diarist's claim that the two sensations are the same, and thus both appropriately called 'E', has meaning only if there is a specifiable respect in which they are 'the same'. It has been argued above that this condition could not be fulfilled if the experience in question were a completely radically private one. The condition is obviously fulfilled by the sensation-words of our common language. But is it fulfilled by the words of our imagined dependent private language? I think that it is in the case of strikingly distinctive internal sensations, and that the fact that the distinctive quality of such sensations cannot be communicated does not rule out our claim to discriminate them. Had Wittgenstein developed some of the hints in Part II of the *Investigations*, he might well have agreed.

It might be thought that the diarist's claim could be vindicated in the future by the discovery that he had a certain type of ulcer, and that others who had this complaint made similar claims about a distinctive sensation. I would regard this as further corroboration, but Wittgenstein's reply is less certain. He would undoubtedly utilise his distinction between symptoms and criteria (*Inv.* 354, 376), from which it would follow that if having this ulcer were a criterion of having the sensations, there is no room for the question whether the ulcers and the sensation are correlated, for this becomes true by definition; whereas if the ulcers are merely a new symptom, having ulcers can only be correlated with having 'E' sensations if there is some reliable way of independently identifying the latter. Whether this is so is just the question discussed above. It is important to realise that we cannot, as Mundle suggests (pp. 114–15 above), just decide to use the principle that similar physiological conditions give rise to similar sensations in different people without producing any confirming evidence. But if we can confirm the principle in those cases where we have expressions of sensation, and can show that we can each identify our own 'E' sensations, then we can reasonably use the principle to confirm that our sensations are similar.

In view of the differences of interpretation already indicated, I find rather more significance in the beetles argument than Mundle does. He acknowledges the beetles-in-the-box model as 'an apt analogy for the situation in which we find ourselves' (p. 114 above), and seems to think that this is how Wittgenstein intended it. But surely it is intended as a *reductio ad absurdum* of the form: if *this* is how you think of sensations, certain consequences follow, in particular that it is impossible to communicate meaningfully about them. Mundle tries to accept the model but deny the consequences, but the form of this denial shows that he does not realise what is involved in accepting the model. For although he accepts that he has no way of verifying that what another person feels when he has a dental abscess is the same as what he himself feels when he has one, he concedes that the behaviour and the descriptions of his feelings given by the other person may leave no room for doubt that he is feeling localised sensations for which he feels a strong aversion. But if the behaviour and the description give grounds as good as this, we are no longer in a situation where the beetles-in-the-box model is appropriate. As Mundle noted earlier, it is one of the features of this model that 'everyone says that he knows what a beetle is only by looking at *his* beetle' (*Inv.* 293, quoted by Mundle on p. 104 above). But Mundle has now conceded that, as things are, we can tell what is in the box by looking outside it. Thus, despite appearances, he is eventually forced to agree with Wittgenstein that our words for sensations are 'tied up with our natural expressions of sensation'. Being in pain is not a separable inner event, independent of the ways in which it is naturally expressed. Cf. *Inv.* 311–12 on what is involved in imagining that one is in pain.) Wittgenstein's thesis is not that there is something apart from behaviour, as if hidden in a box, of which we cannot speak; but rather that by observing how others behave in cases of this sort we *can* discover how they feel. To develop the analogy in an admittedly risky way, the box is at least partly transparent. Wittgenstein seems to think that in so far as it is not transparent, statements about its contents have no meaning; our own view is that some items whose general nature can be displayed to those outside can be discriminated more precisely by the owner of the box.

To summarize: the interpretation of Wittgenstein that I have outlined differs from Mundle's in that it represents him as concerned only to deny what I have called the radical privacy of experience; my own views differ from Wittgenstein's in that while I agree that there can be no completely independent radically private language, I hold that there can nevertheless be a dependent radically private language. I do, then, hold that Wittgenstein's arguments are in need of qualification; but that he was no behaviourist in any important sense is not only compatible with the diary and beetles arguments, but also apparent in various other passages not mentioned by Mundle (e.g. *Inv.* 154; ɪɪ, 186–9), and implicit in a crucial passage (*Inv.* 304–8) which he misinterprets at the beginning of his article.

V The private language argument as a *reductio ad absurdum*

(i) *Hector-Neri Castañeda*

The following essay is only the first study by its author into the connections between consciousness and behaviour, on the one hand, and between language and consciousness on the other. The earlier essays are primarily clarifications of issues and assumptions as well as cumulations of philosophical data. The later essays provide an analysis of the structure of mental concepts and an analysis of certain aspects of the structure of the whole conceptual scheme required for thinking about thinking beings.

The ensuing essay is an examination of what Norman Malcolm has referred to as Wittgenstein's internal attack upon private language. It is complemented by

[1] 'The Private Language Problem', in *The Encyclopedia of Philosophy*, ed. Paul Edwards (New York: Crowell-Collier & Macmillan, 1967) VI, pp. 458–64.

This essay is a complement especially with regard to: (i) the centrality of Wittgenstein's attack on private language in the cluster of Wittgenstein's arguments and views, and (ii) the form of the alleged rules of language. These two essays are supplemented by the examination of what Malcolm has called Wittgenstein's external attack upon private language. This examination appears in:

[2] 'Knowledge and Certainty', *Review of Metaphysics*, XVIII (1964) pp. 529–37.

[3] 'Consciousness and Behaviour: Their Basic Connections', in H.-N. Castañeda (ed.), *Intentionality, Minds, and Perceptions* (Detroit: Wayne State University Press, 1967) pp. 138–45.

These two articles especially complement the discussion with respect to the privacy of sensations and the learning of the use of words. As said in the concluding paragraph, below, of the rejoinder to Thomson, the examination of the private language arguments establishes at least an impasse. And it is incumbent upon philosophers working in the philosophy of mind to erect theories on each side of the impasse. The more diverse and precise the theories we build, the greater the philosophical clarification we produce. A reasoned theory of a non-Wittgensteinian type is outlined in Part 3 of essay [3] above mentioned. The claim is defended that each of the ordinary mental concepts has a complex logical structure and is recursive in character. For instance, the concept of pain is an amalgam of: (i) a first-person private concept, which is observational-like, and is called *plain*; (ii) a third-person theoretical-like concept of *prain* which is part of a causal 'theory' whose observational basis is constituted by plains and behaviour and circumstances; and (iii) a third-person theoretical concept of *peain*, which again is part of a causal psycho-physical 'theory' and presupposes a framework of thoughts. Here an important part of the philosophical task consists in sorting out the different logical and metaphysical presuppositions undergirding ordinary mental concepts.

Prominent among the logical presuppositions underlying our concept of pain are the debated properties of the privacy and incorrigibility of plains, and the corrigibility and inaccessibility of prains and peains. The author's first attempt at cataloguing and formulating precisely such presuppositions appears in section II of the ensuing essay. But, as the reader will note, the very formulation of those presuppositions presents a serious problem. Consider, for instance, the sentence (S) 'The Editor of *Soul* knows at 3 p.m. that *he* has a pain *then*'. The words 'he' and 'then' refer back to 'The Editor of *Soul*' and '3 p.m.' respectively. But they cannot be replaced with the latter, *salva propositione*. The sentence 'The Editor of *Soul* has a pain at 3 p.m.' expresses a different proposition or statement: for clearly, the Editor may very well know that he has a pain at a certain time, without knowing that he is the *Editor* of *Soul* (news of his appointment may not have reached him yet) or that the time in question is 3 p.m. The interesting thing is that the word 'he' in (S) represents *first-person* references that the Editor can make, and hence does not represent any third-person way of referring to the Editor. Similarly, the word 'then' in (S) represents an indexical reference by means of the adverb 'now' that the Editor can make or could have made, and, hence, represents no name or description of the time in question. Both words 'he' and 'then' are examples of what this writer has called *quasi-indicators*. He has argued that quasi-indexical reference is a unique unanalysable way of reference characteristic of conceptual schemes that allow for the possibility of conceiving of other thinking creatures. The arguments and an analysis of the complex structure of quasi-indexical reference appear in the following papers, where [5] contains a general investigation of all indicators and provides an analysis of indexical reference in *oratia obliqua* in terms of both quasi-indexical reference and indexical reference in *oratio recta*:

[4] ' "He": A Study in the Logic of Self-consciousness', *Ratio*, VIII (1966) pp. 130–57.

[5] 'Indicators and Quasi-indicators', *American Philosophical Quarterly*, IV (1967) pp. 85–100.

[6] 'On the Logic of Self-knowledge', *Nous*, I (1967) pp. 9–21.

[7] 'On the Logic of Attributions of Self-knowledge to Others', *Journal of Philosophy*, LXV (1968) pp. 439–56.

[8] 'On the Phenomeno-logic of the I', *Proceedings of the XIVth International Congress of Philosophy* (forthcoming).

In short, the examination of the private language argument led to the formulation of the pain postulates, and the latter in its turn led to the discovery of quasi-indicators and their central place in the conception of other minds.

Note: The prediction argument on p. 151 below was suggested by *Theaetetus* 178 A–E, where Plato is attacking a Protagorean position pretty much like the Wittgensteinian demand upon private language met by that argument.

INTRODUCTION

In the great revolution in philosophy brought about by Ludwig Wittgenstein, a central place is occupied by a cluster of ideas and arguments to the effect that a private language is impossible.

In *Inv.* 250–70, Wittgenstein does seem to be presenting *one* argument against private language in the form of a *reductio ad absurdum*. He writes:

Let us imagine the following case. I want to keep a diary about the recurrence of a certain sensation. To this end I associate it with the sign 'E' and write this sign in a calendar for every day on which I have the sensation . . . . (*Inv.* 258).

He argues that the sign 'E' as described, as a symbol of a private language, has no meaning at all.

Similarly, Malcolm writes at the end of his now classic discussion of those sections:

> The argument that I have been outlining has the form of a *reductio ad absurdum*: Postulate a 'private' language; then deduce that it is not a *language* (p. 48 above, his italics).

I. THE PRIVATE LANGUAGE THESIS

The Assumption for the Reductio ad Absurdum

Wittgenstein's thesis is that a private language is logically impossible. He seems to define a private language by saying: '*The individual words of this language are to refer to what can only be known to the person speaking; to his immediate sensations. So another person cannot understand the language*' (*Inv.* 243, my italics). He means to include not only sensations, but everything that has been called a 'mental act'. He presents himself as attacking the picture of all of them as objects, i.e. as private objects (*Inv.* 207, 222, 293, 304, etc.).

Both Wittgenstein (*Inv.* 243 just quoted) and Malcolm (pp. 41 ff. above) infer from their definition of private language that only the speaker can understand it.

Language

It is nowadays a commonplace (thanks especially to Wittgenstein's own teaching) to say that a language is a system or aggregate of rules, a system or aggregate of linguistic activities. Thus naming, describing, identifying, commanding, questioning, etc., all support one another, in different degrees and ranges, to be sure; but, e.g., *there is no naming in isolation from the rest of a language,* existing as it were in a linguistic vacuum. As Wittgenstein so beautifully puts it: '... a great deal of stage-setting in the language is presupposed if the mere act of naming is to make sense. And when we speak of someone's having given a name to pain, what is presupposed is the existence of the grammar of the word "pain", which shows the post where the new word is stationed' (*Inv.* 257).

Consequently, the assumption for the private language argument cannot be that a man is trying to keep a diary with *only* the sign 'E'. We must assume that he has at his disposal a set of signs interrelated by means of a network of merely linguistic rules and a good deal more, since what Wittgenstein calls 'grammar' includes a lot more than the mere tautologies of a language.

It is not clear that Wittgenstein's is the issue between a public and an *absolutely* private language. Very naturally, one would expect to find many cases of private language all linked up by a series of family resemblances, ranging off from a language *all* of whose individual words refer only to private objects. It is also worth noting that the issue private *v.* public language, as raised, has nothing to do with the extremely difficult problem concerning the *origin* of language. Even if it is a psycho-sociological law that language can be developed by groups only, that law is irrelevant to the present issue. For as Malcolm with characteristic penetration says: 'It is logically possible that someone should have been born with a knowledge of the use of an expression or that it should have been produced in him by a drug' *(Philosophical Review,* LXIII (1954) p. 544).

Private Objects

Wittgenstein's definition makes the privacy of the language depend *solely* on the privacy of the objects the language is used to think about. From that definition, however, it does not follow that, e.g., a private language cannot have a single word in common with a public language. Yet, Wittgenstein himself argues:

> What reason have we for calling 'E' the sign of a sensation? For *'sensation' is a word of our common language,* not one intelligible to me alone. . . . And it would not help either to say that . . . when he writes 'E' he has something. . . . *'Has' and 'something' also belong to our common language. (Inv.* 261, his italics in 'sensation' and 'something' only.)

And Malcolm challenges:

> If I recognise that my mental image is the 'same' as one that I had previously, how am I to know that *this public word 'same'* describes what I recognise? (p. 48 above, my italics).

If Wittgenstein's definition of a private language in *Inv.* 243 is taken as an honest effort at giving the idea of a private language a full run, it must not be understood to deny a private language all logical terms: (*a*) connectives, (*b*) inferential terms, (*c*) copulas, (*d*) quantifiers, (*e*) numerals, etc. Since the meanings of all these expressions have nothing to do with whether the objects talked about are private or public, it is not at all clear why a language about private objects should by that reason alone be prevented from including any of them.

Similarly, to consider a private language as having no propositions in common with any other language is also to deny it all logical signs. If a language has logical terms, then tautological propositions are bound to appear, and sentences expressing them will be translatable into other languages. Thus, a private language is one which has *some* words descriptive or designative of private objects.

Now, there are several senses of 'private object':

(1) one which the speaker alone can (i.e. logically can) have experience of, or be acquainted with;

(2) object whose existence is (logically) determinable by the speaker alone:

   (2a) nobody else but the speaker can think (or say) with original certainty that the object exists;

   (2b) it is logically necessary that if the object exists, the speaker knows that it exists (others may know of the existence of the object, but their knowledge is not a logical consequence of the object's existence);

   (2c) the object's existence is entailed by the speaker's belief that it exists (others' belief that the object exists may be never mistaken, but it does not entail the object's existence);

(3) objects whose possession of some characteristic A is (logically) determinable by the speaker alone:

   (3a) nobody else but the speaker can think (or say) with original certainty that the object is A;

   (3b) it is logically necessary for the speaker, and only for him, that if the object is A, he knows that it is A;

   (3c) the object's being A is entailed by the speaker's, and only by the speaker's, belief that it is A;

(4) objects about which the speaker alone can determine for any first-order statement whether it is true or false of them;

(5) objects about which the speaker alone can make first-order statements, i.e. objects which only first-order predicates which the speaker alone can use, apply to;

(6) objects about which the speaker alone can make any statement at all.

In each alternative, 'can' is a logical 'can'.

The difference between (5) and (6) is that the former does, whereas the latter does not, allow other persons to refer to my private objects indirectly or vicariously, via my statements about them. (6) is a very extreme, empty conception of a private object, not worth discussing.

(1)–(4) do not require fully private predicates; for them it suffices that the predicates in question have only private applications, e.g. after-images and physical surfaces can have the same (or very similar) characteristics of colour and shape. Thus, (1)–(4) can hold in purely private as well as in mixed languages.

What did Wittgenstein have in mind when he attacked private language in order to explode the idea of a private object? Wittgenstein attacks the fundamental idea of a private object ('if we construe the grammar of the expression of sensation on the model of "object and name" the object drops out of consideration as irrelevant', *Inv.* 293; see also *Inv.* 304; II, pp. 207, 222, etc.). Thus it is fair to see him as attacking all types of language which involve the idea of a private object in any of the senses (1)–(6); he particularly attacks mixed languages.

> Or is it like this: the word 'red' means something known to everyone; and in addition, for each person, it means something known only to him? (Or perhaps rather: it *refers* to something known only to him.) (*Inv.* 273.)

Final Statement of the Assumption for the Reductio
We are then to assume that a certain person (to be called *Privatus*) speaks and writes a language (hereafter called *Privatish*) which is private. *Privatish contains several logical signs, which we shall assume to be identical with those of ordinary English.* In some cases we shall assume that Privatish includes *a public sub-language* of the relevant kind, whose purely public words will be supposed to be identical with their English counterparts.

II. Some Counter-Examples

Privately Experienceable Objects
If Wittgenstein conceived of private objects in sense (1), his thesis seems to admit of an obvious counter-example. Many philosophers

and non-philosophers alike have held that one cannot (logically cannot) be acquainted with, or have experience of, someone else's sensations or after-images. These are all regarded as private in sense (1).

Privately Ascertainable Objects: Pains
If Wittgenstein and his followers have senses (2) and (3) of 'private object' in mind, then the private-language thesis is amenable to refutation by existing counter-examples. Ordinary pains and after-images are private in those senses.

The ordinary language of pains which I employ is such that the following propositions are all logically true (or true *ex vi terminorum*):

Meaning Postulates of Pain:
A. *(Postulate of Subjectivity.)* If X has a pain Y at time t and is not distracted from it, he feels Y at t.
B. *(Postulate of Subjective Ownership.)* If X feels a pain Y at t, X has Y at t.
C. *(Postulate of Direct Access.)* If X feels a pain Y at t, and at t he is capable of thinking that he has a pain at t, and is attending to his feelings (or his mental goings-on), then at t X knows that he has Y.
D. *(Postulate of Incorrigibility.)* If X thinks attentively at t that he has a pain Y at t, then X knows that he feels Y then.
E. *(Postulate of Subjective Thought.)* X thinks at t that he has a pain Y if and only if at t he thinks that he feels Y.
F. *(Postulate of Corrigible Access to Others.)* It is logically possible that everybody else thinks attentively at t that X has (had or will have) a pain Y at t_1 without having Y at t_1.
G. *(Postulate of Indirect Access to Others.)* It is logically possible that X has a pain Y at t without anybody else knowing at any time that X has Y at t.

The following propositions can be derived from the postulates:

J*. *(Theorem of Limited Private Access.)* There are some kinds (or predicates) ϕ such that if X has a pain Y of kind ϕ at t, nobody else knows that X has Y at t.
J^a. *(Theorem of Qualified Private Access.)* If X has a pain Y at t, nobody else knows, whatever the time, that X has Y at t, *in the same way* that X knows that he has Y at t.

Proposition J* makes of the ordinary language of pains (as I understand it) a private language. According to it, the speaker alone can determine whether a pain of kind ϕ exists or not and, of course, whether the pain (in case it exists) is ϕ or not. Thus, pains are private in senses (2a) and (3a).

Postulates C (of Direct Access to One's Own Pains) and G (of Indirect Access to Others' Pains) entail that ordinary pains are private in sense (2b). One knows, according to them, of his own pains by merely having them. That is, one knows of them privately. Likewise, postulates D (of Incorrigibility Concerning One's Own Pains) and F (of Corrigibility Concerning Others' Pains) entail that pains are private objects in sense (2c). Therefore, the ordinary language of pains is a counter-example to Wittgenstein's thesis, if interpreted as the claim that a language employed to think about private objects is of type (2).

Finally, the same postulates C and G, or D and F entail that the speaker is, of logical necessity, in a privileged position to determine whether or not a certain predicate applies to a pain he feels. Pains are, then, private objects in both senses (3b) and (3c).

Some Wittgensteinian Arguments

Wittgensteinians hold the view, W, that 'I know that I am in pain' is either senseless or a verbose synonym of 'I am in pain'. W suggests a reply to my claim that pains are private objects in senses (2) and (3). A Wittgensteinian may say that since it is senseless to say 'I know that I am in pain' it is senseless to say that one's own pains are objects which one alone can *know* in either sense (2) or (3); hence, it is senseless to say that one's language about one's own pains is private. Wittgensteinians have offered four arguments in support of W. The ensuing discussion of these arguments should be understood as making its points cumulatively.

(*a*) The first argument runs: If a proposition is contingent, it is logically possible to believe falsely that it is true. If 'I am in pain' expressed the contingent proposition we normally take it to express, one could believe that one is in pain without being in pain. This is impossible, hence there is no such proposition that one can believe or know.

This is a howler. From 'It is impossible to believe falsely that one is in pain' it follows that it is necessary that if one believes oneself to be in pain, one's belief is true. Since 'I am in pain' cannot but be contingent, the major premise of the argument is false.

Probably Wittgensteinians mean to argue: A contingent propo-

sition can be believed falsely to be true: if 'I am in pain' expressed
a contingent proposition as we normally take it to do, the sentence
'I believed falsely at time t that I was in pain at t' would be meaningful. It is not, hence there is no such proposition.

But obviously 'I believed falsely at t that I was in pain at t' is
meaningful. Indeed, it is meaningful even in the disputed sense that
it can express a false proposition, for pain postulate D leaves it open
to believe falsely, when inattentive, that one is in pain. In any case,
the conclusion of the argument is false. 'I am in pain' uttered by me
expresses the same truth value as 'Castañeda is in pain' uttered by
you, which expresses (or is) a proposition. In short, 'I am in pain'
expresses something which is true or false, which can be contra-
dicted, that has entailments, and appears as a premise in arguments. These four features together are sufficient to make the utterances of 'I am in pain' the expressions of propositions.

(*b*) The second argument for W runs: It is odd and out of order
in ordinary language to say that one believes or thinks that one is
in pain. 'I believe that p' is used to make weak assertions that p,
i.e. to suggest the possibility of a mistaken belief or a doubt. There
is no room for doubt or mistaken belief about one's own pains.
Hence, 'I believe that I am in pain' is senseless and so is 'I know
that I am in pain'.

This argument is invalid, unless 'senseless' means 'out of order
or odd'. Once again, from 'There is no room for a mistaken belief'
it follows that if one believes that one is in pain one's belief is true.
And this explains fully why it is odd to say merely 'I believe that
I am in pain', given that this assertion suggests the possibility of a
mistake.

(*c*) The third argment for W: In ordinary language it is odd and
out of order to ask a person who has declared that he is in pain
'How do you know?' Hence, it is senseless to say 'I know that I am
in pain', unless this just means 'I am in pain'.

This is an inconclusive argument, even if 'senseless' means 'odd
or out of order'. Given the fact that, when attentive to one's
mental goings-on, one cannot be mistaken about one's pains, the
senselessness of the question amounts to the pointlessness of asking
a person for an answer which the person knows that one already
knows. The only answer to 'How do you know?' is here: 'By having
the pain' or 'By attending to my feelings'. Since both persons know
that they know the meanings of 'pain', 'know', etc., the question is
quite pointless and out of order.

Nothing in the argument shows that it is even pointless – let alone nonsensical – to speak of knowing one's own pains. In making an inventory of the ways of knowing, one lists physical objects as known by perception, pains as known by feeling or introspection, mathematical theorems as known by deduction, etc. This also refutes the fourth argument for W, which is:

(*d*) It is correct to speak of knowledge only when there is a question of finding out, of checking and testing. But it is absurd to suppose that one can make tests for finding out whether one is in pain or not.

Since it is correct to speak of knowing one's own pains, the major premise is false.

In sum, it is odd, because pointless, to inform another person that one believes or thinks that one is in pain, or to insist that one knows that one is in pain. But this fact about ordinary *reporting* in no way shows that there are no facts that would not be reported if one were to make pointless assertions. The pointlessness of the assertions is not only compatible with their intelligibility, but even *presupposes* it: I conclude, therefore, that the ordinary language of pains is still a mixed private language in several senses and remains, therefore, a counter-example against some interpretations of Wittgenstein's thesis.

III. THE PRIVATE LANGUAGE ARGUMENT

The Charge: Possibility of Mistakes

From the assumption formulated above we are, according to Malcolm, to deduce that Privatish is *not* a language. Since a language is an aggregate of rules, it would suffice to show that in using Privatish, Privatus cannot be following rules.

Wittgenstein's argument is very compact, but the following unpacking seems to be true to what he had in mind. A rule is essentially the sort of thing that can be followed (obeyed or satisfied) or not, and also the sort of thing that can be misapplied; a person trying to follow a rule can make a mistake and end up by not following it. Thus, the possibility of not acting in accordance with a rule is of the essence and substance of a rule. Hence it must be possible for Privatus to make mistakes in the exercise of the rules constituting Privatish. If there is no way in which Privatus can misapply the signs belonging to Privatish, then this is not made up of rules and is, therefore, not a language. Naturally, Wittgenstein does claim that it is impossible for Privatus to make mistakes in using the (so-called) signs belonging to Privatish. This claim has been rounded out by Malcolm as follows:

1. Now how is it to be decided whether I have used the word consistently [i.e. correctly]?
2. What will be the difference between my having used it consistently and its *seeming* to me that I have?
3. Or has this distinction vanished?
4. 'Whatever is going to seem right to me is right' (*Inv.* 258).
5. 'And that only means that here we can't talk about "right".' (Ibid.).
6. If the distinction between 'correct' and 'seems correct' has disappeared, then so has the concept *correct*.
7. It follows that the 'rules' of my private language are only *impressions* of rules (*Inv.* 259).
8. My impression that I follow a rule does not confirm that I follow a rule, unless there can be something that will prove my impression correct.
9. And the something cannot be another impression – for:
10. This would be 'as if someone were to buy several copies of the morning paper to assure himself that what it said was true' (*Inv.* 165).
11. The proof that I am following a rule must appeal to something *independent* of my impression that I am.
12. If in the nature of the case there cannot be such an appeal, then my private language does not have *rules*.

These are Malcolm's sentences and quotations, in sequence (pp. 42–3 above), but the numbering is mine.

The first remark to be made is that Wittgenstein's and Malcolm's discussions relate to the assumption that Privatus wrote the isolated symbol 'E' on a calendar, while he is not given the privilege of using the rest of Privatish. As we said this is an unfair *reductio ad absurdum*.

The second remark is that the quotation from Malcolm does *not* prove that in a private language the distinction between 'correct' and 'seems correct' is missing – except in as much as this follows from sentences 8 and 9 or 11 and 12. The first three sentences are questions, *not* reasons, which simply formulate the issue in slightly different ways. Sentence 4 formulates, precisely, the *conclusion* to be established ('Whatever is going to seem right to me [or Privatus] is right'). Sentence 5 is a consequence of the fourth one – but it cannot be asserted unless the fourth is established. The next assertion, in sentence 6, follows from the preceding one, and so depends on the thesis formulated in sentence 4, which *still* is to be proven. Sentence 7, I think, is a logical truth ('It follows that . . .') viz., that something follows from sentence 6; but what comes after the word 'follows' is still hanging in mid-air, and will be there, until what the fourth sentence asserts is shown to be true. The next two assertions, in sentences 8 and 9, can be taken to constitute the premises of an argument. The tenth sentence gives, as a reason for the ninth, an analogy, which by itself proves nothing. Sentences 11 and 12 look like a repetition of sentences 8 and 9. But there is a difference.

Thus, to examine Malcolm's and Wittgenstein's argument in their *reductio ad absurdum*, we must first focus our logical microscopes on 8 and 9:

8. My impression that I follow a rule does not confirm that I follow a rule, unless there can be something that will prove my impression correct.
9. And the something cannot be another impression.

Clearly, these two assertions by themselves do not entail that a private rule, or a private language, is impossible. To prove this we need a minor premise.

9A. The user of a private language can avail himself of impressions only.

Unfortunately, 9A is far from being obviously true. It might be thought that all private objects are impressions. But even if this were to be granted, 9A would still be true only of the purely private languages. With the equation of private object and impression, propositions 8 and 9 would then amount to the statement that the user of a purely private language cannot resort to his private objects to check whether he is following a rule of his language. But neither this proposition nor the equation of impression and private object is self-evident. It is not even clear how one should attempt to prove them. At any rate, the argument so produced would not exclude the possibility of a mixed language.

Let us turn now to the alternative premises:

11. The proof that I am following a rule must appeal to something *independent* of my impression that I am.

12. If in the nature of the case there cannot be such an appeal, then my private language does not have *rules*.

Sentence 12 seems to be saying essentially the same as 8, but the meaning of 12 is clarified by 11, which differs from 9, which supplements the meaning of 8. Sentences 11–12 do not forbid Privatus to check whether he is following a rule of Privatish by means of other impressions of his; they only require that he make use of impressions which are independent of his impression that he is following the rule (correctly). They do not beg the question against a purely private language. In short, 11 and 12 are very reasonable; the only restriction one should impose on them is *that they must also hold for public languages* – if the alleged *reductio* is to be genuine.

No doubt, from 11 and 12 it does follow that Privatish is not a language – provided that we can establish the antecedent of 12:

12A. In the nature of the case there cannot be an appeal to something independent of Privatus' impression that he is using a rule of Privatish correctly, to check whether his use is in fact correct or not.

But this proposition must be established. Indeed, given the direction of the argument, it is precisely the substance of Wittgenstein's thesis.

The Charge Reformulated: self-correction

Can Privatus avail himself of something independent of his impression that he is following a rule of Privatish to check whether he is in fact following it? If there is something which meets the requirements, then the argument of Wittgenstein and Malcolm cannot succeed, unless it follows some line different from the one now being discussed.

Before proceeding any further, it should be noticed that the above formulation of the issue is misleading and biased. It presents Privatus as deciding whether a certain utterance of his accords with a certain rule. The contention is that the utterance is arbitrarily chosen so that it is legitimate to generalise to all utterances in Privatish. But the initial set-up is distorted. We cannot require Privatus to know the formulation of the rule in question.

There is an insight in saying that language is a set of rules; but it is misleading to say that to use language is to *obey* or *follow* rules. For the most part one's actions exhibit certain regularities, which one would describe as actions in accordance with certain rules. But one is not obeying or trying to follow a rule. If an action is successful, i.e. if there are no unexpected obstacles, there is no question about having followed a rule correctly. Inasmuch as it makes sense to say that when a person speaks or writes he applies the rules governing the use of the expressions he employs, *linguistic rules have to be precisely rules which are much more often than not applied correctly without their correct application being an issue at all*, as Wittgenstein well knew (cf. *Inv.* 207). If every sound or word were uttered from the conception of its rule, we would have to be aware of the rules in question in a language or in words (including the logical words), altogether different from the language or words we are to use in following those rules. But we would need another language to formulate and try to obey those rules, if every use of language is a case of obeying rules, and so on *ad infinitum*. This is a platitude, but it is worth emphasising, for it would be bad logic to suppose that Privatus must decide for each rule he abides by in making a Privatish utterance, that he is following it. He should be supposed, like any speaker of a public language, both.

(*a*) to be using Privatish words (correctly or incorrectly) without having *to think*, let alone decide, that each one is used correctly;

and

(*b*) to be using most of them correctly as a matter of course.

As Wittgenstein has greatly emphasised, a language (and, naturally, he is speaking of a public language) has to have 'enough regularity' (*Inv.* 207), i.e. people cannot always be mistaken in their use of words; for the most part they must get to use them rightly (see also *Inv.* 222–4, 245). Indeed, as he goes on to stress: 'If language is to be a means of communication there must be agreement not only in definitions but also (queer as this may sound) in judgments ... what we call "measuring" is partly determined by a certain constancy in results of measurement' (*Inv.* 242).

Thus, in the case of Privatus and Privatish it is fair to assume, in so far as for the purpose of our *reductio ad absurdum* we are assuming that Privatish is a language, that Privatus is for the most part consistent in his use of Privatish, that his use of signs possesses 'enough regularity', and also that he holds certain true beliefs about his private objects, which beliefs are the counterparts of the judgments agreed on in the case of a public language.

Wittgenstein or Malcolm cannot imply that Privatus must decide whether each word is used correctly or not. All that they may argue is: (i) that it must be *possible* for Privatus to misapply the rules of Privatish, (ii) that it must be *possible* for Privatus to know that he has made a mistake, and (iii) that he must know how to correct some of his mistakes.

Examination of the Charge

Now Privatish is not a language, if Wittgenstein's and Malcolm's contention is true that Privatus cannot appeal to something independent of his impression that he is following a rule to check whether he is in fact following it or not. But is this contention true?

It is false. Privatus can resort to practically all the 'things' to which the speakers of public, or of ordinary, languages have recourse – he can do this even in the case in which Privatish is a *purely* private language. In general, to determine whether or not a word has been correctly used, we resort to the objects of our experience, the noises or marks which constitute our language, the memories of past utterances, the entailments among our concepts, and the generalisations which relate different kinds of objects. In the case of a public language, we can ask a fellow speaker, or we can receive his unsolicited corrections. This is, of course, not open to Privatus. Yet that circumstance cannot be at this juncture an objection against Privatish being a language. The very issue is, in part, whether that circumstance *is* a necessary condition for a language.

One thing, however, is definitely clear, namely, *that a person possesses a language only inasmuch as he is capable of self-correction.* A person has not learned colour words or English, unless he is able to use his symbols independently of another's approval; but then he will know how to correct his occasional mistakes.

Privatus *qua* speaker of Privatish has his experiences and the objects, private or public, which he apprehends in them, his memories of previous utterances, the words of Privatish, the logical connections among these, and the generalisations which link some objects to others. Clearly, most of them are independent of his impression that he is using a certain word correctly. Even his memory images that on, say, five occasions in the past he described a private object as A may be wholly independent of his present impression that 'A' applies to the same or some similar object.

Privatus can correct his mistaken uses of words in essentially the same way in which we normally correct our linguistic errors. For instance, an English speaker can correct his misapplication of a word simply by noting that the object is not what he called it; he may say: 'That red,... I mean, brown chair...' Here we have a linguistic self-correction. If a rule of language was not followed (I suppose, the one governing the use of the expression 'red' or 'brown') and a correction was made, then Privatus may be correcting his having not followed a linguistic rule of Privatish in a case in which he says: 'This A, that is, this B...', where 'A' and 'B' may very well be private predicates. Often, in the English example, the speaker knows of his slip on hearing his utterance of the word 'red', and clearly, both his hearing of it and the noise he hears are independent of his impression that he was using the correct word. Exactly the same can be said of Privatus and his Privatish expressions 'A' and 'B'. The possibility of such a case provides a counterexample to Wittgenstein's and Malcolm's contention.

It may be argued that the English speaker can correct himself without having anything at all independent of his impression that he used the word 'red' correctly, that he can correct his slip without hearing his words, etc. Then it is argued that in the case of an ordinary language, which is assumed to be public throughout, since private languages are claimed to be impossible, a person can correct himself without the aid of anything independent of his impression that he has used a word correctly. *But then it is bad logic to require a private language to meet qua language a condition which is not regarded as necessary for language.* It may be replied that in the English case, others can in principle correct the speakers. This is certainly true. But it cannot be adduced as a reason by itself, for the argument is precisely intended to prove that *because* of the fact that others cannot correct him Privatus cannot correct himself. The fact in question has been assumed from the very beginning; the issue is the *because*.

To belabour the point, let us consider another situation. A person can become aware of, and correct, a slip thanks to his wanting to make a certain inference and finding himself using the right generalisation. For instance, one may say 'This is an elephant; since every rhinoceros has a horn on its nose, this, I mean, this rhinoceros, not this elephant, will have a horn on its nose.' Here the items independent of the impression attached to the first use of the word 'elephant' that it is a correct use are (or may very well be): the desire to make the reasoning in question valid (which requires the premise 'This is a rhinoceros'), the awareness of uttering or thinking that every rhinoceros has a horn on its nose, the utterance, the uttered premise 'This is an elephant' (whose lingering presence to the mind is necessary as part of the inference), the awareness (or 'feeling' or impression) that the validity of the inference requires the two premises to have a common term at those places, etc. These are not all impressions (in any normal sense of the word), but even if impressions, they are independent of the impression that the word 'elephant' was used correctly. There is nothing in the case which requires that other persons can correct the speaker, even if merely in principle. Privatus may do exactly the same while using Privatish.

Furthermore, on the assumption, as presented in the final statement of the assumption for the *reductio*, that Privatish is a private language, Privatus is automatically allowed to avail himself of other items which are independent of his impression that he has used a certain term correctly. He may write one afternoon, under our telescopes:

> (α) This is an E. Since all E's are followed by B's, this A will be followed by a B.
> There is a B.

Suppose, in accordance with the assumption *to be shown* to be self-contradictory, that 'A', 'E' and 'B' are purely private predicates. Clearly, Privatus can a few minutes later (as measured by our clocks) read the entry (α) in his diary. He reads it aloud, stops at the symbol 'A', scratches it off and writes just above it the symbol 'E'. Here, in addition to the items mentioned above, he has the written text and his visual perceptions, which are certainly independent of his impression that he used the word 'E' correctly.

I conclude, then, that if for the purpose of a *reductio ad absurdum* it is fully assumed that Privatus possesses a private language, i.e. a whole system of symbols whose use is interrelated, habits of using such symbols, and enough private objects which manifest sufficient regularities, then Privatus has everything necessary for linguistic self-correction, which after all is really the necessary condition at issue for the possession of a language. The symbols of the language, the private objects themselves, the logical or grammatical interrelations among the former, the empirical generalisations linking the latter, the memories of previous uses of language, are all available to the speaker of a private language. Hence, the important premises 9A and 12A quoted above (under 'The Charge: Possibility of Mistakes), necessary for the success of the Wittgenstein–Malcolm argument under discussion, cannot be established.

First Rejoinder: Infinity of Doubts

It is sometimes argued that the speaker of a private language can never be sure that he is using a (private) sign correctly, even if he has something with which to test his use of the sign for correctness. Suppose Privatus has something, say B, against which he can test his present use of the sign 'A'; surely, he can misinterpret B; so he can be in doubt as to whether he is using B correctly; thus he would have to appeal to something else, say C, to test the correctness of his application of B; but again, he can misinterpret or misapply C, and so on *ad infinitum*.

The argument is a telling one. It shows that there can be no *logical* certainty that a descriptive word has been used consistently throughout. *But this is also true of public languages.* If I say 'This is red', and you tell me that it is blue, to be sure that my use of 'red' is incorrect I must be sure that your use of 'blue' is correct. But to be sure of that I must be sure that it is true that you have in fact said 'No, it is blue'; and for this I must be sure that you are there, are not a deaf-mute, were talking to me, etc. And each of these *can* also be subjected to a doubt. So, if to be certain that a word has been used correctly (or incorrectly) I must reach a point where no doubt is possible, then public languages also fall under the axe of the present argument. This is a *reductio ad absurdum* of the rejoinder.

Second Rejoinder: 'Mistakes, not Slips'

Often a defender of Wittgenstein's thesis argues that the issue whether or not Privatus can misapply the rules of Privatish and correct himself has not been touched by such discussion. He insists that a relevant mistake and a relevant correction are a mistaken belief of Privatus and his correction of such a belief about his private objects or about the rules of Privatish. The Wittgensteinian often argues that whatever Privatus believes to be A will have to be A, for it is so for him and he has nothing independent against which to check his *belief*.

A verbal slip is as good as any other case of not doing what the rule prescribes. The essential feature of rules, which distinguishes them from descriptions of action, is that they can hold (be true or valid) regardless of what the agent (for whom they prescribe some action) performs, while at the same time they differ from grammatical or analytic statements in that they can be fulfilled (satisfied) or not. Whether it is because of a slip or a misinterpretation or something else that an agent does not satisfy the rule is completely immaterial.

Is it not true that if Privatus follows the rules of Privatish, he calls every case of A 'A'? Then, since in the case of a slip he calls an instance of A 'E' and not 'A', he did not follow, or write in accordance with, all the rules of the Privatish language.

Let us accept then that the possibility of verbal slips is not enough to show that Privatish conceived as having objects of type (6) or type (5) – as we listed them at the outset – is a language; let us take it as established the Privatish must allow Privatus the possibility of holding some false belief. As in the case of mistakes in doing something in accordance with a rule, we must concede: (i) that Privatus must be in a position to have some false beliefs, even if in fact he never does; (ii) that Privatus must be in principle capable of knowing of some of his false beliefs that they are false; and (iii) that Privatus must be able to correct some of his mistakes in belief.

It is quite apparent that Privatus can make predictions about his private objects, and those predictions can turn out to be false. Hence, Privatish does not prevent Privatus from entertaining false beliefs.

Suppose that Privatus calls an object a 'B' if it is M and becomes P while remaining M. Then he can be mistaken and find out that he is mistaken when he says that a certain object is a B on the evidence that it is M. However, it may be replied that Privatus cannot be mistaken about something being M, provided that he is using the term 'M' correctly.

Suppose that Privatus cannot have a false belief about his present directly experienceable private objects or pains, unless he has forgotten the meaning of the relevant terms. But even this is not so simple as it looks. The application of every predicate involves an implicit comparison with both previous and later applications, as well as an implicit connection between the predicate in question and other predicates. Thus, one can be mistaken about those implicit features which constitute the grammar of the predicate. Privatus can have a doubt as to whether something he is experiencing is an M or not only because he has forgotten the meaning of 'M', without this entailing the absurdity that he lacks even the faintest idea of what an M is like while he can formulate his doubt about the object being M or not. Forgetting the meaning of 'M' is not a black-or-white situation. One may have forgotten the meaning of 'orange' *enough* so as not to be able to tell whether a given object is orange or not; but one can have the doubt because one knows that orange is a colour and knows that it keeps certain similarities to red, for instance. One can even resolve one's doubt by testing for the appearance of the colour of the object in question by mixing red and yellow pigments, if one remembers that orange is thus producible. And this need not involve the claim that orange is defined as the colour obtained by mixing red and yellow pigments. All that one needs is to hold fast to the generalisation that orange is as a matter of empirical fact so produced. *It is an essential part of the meaning of an empirical word that it must enter into well-grounded generalisations.* Likewise, one may even decide whether a certain sensation is of pain or not by cutting oneself and experiencing a typical case of pain. Again, here it is only necessary that the empirical link between pains and wounds of the relevant sort be well established.

Once again, we find that if Privatus is allowed to support a given application of an expression of Privatish with the rest of the Privatish language, he can avail himself of the objects of his experience, the other expressions, the entailment relationships, and the empirical generalisations, and thus he can check whether *some* of his beliefs are true or false.

The rejoinder, then, is met. Privatish allows Privatus to have some false beliefs, to experience some doubts about certain facts (or propositions) formulable in the purely private part of Privatish, and to resolve some of those doubts.

Further Rejoinder: Other Persons' Corrections

We have encountered the suggestion that other persons' corrections are (in principle) necessary for the acquisition of the concept of *correct*. At some place Malcolm, for instance, alleges that 'on the private-language hypothesis, no one can teach me what the correct use of "same" is' (p. 47 above). Wittgenstein expresses himself in the same vein:

> 'Before I judge that two images which I have are the same, I must recognise them as the same.' And when that has happened, how am I to know that the word 'same' describes what I recognise? Only if I can express my recognition in some other way, and *if it is possible for someone else to teach me that 'same' is the correct word here.* (*Inv.* 378, my italics.)

Here the argument is not that Privatus *has* not learned from others the correct use of a word, but that he *could* not have learned it from others.

It is true that in the case of a purely private language nobody else can teach the speaker how to use a private predicate. This is a trivial consequence of the definition of 'private language'. But the major premise of the argument is not obvious at all: that if nobody else can teach Privatus the use of some word he does not know how to use it. Indeed, the argument along the present lines just reduces to the proof of that conditional. We have a right to expect an argument to show that if other persons' corrections are not available, the whole idea of *correct* is not available, either.

The Need for Others' Corrections

Even though neither Malcolm nor Wittgenstein has proved that Privatus' concept of correct use must come from outside Privatish, may this not be so? Our discussion (in 'The Charge Reformulated: Self-correction', and later) seems already to show that it need not be so. Nevertheless, somebody may stress that if it is *logically* impossible for another person to correct Privatus' use of language, then he cannot tell whether his use is correct or not. But 'Nobody else can correct Privatus' does *not* entail 'Privatus cannot correct himself', regardless of whether 'can' expresses here a logical modality or not.

It seems strange that a *mere* logical possibility of being corrected by somebody else could serve as an antidote against Privatus' mistakes. To know that he has made a mistake and to know how to correct it require a good deal more than the purely abstract possibility that if somebody were to speak Privatus' language such a person could tell him what he did wrong and why. If nobody is *in fact* around to correct Privatus' mistakes, or if nobody can correct his mistakes simply because nobody around him speaks his public language, then he will be in just as bad a predicament as if his language were private (in the sense characterised in *Inv.* 243). He would be left entirely to himself and his mistakes, without any help which could in fact enable him to distinguish the correct from the incorrect. As I see it, if it were legitimate to require seriously the possibility of other persons' corrections, it would be impossible to have the case of a single person speaking a public language, e.g. Dalmatian or ordinary English. Yet at the end of the nineteenth century there was just Antonio Udina who spoke Dalmatian, and it makes sense to suppose that World War III may leave on earth exactly one English speaker with no knowledge of any other language. Obviously, whatever the last speaker of English were to say would be right – in so far as nobody else could correct him. It would be of no avail to say 'Well, if there were another English speaker near him, such a speaker *could* correct him.' The issue is not whether he *could* have a language, but whether he *has* one. The point is that he would in fact be uttering sounds under no checks whatever – except what he remembered and what he experienced.

Indeed, it is not even clear that a person who spends some time in isolation would be actually using rules – if we are to require that other persons' checks be necessary. Clearly, the longer he remains alone the greater are his chances of making mistakes, and, once again, the *mere* abstract logical possibility of another person's corrections is too tenuous to be of real help. It is very difficult to see how the mere fact that *if* another person were beside the isolated speaker he could correct him, provides that speaker with checks and criteria and the conception of *correct* and the conception of *true*, even though *in fact* there is nobody beside him and he hears no voices approving of his use of language or confirming his beliefs! The only positive way in which the isolated speaker can detect and correct his mistakes is by actually checking his assertions or beliefs against the objects as they appear to him or as he remembers them – exactly as Privatus has been doing all along while using Privatish.

It may be adduced that there is a difference between Privatus on the one hand, and on the other Antonio Udina (when he became the last speaker of Dalmatian), Robinson Crusoe, and an isolated speaker of, say, Spanish. These persons have all *acquired the concept* of correctness from their elders, whereas Privatus did not; and it may be alleged that the issue is not whether a person's uses of words are corrected or not, but whether the person has come into possession of the concept of correctness. Thus, according to this allegation, Antonio Udina's knowledge of Dalmatian may deteriorate if nobody can in practice correct him, but since he has acquired the concept of correct use he can go on speaking Dalmatian indefinitely. This is an exciting line of argument, but it is irrelevant to the private language issue. As noticed at the beginning, the mode of acquisition of the use of words, i.e. of a concept, is not a characteristic feature of language: 'It is logically possible that someone [why not either Privatus or Antonio Udina indifferently?] should have been born with a knowledge of the use of an expression or that it should have been produced in him by a drug' (*Philosophical Review*, LXIII (1954) p. 544).

(ii) *V. C. Chappell*

Castañeda's paper contains a good deal that I cannot accept, and my general judgement is that though he makes a number of valuable points in his examination of what he calls 'the private language argument', his case against Wittgenstein and Malcolm is, as a whole, unsuccessful.

I shall comment on two things specifically: (A) what Castañeda calls 'the assumption for the private language argument', or in other words what he claims the expression 'private language' means for Wittgenstein and Malcolm and hence what he claims is the view that Wittgenstein and Malcolm, in their arguments against a private language, are attacking; and (B) Castañeda's own attack upon the private language argument, as he understands it, which argument he ascribes to Wittgenstein although it is Malcolm's statement of it that he actually discusses. I shall claim, regarding (A), that there is no warrant for attributing Castañeda's 'assumption' to Wittgenstein and Malcolm and in fact good reason for denying that they do or would accept it; and, regarding (B), that Castañeda's main counter-argument to Wittgenstein's (or anyhow Malcolm's) argument, even given his interpretation of it, is faulty.

(A) According to Castañeda, 'Wittgenstein's thesis is that a private language is logically impossible' (p. 135 above). This thesis, he says, is supported by an argument of the *reductio ad absurdum* form, and he approves Malcolm's characterisation of Wittgenstein's procedure: 'postulate a "private" language; then deduce that it is not a *language*'. But what is this 'private language' that is so postulated? Castañeda cites a passage from the *Investigations* in which, he says, Wittgenstein 'seems to define a private language': 'The individual words of this language are to refer to what can only be known to the person speaking; to his immediate private sensations. So another person cannot understand the language' (*Inv.* 243). But this definition, if it is that, may not be complete; as Castañeda notes, this passage does not make altogether clear what the 'language' in question is. So this remains to be determined. Wittgenstein himself is of little help here, though he does refer again to the 'language' of 243 in later passages. In *Inv.* 256, e.g., he considers 'the language which describes my inner experiences and which only I myself can understand.' But he really tells us no more about this 'language' in this passage; he only makes more explicit what

was surely explicit enough in 243, that not being understandable by anyone other than the speaker is a necessary condition for
something's being a 'private language'. Again, in 258 Wittgenstein
presents a case which is plainly meant to be an example of the
'language' referred to in 243 and 256. This is the case in which I
'keep a diary about the recurrence of a certain sensation', making
use of the 'sign "E"'. But here again, the only thing that is clear
from the text about the 'language' which my use of 'E' constitutes
or perhaps belongs to is that I alone am capable of understanding
it. And I think there is no other passage in the *Investigations* in
which any more than this is said about the postulated 'language' of
243 and following.

Perhaps then Wittgenstein intended the condition stated in these
passages to be sufficient as well as necessary for something's being a
'private language'. This is, I think, the most plausible view to take,
and I believe it is the view that Malcolm takes. The specification
given *is* complete; what is said is all that is meant to be true of the
postulated 'language'. Castañeda, however, thinks otherwise. Our
assumption regarding the diary keeper of *Inv.* 258, he says, 'cannot be
that [he] is trying to keep a diary with *only* the sign "E"'. Rather 'we
must assume that he has at his disposal a set of signs interrelated by
means of a network of merely linguistic rules and a good deal more'
(pp. 135–6 above). But why must we make this assumption? The
nearest thing to an explicit answer to this question that I can find in
Castañeda's text is this, that if we did not we should not be taking
the 'definition of a private language in *Inv.* 243 . . . as an honest
effort at giving the idea of a private language a full run' (p. 136
above). Or as he later puts it, the *reductio ad absurdum* would, in
this case, be 'unfair' (p. 143 above). Castañeda's reasoning seems to
be as follows. A private language is, after all, a language; that is
what it is *called*. And a language, as Wittgenstein himself has
taught us, 'is a system or aggregate of rules, a system or aggregate
of linguistic activities' (p. 135 above). Hence the postulated 'private
language' must be such a system or aggregate, and this means that
it must not be denied 'all logical terms' and must not be considered
'as having no propositions in common with any other language'
(pp. 136–7 above).

Now this reasoning, I submit, is inconclusive at best. To 'postulate' something for the purpose of reducing it to absurdity is not, or
not necessarily, to suppose that it *is* what it is *referred to as*; it is not
to attribute to it all of the features which things correctly called by
its name do or must have. One does not confer existence or a nature

upon something by 'postulating' it in this way, any more than one confers existence upon something by mentioning it; we have only to recall Russell's and Quine's worries about negative existential statements to be clear about this. Thus, the barber who shaves all and only those who do not shave themselves is not a man, nor is he not a man. To argue that he must be a man is like arguing that Hamlet's grandfather must have been a Dane or that the Loch Ness Monster must have a tail. In each case the question as to what the mentioned subject is or has simply does not apply. Of course there must be some warrant for referring to a postulated entity in the way that one does, for calling it by that name rather than some other. But this may be provided if the entity be given some of the features necessary to the things that are normally and correctly called by that name; it need not be given all of them. Typically, indeed, a *reductio ad absurdum* argument proceeds as follows: a postulated entity, referred to as it is because it has some of the features necessary to the actually existing things that are (correctly) referred to in this way, is shown not to have certain further features necessary to such things because the features which it is postulated to have logically rule out its having these further features. Wittgenstein's private language argument, as I see it, conforms to this pattern. A private language is postulated; we call it a language because it is supposed to have words, and these are supposed to be used to refer, a linguistic activity. But, so the argument runs, because the supposed referents of these supposed words are 'private', in a certain special sense, reference to them is in fact impossible, and the supposed words are not words at all, from which it follows that the supposed language which they constitute or belong to is no language after all.

It is clear, I think, that Wittgenstein *is* merely 'postulating' a private language in the *Investigations* passages to which Castañeda refers. In the portion of *Inv.* 243 immediately preceding that in which Castañeda finds his 'definition' of a private language, Wittgenstein says that we are to consider whether a private language is 'thinkable' – or, in Miss Anscombe's translation, whether we could *imagine* any such thing – in other words, whether any such thing is possible. There is no question here of some *existing* thing's *being* a language, or of its *not* being one. The question rather is whether any *such* thing as a private language *could* exist – and the content of the 'such' here is given in the immediately following 'definition'.

If Wittgenstein does argue as I have suggested, then not only is the attribution to him of Castañeda's 'assumption' unwarranted, it is positively implausible. For if Wittgenstein does want to show that the postulated private language cannot have certain features that any language must have, then it would certainly be odd for him to build those very features into his conception of a private language. And yet this is what he would be doing if Castañeda were right. For it is (roughly) just the absence of 'logical terms' and of what, in Castañeda's view, this entails that makes the postulated private language not a language, according to Wittgenstein. Besides which, there is a passage in the *Investigations* which strongly suggests, if it does not quite state, that the diary keeper's 'language' is to have no terms in common with 'our common language', including, one would think, Castañeda's 'logical terms'. This is *Inv.* 261, which Castañeda quotes (p. 136 above), oddly enough, without grasping its import for his interpretation of Wittgenstein's position.

But this is not the worst of it. As far as I can see, Castañeda, by attributing his 'assumption for the private language argument' to Wittgenstein, all but begs the main question of his paper, the question of the cogency of Wittgenstein's argument. For Castañeda rests his case against the argument primarily on the premise that the postulated private language does have 'logical terms', with all that he thinks this entails – which, by the time the fray is actually joined, has become a good deal: when 'for the purpose of a *reductio ad absurdum* it is fully assumed that Privatus [the diary keeper] possesses a private language, [what is assumed is that he has] a whole system of symbols whose use is interrelated, habits of using such symbols, and enough private objects which manifest sufficient regularities' (p. 149 above). I shall argue shortly that Castañeda's case is faulty even on this premise. But that aside, his case is surely not successful if the premise in question is not Wittgenstein's. And in the absence of any convincing reason for thinking that it is. Castañeda's mere claim that it 'must be' smacks strongly of a *petitio*.

There is one curious statement in Castañeda's paper which bears on this point. On p. 143 above, after quoting the passage in which Malcolm states (what Castañeda accepts as) Wittgenstein's argument, Castañeda says that 'Wittgenstein's and Malcolm's discussions relate to the assumption that Privatus wrote the isolated symbol "E" on a calendar, while he is not given the privilege of using the rest of Privatish [i.e. the private language conceived in accordance with Castañeda's "assumption", which is to say as containing "logical terms"]. As we said, this is an unfair *reductio ad absurdum*.' The curious thing is that Wittgenstein and Malcolm should not be trusted to determine what should and should not be allowed to

Privatus – as if it were not they who introduced the notion of a private language in the first place! Castañeda here, I think, gives away the show.

In any case, I conclude that Castañeda's attribution of his 'assumption for the private language argument' to Wittgenstein and Malcolm is both unwarranted and implausible, and besides begs, or comes close to begging, the larger question of the soundness of the private language argument, at least as Wittgenstein and Malcolm themselves understand it.

(B) If the argument that Castañeda attacks is not the argument that Wittgenstein and Malcolm have in mind, then Castañeda has no case against *them*, whether or not he begs any questions in attributing his version of the argument to them. But I want now to show that Castañeda's case is not even successful against his own version of the private language argument, and hence that his attack on Wittgenstein and Malcolm miscarries twice over.

The crux of the argument, as Castañeda understands it, is the claim that 'it is impossible for Privatus to make mistakes in using the (so-called) signs belonging to Privatish' or 'in the exercise of the rules constituting Privatish' (p. 143 above). Castañeda grants (what he takes to be Wittgenstein's view) that 'if there is no way in which Privatus can misapply the signs belonging to Privatish, then this is not made up of rules and is, therefore, not a language' (ibid.). Castañeda also grants that Privatus cannot misapply the sign 'E', e.g. if it is not possible to prove that his use of 'E' on a given occasion is or is not correct, and if it is not possible for him to know that he has misapplied 'E' and correct his mistake. Wittgenstein and Malcolm argue that no proof of the correctness of any use of 'E' is possible and that the user of a private language can neither know of nor correct linguistic mistakes; the very notion of correctness is out of place here. It follows, so their argument concludes, that the user of a private language cannot make mistakes. It is this argument, specifically, that Castañeda attacks. One of its necessary premises, he says, 'cannot be established' (p. 149 above). In fact what he claims is that the premise in question is *false*. In either case, what he should claim thence is that Malcolm's and Wittgenstein's conclusion is without warrant, but again, what he does claim is that the conclusion is false: Privatus *can* make mistakes. Castañeda does not, so far as I can tell, argue explicitly for this stronger claim, but his reasoning seems to be this: what makes the Wittgensteinian–Malcolmian premise referred to false is the (alleged) fact that Privatish is just like our ordinary language in certain respects. In particular, Privatus 'can resort to practically all the "things" to which the speakers of public, or of ordinary, languages have recourse' in order to prove the correctness of some one of his uses of 'E' and to recognise and correct any linguistic mistakes he might make. Since, then, it is possible for the speaker of ordinary language to make linguistic mistakes, so too is it possible for Privatus to do so.

It is precisely here that Castañeda seems to me to beg the question as to the soundness of Wittgenstein's and Malcolm's argument. His claim that Privatus 'can resort to practically all the "things" to which the speakers of public, or of ordinary, languages have recourse" (p. 147 above) seems to me to be founded directly and only on his 'assumption' that the private language discussed by Wittgenstein, being a language, has 'logical terms'. And this assumption, as I have indicated, seems to me to have no other basis than that Castañeda's critique of Wittgenstein requires it. But it is not this point that I am trying to establish now. Rather, what I now want to show is that the 'things' to which, according to Castañeda, Privatus 'can resort' are such that *either* an appeal to them would not prove the correctness of anything, *or* the claim that Privatus can resort to them is inconsistent with the original and explicit stipulation regarding the use of the sign 'E', e.g. that 'E' be used to refer to a 'private' object and that it be intelligible to no one but its user. In other words, I want to show that Castañeda's case against Wittgenstein and Malcolm is faulty even if they do hold the view that he ascribes to them, of what a private language is or could be. For whether or not this language includes 'logical terms', with whatever else this entails, some of its terms must be such that no one but the speaker can understand them, and this because they are used to refer to objects which only the speaker can know about. This much Wittgenstein says, explicitly; it is the presence of such 'private' terms, after all, that makes Privatish a private language. Hence it is Privatus' use of *these* terms that must be subject to mistakes, correction, and proof of correctness, whatever other terms Privatish contains and whatever is true of these. My claim will be that recourse to the 'things' to which Castañeda says Privatus can have recourse, in order to prove the correctness or incorrectness of some application of a term, is either fruitless or impossible when the term in question is private, and hence that, at the very least, Castañeda has not established that Privatus can make mistakes in using the private terms of Privatish.

How do Wittgenstein and Malcolm back their claim that the

user of a private language cannot make linguistic mistakes, that,
e.g., the diary keeper of *Inv.* 258 cannot misapply the sign 'E'?
Castañeda confines his attention to the sketch of Wittgenstein's
reasoning that is given by Malcolm (pp. 42–3 above). According to Malcolm, to misapply a word is to violate the rule which
governs its (correct) application. In the case of 'E', the rule
can only be that 'E' be used consistently, i.e. used for the same sort
of thing on each occasion; since 'E' is a private word, the question
of whether the speaker's use of it agrees with others' use of it cannot
arise. But now a rule cannot be violated, or indeed followed, unless
it is possible to prove that a given use of language does or does not
conform to it – in the case of 'E', unless it is possible to prove that
the diary keeper's application of 'E' on a given occasion is consistent, or inconsistent, with his previous applications. But how is this
to be done by the user of a private sign? What does the diary keeper
have to go on? He may be convinced that he is using 'E' in the
way he has done, but his conviction, or as Malcolm says, his impression, that he is following his rule for 'E', by itself, is insufficient.
For my conviction or impression that such and such is so, counts for
something only in case it is possible to distinguish my *being* right in
thinking what I do, from its *seeming* to me that I am right; otherwise the very notion of 'right' does not apply. In Malcolm's words,
'My impression that I follow a rule does not confirm that I follow a
rule, unless there can be something that will prove my impression
correct. And the something cannot be another impression – for this
would be "as if someone were to buy several copies of the morning
paper to assure himself that what it said was true" (*Inv.* 265). The
proof that I am following a rule must appeal to something independent of my impression that I am. If in the nature of the case there
cannot be such an appeal, then my private language does not have
rules, for the concept of a rule requires that there be a difference
between "He is following a rule" and "He is under the impression
that he is following a rule"' (pp. 42–3 above).
   Castañeda claims that two different arguments are stated in the
passage just quoted, one in the first two sentences, the other in the
last two. He also claims that a necessary premise has been omitted
in both cases. Neither claim, I think, is quite correct. Malcolm is
not so much rigorously stating as sketching Wittgenstein's argument
in the passage in question, and there is considerable looseness in his
presentation of it. I believe the same point is made in the last two
sentences quoted as in the first, and the missing premise is clearly
implied, if not quite stated. Castañeda, I think, has been over-

literal in his reading of Malcolm. If the two pairs of quoted sentences are put together and the implied premise made explicit, Malcolm's argument runs as follows. The proof that someone is following a rule must appeal to something independent of his impression that he is. This something cannot be another impression of his, or anything like an impression – a conviction, an idea, an image, an inclination, or a memory (i.e. a memory-image or memory-belief). The proof must indeed appeal to something outside the subject's mind altogether, something 'non-subjective' (cf. *Inv.* 265). If in the nature of the case there cannot be such an appeal, then no rule is being followed, and hence no language is being used. Now in the case of the user of a private sign or language, in the case of Privatus or the diary keeper of *Inv.* 258, there cannot be such an appeal. Hence a private language is no language, the sign 'E' is no sign, and the use of 'E' is no linguistic activity.

If this is Malcolm's argument (and it seems to me certain that it is) then Castañeda's quarrel with it comes to this: the premise stated in the penultimate step (he would say) 'cannot be established'. It cannot be established because it is, in his view, false. And it is false because the speaker of a private language 'can resort to practically all the "things" to which the speakers of public, or of ordinary, languages have recourse', 'most' of these things being 'independent of his impression that he is using a certain word correctly', so that he is able thereby to 'correct his mistaken uses of words in essentially the same way in which we normally correct our linguistic errors' (p. 147 above). What are these 'things', and how is Privatus, by 're-sorting' to them, able to correct his linguistic errors? Castañeda here, unfortunately, is less than clear. He gives several lists and examples of such 'things', and of ways in which Privatus can correct himself, but the relation between these various lists is obscure and it is uncertain, often, what a proffered example is supposed to be an example of. There is one list, however, which does appear, with minor variations, three different times (p. 147 above twice, p. 149 once), and which appears a fourth time (p. 152 above) with one item omitted, so I shall take this as canonical and give most of my attention to it.

Five 'things' are listed: 'Privatus *qua* speaker of Privatish has (i) his experiences and the objects, public or private, which he apprehends in them, (ii) his memories of previous utterances, (iii) the words of Privatish, (iv) the logical connections among these, and (v) the generalisations which link some objects to others' (p. 147 above, my numbers inserted; earlier on page 147 above (iii) is 'the noises or marks which constitute our language'). I shall now try to show that, of these five things, (i), (ii) and (iii) are such that recourse to them would in no way prove the correctness of any use of language, much less the use of a private term, and (iv) and (v) are such that recourse to them in order to establish the correctness of the application of a private term is logically ruled out by the very fact that the term in question is private. I shall consider each of these five things, briefly, in turn.

(i) How could an appeal to an 'object of our experience' (p. 147 above), especially a private object, provide a proof of anything? The task would be to prove that my use of a certain word, indeed of a private word, as the name of some private object now present to me is consistent with my past use of the same word; i.e. that I have used this word to refer to and only to objects of the same sort as that to which I am now using it to refer. The object or objects to which I may appeal would also, presumably, be now present to me, either the object to which I am referring or some other. But now if the latter, how would an appeal to it have any bearing on my use of the word in question? The only objects in any way relevant to that, surely, are that present object to which I now refer and those past objects for which I have used the same word. And if the object I appeal to is the object I refer to, it is hard to see how that could prove my use of that referring word for it to be correct. Perhaps I am to scrutinise it very closely, examine it more carefully than I did at first. But I am not sure that the idea of scrutinising or examining a private object has any sense. And even if it did, what could such scrutiny establish? Something about the object as it revealed itself to my first careless glance led me to use this word for it in the first place. A closer look might convince me that the object really is as I first thought it was, and hence that this is the right word. But that only touches my *conviction*; the question is whether I am *right*, which is to say, whether this *is* the word that I have used for this sort of object in the past. Closer examination of something in the present decides nothing concerning that. Perhaps Castañeda, misled by Malcolm's word 'impression', has something like this in mind: I have the impression that my use of this word for this object is correct; my impression can be confirmed, its correctness proved, by 'having recourse to' the objects of this impression (an impression is an impression *of* something); I check the impression against these objects, determine whether they match, and so on. But this is hopelessly misguided. In the first place, the impression that Malcolm is speaking of is not an impression *of* but an impression *that*, and as such has no object or archetype. Secondly, even if there were an object or archetype, something of which the impression were somehow an image or copy, the notion that I can compare the two is without sense. If I were capable of getting at the object, directly, as it were, there would have been no need – and no room – for the impression in the first place. And if I am not so capable, the best that I can do is compare the original impression with another impression, or something like an impression, be it memory, perception, or whatever, in that it, too, is just an image or copy of the object. This amounts, I think, to a *reductio ad absurdum* of the view that there are such impressions, and in general of what Reid called the idea theory of perception and thought. (I do not say that Castañeda holds this view.)

(ii) What does Castañeda mean by 'memories' in 'memories of previous utterances'? If he means 'memory impressions' or 'memory beliefs' then (ii) reduces to (i), and the same sorts of points made against it apply here as well. If, on the other hand, Castañeda means by 'memories' 'correct memory impressions' – if, i.e., he intends the use of 'memory' which goes with that use of 'remember' whereby 'I remember that p' implies that p – then his saying that Privatus can resort to his memories of previous utterances, and so prove that his present use of language is correct, clearly begs the question. In either case, an appeal to one's memories proves nothing.

(iii) There is an important difference between the words of a language and the 'noises or marks which constitute' a language, at least as these expressions are normally understood. Among other things, the former are types, the latter tokens – unless Castañeda does intend the two expressions to be equivalent, in which case I cannot tell which way he means them to be taken. But it really makes no difference, for the result is the same in either case. How is one to appeal to a *word* in a language at all, taking 'word' in the type sense? And even if this could be managed, what would any such appeal prove regarding, say, our diary keeper's use of the sign 'E'? Let us imagine him wondering whether 'E' is the right word for the private object now before his mind, or trying to confirm his impression that it is. It is hard to see how an appeal to any other word of his private language besides 'E' would have any bearing on this question. And it is equally hard to see how an appeal to 'E' would accomplish anything, beyond convincing him that it is the word 'E' that he is now concerned about. Let us suppose, then, that our diary keeper appeals to some noise or mark which 'constitutes' a word, i.e. to some token. Again, an appeal to a noise or mark constituting (some utterance or inscription of?) any word other than 'E' would have no relevance to the task at hand. And an appeal to a noise or mark for 'E' would reveal nothing as to the consistency of this present use of 'E' with past uses – which is, after all, what is in question. Besides which, a noise is something heard and a mark something seen, which means that both are objects of experience. Hence the difficulties noted in the discussion of (i) above apply here as well.

(iv) I have been willing to suppose for the sake of argument that Privatish may have 'logical terms' as well as private ones, although I actually believe that the Wittgenstein–Malcolm view excludes this. If then there are these logical terms, so will there be 'logical connections' among them. But our task is not to prove some application of a *logical* term of Privatish correct; it is the private terms that concern us. The question is, then, whether the private terms of Privatish also exhibit logical connections among themselves and with the logical terms. If so, then I believe it would be possible, in principle, to check the use of a private term by appealing to such logical connections, though the details of how this would be done remain to be worked out. But in fact the private terms of Privatish cannot, I think, be logically related, either to other, non-private terms, or among themselves. For if they were so related, then they would not be private, understandable to no one but their user. This is clearly true in the case of relations to non-private or logical terms. For such terms can be understood by persons other than their user, and this means that another person could deduce and hence understand the meaning of a private term via its logical connections with terms whose meanings are, in principle at least, known to him. The same is true, I think, for the case in which a private term is logically related only to other private terms, although I am not quite clear about this. For it seems to me that a term must have a certain stability, as it were, an established use, in order to sustain logical relations to other terms at all, and such stability is just what is ruled out by the term's being private. Or perhaps 'ruled out' is too strong here; perhaps I should say that it is just such stability which is in question in the case of private terms, so that to suppose such a term to have this stability is to beg the question of its being a proper term, or element of language. In any case, an appeal to the logical connections of the private terms of Privatish cannot serve the purpose which Castañeda says it does.

(v) The generalisations to which Castañeda alludes are to 'link some objects to others' and they are also to be empirical (pp. 147 and

149 above). I agree that if there were such generalisations linking private objects with non-private or even other private objects, they could be used to prove, or anyhow to make probable, that the use of a certain word for some private object so linked was or was not correct. But how are such generalisations to be established? Presumably, since they are empirical, by observation (or the like) of the objects to be linked. But as I have already indicated, the idea of observing a private object seems to me not to have any sense. More importantly, one can hardly establish or even undertake to establish a general truth about a thing or sort of thing unless one can refer to that thing or sort on different occasions and know that he is referring to the same thing or sort each time. Hence, to establish generalisations about a private object one would have to know that one's intended references to that object were all, or mostly, in fact references to that object; one would have to know, in other words, that one's use of one's private word for that object was consistent. But this knowledge, of course, is just what an appeal to such generalisations is supposed to provide. In short, generalisations about private objects presuppose, and hence cannot provide, the possibility of proving the correctness of references to such objects. And even if the privacy of private objects does not rule out the existence of such generalisations, as I believe it does, it is at least clear that nothing can be proved by them, or nothing to the purpose at hand. I conclude that Castañeda is no more successful with this item than he is with the other four.

I will comment briefly upon a few of the other alleged things by which, or ways in which, Privatus can, according to Castañeda, prove the correctness of his uses of words and correct his linguistic mistakes. Castañeda says that 'an English speaker can correct his misapplication of a word simply by noting that the object is not what he called it', and that Privatus can do the same (pp. 147–8 above). But how is one, or how is Privatus, to 'note' any such thing? He has his initial impression that the object is what he called it; is he now supposed to dispense with this impression and grasp the object directly? But if he can do this now, why didn't he do it in the first place? And even if he does get past or go around the impression and get to the object itself, what shows or indeed could show that he 'notes' it correctly? Or doesn't this question arise? Castañeda cannot, I think, get any mileage out of this suggestion at all.

On p. 148 above Castañeda notes that an English speaker who makes a linguistic mistake often 'knows of his slip on hearing his utterance of the word [in question], and clearly, both his hearing of it and the noise he hears are independent of his impression that he was using the correct word'. 'Exactly the same', he then says, 'can be said of Privatus.' This, I think, is true. But the English speaker knows *on* hearing, not *by* hearing, and certainly not by *his hearing* or by the *noise*, and it is 'by', not 'on', that Castañeda needs. How could one know or prove or correct anything *by* his hearing or *by* a noise in any case? Also, the sense in which Privatus' hearing himself speak is *independent* of his impression that he is speaking correctly is not the sense that Malcolm and Wittgenstein intend when they say that a proof must appeal to something independent, as I noted earlier. The noise that Privatus makes may be independent in the required sense, but a noise, surely, cannot be used to prove anything.

Finally, in the case that Castañeda describes on pp. 148–9 above, involving an inference, the following are among the items cited as being 'independent of the impression attached to the [speaker's] first use of the word [in question] that it is a correct use': 'the desire to make the reasoning in question valid', 'the awareness of uttering or thinking that' the major premise of the inference is true, and 'the awareness (or "feeling" or impression) that the validity of the inference requires the two premises to have a common term'. Surely, none of these is *either* independent, in the required sense, of the speaker's mind *or* capable of proving the correctness of anything.

I conclude, therefore, that Castañeda fails to make his case against the private language argument even on his own interpretation of it. He has not shown that a necessary premise of the argument cannot be established. Rather, his own contention that the premise is false has not been established.

Castañeda's case against the private language argument is unsuccessful, and doubly so. But is the argument then sound? I do not know, but I think this question ought not to be raised until we understand more clearly just what the argument is. Castañeda, I am sure, has not got it right, but knowing this is far from knowing what the correct formulation would be. I will make only one general suggestion on this point. It seems to me that Wittgenstein's essential target in the argument is a certain conception of sensations and feelings, or more generally, the notion of a necessarily private object, one the 'possessor' of which alone can possibly know about. Wittgenstein seeks to reduce this notion to absurdity, as I see it, by appealing to linguistic considerations. This of course requires certain premises concerning the relation of language to existence and to knowledge, and concerning the nature of meaning and reference, and hence the argument does throw light upon these subjects. But this, I believe, is incidental to Wittgenstein's main purpose. He is not trying to show something about language but rather about sensations or mental phenomena. Linguistic considerations are the means, but an understanding of the latter is the end. An appreciation of this fact is, I believe, the necessary first step to a full and accurate understanding of the private language argument.

(iii) *J. F. Thomson*

It is, as Professor Castañeda says, widely held that Wittgenstein demonstrated the impossibility of a private language. Castañeda does not share that view. He undertakes to examine the Private Language Argument as it is sketched, on Wittgenstein's behalf, by Professor Malcolm, and he claims that when the Argument is properly set out it is seen to be either question-begging or inconclusive. Independently of this (if I understand him properly) he thinks that the Argument could not succeed anyway, since its conclusion is false; private languages exist, hence are possible.

I agree with Castañeda that it is not clear at all what the Private Language Argument is supposed to come to or what its assumptions and its reasoning are. But I think that the difficulties in coming to an understanding of it are much greater than he allows for.

1. Castañeda begins by maintaining that if the notion of a private language is to be given a run for its money, we must be allowed to consider the possibility of 'mixed' languages, languages which contain private sub-languages. A language or sub-language is defined to be private if it contains designations for private objects, where these latter are things which satisfy one or more of the conditions on p. 137 above. He now remarks that English contains a private sub-language, since English-speakers talk about their pains and aches and after-images, and these are private objects in one or more of the required senses. He concludes that English is a counter-example to the thesis that a private language is impossible.

Castañeda supposes then that a private language can be taken as one which contains designations for private objects in his, Castañeda's, sense. I do not think it can.

Wittgenstein asks (*Inv.* 243) whether there could be 'a language in which a person could write down or give vocal expression to his inner experiences – his feelings, moods, and the rest – for his private use'. He makes it plain that this language is not to be 'our ordinary language', but rather one whose words refer 'to what can only be known to the person speaking: to his immediate private sensations'. The German here has 'wissen' – 'Die Wörter dieser Sprache sollen sich auf das beziehen, wovon nur der Sprechende wissen kann' – so that the idea is that the words of the language are to refer to that about which only the speaker of the language can have knowledge. Wittgenstein adds, 'So another person cannot understand the language.' The question whether such a language is possible is returned to in *Inv.* 256: 'Now what about this language which describes my inner experiences and which only I understand?' Wittgenstein at once makes the point that if there were such a language, a connection would have had to be set up between the words of it and the sensations they stood for. But *how*, he asks, would the connection have been set up? Would it have been set up in the same way as the connection is set up between the English word 'pain' and pain? Then, he replies, the language would not be a private one. For the connection between 'pain' and pain is set up via the natural expression of pain. And because of that, 'someone else might understand it [i.e. the language] as well as I'.

What then, for Wittgenstein, makes a language not private, is that there is the possibility of its being understood. And that English is a private language in the relevant sense is something quite implausible.

Wittgenstein says that the words of the (hypothetical) private language are to refer to things that only the speaker can know about, and seems to take this to be much the same as saying that they are to refer to his immediate private sensations. Castañeda restates this in terms of designations for private objects. But then he is not at liberty to put his own interpretation on 'private object'. He has a rather easy job making it out that pains are private objects in his sense. But to show that a pain is a private thing in the sense of *Inv.* 243 he would, I think, have to be able to show something like this: if a man has a pain it is possible for him to know something about his pain which it is impossible that anyone else should know. This condition is stronger than any condition to the effect that if a man has a pain then he has a way of getting to know about his pain which it is impossible for anyone else to have. (Compare Castañeda's conditions 2a and 3a for something to be private, and also what he says on p. 140 above about knowing of a pain privately, apparently just by having it.) It is a stronger condition than is indicated by any of his postulates A through G on p. 139 above, or by J^a. And I conclude that it is also stronger than J*, since he says that J* can be derived from A through G. Now that pains are private in this stronger sense is certainly not obvious, nor would Wittgenstein have admitted that it was true (see *Inv.* 246). So I cannot see that Castañeda's counter-example is anything more than an *ignoratio elenchi*.

It is also a surprising one. Castañeda explicitly notices that Wittgenstein infers from his definition of a private language that only its speaker can understand it. It is strange that he never raises the question whether that inference is a correct one. For, of course, if it is, and if English is a partly private language in the relevant sense, then it seems to follow that someone who says 'I have a toothache' says something which cannot be understood by his dentist or his wife. Does Castañeda accept that conclusion, I wonder?

2. But I now want to make something of the fact that Wittgenstein does not explain or discuss that inference either.

It is usual in this kind of discussion to emphasise that the philosophical question of a private language is of a language which is, as a matter of logical necessity, unintelligible to anyone except its speaker. But this does not by itself explain what the question is. For what would make a language of such a kind that it was logically impossible for anyone but its speaker to understand it? What kind of language is here being envisaged?

Well, as Professor Ayer reminds us (p. 51 above), Professor Carnap once held that if a thirsty man says 'Thirst now' and is held to be referring to his sensations(s) of thirst, it follows that what he says cannot be understood by his hearers. (Or perhaps it cannot be fully or properly or completely understood.) Carnap concluded that 'Thirst now' does not refer to the speaker's sensation but is rather equivalent to some sentence or set of sentences about his body (Physicalism). Let us try to reconstruct the argument here. Given (A) 'If X says "Thirst now" he says something which if true is made true by his having a sensation of thirst', and (B) 'No one but X can know whether X has a sensation of thirst', it does not yet follow that (Z) 'If X says "Thirst now" no one else can understand what he says.' We need some extra premises. It is a reasonable guess that Carnap would have offered something like (C) 'It is possible for Y to understand a sentence only if it is possible for Y to come to know whether the truth-conditions of that sentence are fulfilled.' (C is either a statement of or a consequence of some statement of Verificationism.)

What now about the inference recorded by Wittgenstein in *Inv.* 243, 'So another person cannot understand the language'? How is that inference to be explained? Of course we are not now concerned with 'our ordinary language', but with some hypothetical language. But we still need to have it explained what is supposed to make that hypothetical language unintelligible to anyone but its speaker. All that we are told is that the words of the language are to refer to the immediate private sensations of the speaker, these being apparently things about which he alone can have knowledge. Perhaps then the operative words here are 'immediate' and 'private'. And perhaps Wittgenstein would have offered some argument like the one above, but with the word 'sensation' in A and in B replaced by 'immediate private sensation' to yield two statements which we may call A' and B'. But A' and B' do not entail Z. We need still a third premise. Would Wittgenstein have offered Carnap's verificationist premise C? This may be doubted (at any rate it will be denied). But then what third premise are we to supply? For we still need one – for example a premise spelling out the notion of a sensation's being immediate and private.

If we suppose that by the phrase 'immediate private sensations' Wittgenstein means just *sensation*, then the negative side of what Wittgenstein says is barely distinguishable from the negative side of what Carnap says. On this interpretation Wittgenstein would be denying (or would anyway be committed to denying) that we do ever, in any straightforward sense, report on or talk about our sensations at all. (Cf. Professor Strawson's doubts on this very point in *Mind*, 1954.) Their positive suggestions are of course different. Carnap, unwilling to accept Z, rejected A and adopted physicalism. Wittgenstein, on this way of reading him, also rejects Z and therefore A' (which is now the same as A), adopting rather the view that the relevant sentences are to be seen as avowals, pieces of linguistic behaviour which replace certain kinds of unlearned behaviour. I say 'on this way of reading him', and of course this way of reading him may be wrong. But the alternative is, I think, that Wittgenstein has no coherent view at all. It is clear that throughout these sections of the *Investigations* he is trying to characterise and expose some way of thinking about sensations, some way which makes them out to be 'private objects'. It is to this way of thinking about them that he opposes the reminder about how sensation-words are in fact learned, and the connected idea of avowals. But he does not, I think, ever make it clear what is the way of thinking that he wants to expose and discredit. So the alleged disease and the alleged specific pass each other by.

At all events I am inclined to think that the question raised in *Inv.* 243 is obscure. It is obscure because we are not told what is supposed to make the private language a private language. And that surely needs to be explained. For what otherwise can we make of the idea of a private language, a necessarily private language? And, incidentally, if the question whether a private language is possible is an obscure one, mustn't the claim that Wittgenstein answered it be at least as obscure?

3. When Castañeda turns to examine the Private Language Argument, he proceeds by supposing someone – Privatus – to be speaking or writing a private language, and then asks what objections can be brought against the consistency of that supposition. He considers some objections which are suggested to him by Malcolm's discussion, and concludes that these objections are either inconclusive or question-begging.

I shall not discuss this part of Castañeda's paper (although I am in agreement with much of what he says). This is because, for one thing, I do not see that there is anything in his supposition about Privatus to make Privatus' language a private one in any interesting sense. But, for another, I think that Castañeda has failed to notice that he and Malcolm are likely to be at cross-purposes.

Malcolm does indeed claim to have sketched a proof by *reductio ad absurdum* that a private language is possible, in some unexplained sense of 'private language'. But how seriously does Malcolm himself take that claim? Having sketched the line of argument which Castañeda examines, he imagines an objector to say:

'Even if I cannot prove and know that I am correctly following the rules of my private language, . . . still it *may* be that I am. It has *meaning* to say that I am. The supposition that I am makes sense; you and I *understand* it.'

Malcolm says that Wittgenstein has a reply to this. The reply consists in likening the sentence 'I am following the rules of my private language' to such sentences as 'The stove is in pain'. These 'call up a picture in our minds', and that is about all. So I suppose that if Castañeda were to say, 'Even if we cannot prove and know that Privatus is following rules, perhaps all the same he is; the supposition that he is makes sense', then Malcolm's reply would again be the same.

What Malcolm treats as an objection to his view is of course no more (though equally no less) than a rhetorical restatement of the point at issue. So the 'reply' to it should consist of or appeal to a complete argument against the possibility of a private language. But it doesn't. It amounts to the *assertion* that the supposition of a private language is not a genuine supposition, or is at least in need of explanation. To be willing to make that reply is not (I would have thought) to be even trying to offer or explain a proof of impossibility. It is rather like offering a challenge: 'Make me understand what it would be like for someone to be speaking a private language.' It is rather obvious that Castañeda may now issue a challenge of his own: 'Make me understand what your difficulty is and that it is a real one.'

What future there is for that kind of debate I do not know. But it does seem that Castañeda is writing (not indeed without reason and excuse) as if Malcolm had assumed the burden of proof, and that Malcolm is writing as if the onus of proof or of clarification were on his opponents. If that is so, there is all the more reason for having the terms of the dispute about private languages made clear – or for giving up the whole thing as a mare's nest.

Let me end by stressing the amount of my agreement with Castañeda. (1) It is widely held that Wittgenstein showed something important about the notion of a private language. (2) When we look into this claim, it is not obvious that he did anything of the sort. My disagreement with Castañeda arises over the question whether any clear claim at all has ever been made on Wittgenstein's behalf.

(iv) *Hector-Neri Castañeda*

I

Concerning Professor Chappell's Comment (A)
Although I do not think Chappell has described in general what a *reductio ad absurdum* properly is, I shall not examine his views thereof. I wish to start with two points which especially need emphasis in the issue between us:

(1) in the reduction of a conjunctive concept P&L to absurdity one can distinguish two cases: (a) there is a concept L' which is a conjunction of only some of the necessary conditions constituting L such that P&L' can also be reduced to absurdity; (b) there is no concept L' as described. In case (a), which seems to be the only one that Chappell allows for, there is, however, *no mistake* in deriving an absurdity directly from P&L. Obviously, since being P&L entails being P&L', if P&L' implies an absurdity, so does P&L. In case (b), the *only* correct procedure for the *reductio* is to reduce the whole of P&L itself to absurdity. Therefore it is *never* a mistake to spell out *all* the necessary conditions of L when one is trying to reduce some concept P&L to absurdity, and sometimes it is even necessary to do so. Chappell seems not to recognise this.

(2) Let S be a necessary condition for L, and let L* be exactly like L except that L* has S* *instead of* S as a necessary condition. Suppose that P&L* is reduced to absurdity. Clearly, from this alone we cannot correctly infer that P&L can be reduced to absurdity. Furthermore, if the reduction to absurdity depends necessarily on the presence of S* instead of S, then the argument, however conclusive, proves nothing about P&L. Hence, demanding that a private language meets *qua* language conditions not required of public language in order to reduce the idea of private language to absurdity is simply an outrageous howler.

Certainly Wittgenstein is entitled to define 'private language' as he pleases. And if on his definition a private language has no logical words, or only a sign 'E', I agree that private languages are impossible. But from this it does not follow that private languages are impossible in the sense of *Inv.* 243 – languages whose 'individual words refer to what can only be known to the person speaking'. Of course, Wittgenstein may conjoin these two features into one definition of private language. But Wittgenstein cannot decide that the possession of one feature entails the possession of the other. Now I claim not to know what Wittgenstein meant to do. But I am anxious to discover whether or not, as Malcolm claims, private languages in the sense of *Inv.* 243 are impossible. Clearly, once we have settled on this definition, neither Wittgenstein nor Malcolm has a right, nor do I, to 'determine what should and should not be allowed to Privatus' (p. 158 above) by way of a different definition of private language. Chappell simply overestimates the rights accruing to Wittgenstein and Malcolm in having 'introduced the notion of a private language in the first place'.

Now if, as Wittgenstein claimed (correctly in my view), a neces-

sary condition for a language is the possession of a systematic structure, then to show that a private language* (i.e. a language deprived
of its systematic structure) involves an absurdity is *not* to show that
a private language involves an absurdity.

The point is of such importance that I wish to put it over again
in another way. Suppose that a language need not have a systematic
structure. Then there are two species of private language: (*a*) one
with a systematic structure and (*b*) one without it. It should be
obvious that to show that species (*b*) *qua* species (*b*) cannot have
instances, is not to show the impossibility of instances of species (*a*).

I concede that Wittgenstein's suggested arguments are effective to
show the absurdity of private languages of certain species: with no
logical terms, with only one rule, with only one sign 'E', etc. But
by (1) and (2) above it is a mistake to conclude from this alone that
those arguments dispose of the other species, or that there is no other
species to consider. And it is of high philosophical importance to
determine whether or not another species can have instances – even
if Wittgenstein and Malcolm denied them, or never dreamed of
them.

Concerning Chappell's Comment (B)

By (2), 'Privatish is a private language' is not to be reduced to
absurdity by replacing necessary conditions for the existence of a
language by conditions which are not necessary. If the having of a
criterion for proving that the application of a term of L is correct,
is not required for L to be a language, then it is a mistake to object
that in a private luuage there are no criteria for proving that
certain applications of its private terms are correct. In accordance
with (2), my argument is intended to show either that Privatus while
using Privatish has most of the ways of correcting his uses of words
available to a speaker of a public language *or else that there is
nothing that either speaker has by which he can correct his uses of
words*. The latter disjunct is precisely the theme of my insistence on
a 'fair *reductio*', which insistence did strike Chappell's attention.
Now Chappell agrees that, say, General Eisenhower knows of his
slip in English 'This green . . . I mean red chair . . .' on hearing the
word 'green', just as Privatus could know of a slip involving a private word. But Chappell stresses that the speaker knows *on* hearing,
not *by* hearing, and claims that my argument requires that Privatus
corrects himself *by* hearing his word. By (2) this claim is not entirely
true. Yet Chappell does not consider that Eisenhower also has
nothing *by* which to correct himself, if his identification of the

colour (on a par with Privatus' identification of the properties of his private objects) is not to count as a criterion. Doubtless Mrs Eisenhower might, correctingly, have said: 'Not green, but red, Ike.' But this is not a criterion *by* which Eisenhower is to correct himself. He has to hear Mrs Eisenhower's utterance. But the *hearing* of her utterance is not a criterion by which Eisenhower is to correct himself, either. He must understand the utterance; he must understand that it was meant as a correction. And all of this presupposes that he can identify the words of the utterance without criteria; that is, his second-person's or addressee's use of the second-order words 'not', 'green', 'but', 'red', and 'Ike' *involves no criteria.* Yet this is not enough. Eisenhower must have strong reasons for supposing that Mrs Eisenhower is right. But the best reasons he can have are only inductive and would *not*, to use Chappell's term, 'prove' that Eisenhower's use of the term 'green' was incorrect. Even if the largest crowd of English speakers joined in saying 'Not green, but red, Ike', the situation remains unaltered. The choral utterance is not a criterion for Eisenhower; he has both to hear it and to be sure that they have not connived to deceive him, or that each person did not suddenly get an impulse to trick him, etc. There is nothing by which he can *prove* that his utterance of 'green' is incorrect. (If one says that others' correcting utterances function as a criterion because they are *causally* efficient in correcting the speaker of a public language, then one gives up the claim that Privatish fails to be a language in failing to have proofs of correctness or incorrectness. Besides, many different natural events not involving other people may very well cause Privatus to make the necessary linguistic self-corrections to keep up Privatish.)

In Regard to Chappell's Paragraph (i)

I have only two counter-comments. On the one hand, Chappell fails to note that most of what he says in (i) applies also to the use of words referring to non-private objects. His conclusion about private language is, by (2), at least over-hasty. On the other hand, Chappell fails to realise that there is nothing in the characterisation of private objects (*Inv.* 243) that requires them to be ephemeral and non-coexistent. He argues that Privatus cannot determine whether or not a private object is truly describable, e.g., as W on the grounds that the past W's provide no useful comparison, while *the* present object is precisely the one whose W-ness is at issue. This is an incomplete disjunction. Even if we assume that comparisons are required, there is no reason to suppose that Privatus' paradigm of W is not a long-lasting private object steadily present in Privatus' experience with which all objects coexist. For that matter, the paradigm of W can very well be a series of longer-lasting overlapping W's. Thus, Privatus could compare his private (or public) objects with his paradigm of W and determine whether his use of the word 'W' is correct or not. Of course, if paradigms for comparison do not consitute or provide criteria of correctness, they also do not in public languages; thus, by (2), we have here nothing against private languages.

In Regard to Chappell's Paragraph (ii)
The case of memory is just as difficult for public as for private languages. The point is that without being in a position to *prove* that our memory impressions or judgments are correct or true, we *de facto* get some of them right, and it is this fact, without a proof, which is a necessary condition for the existence of language, public or private.

In Regard to his Paragraphs (iii) and (iv)
As I have argued, we must consider private languages with systematic structure. Thus, (a) some words of Privatish may be definable in terms of others, and (b) some words, though indefinable, have entailment relationships, just as the indefinable 'red' stands, to the term 'extended', in the entailment relationship exposed by 'Everything red is extended'. In case (a) Privatus can determine whether or not a term or its negation applies to an object; in case (b) he can determine only whether or not one of the two terms applies. Chappell seems to grant this, but he reasserts that a term involved in logical relations is not private, i.e. not understandable to the speaker alone. This time he gives a reason: 'a term must have stability ... in order to sustain logical relations to other terms at all, and such stability is just what is ruled out by the term's being private ... to suppose a (private) term to have this stability is to beg the question of its being a proper term, or element of language' (p. 165 above). Now, this reason is not very persuasive; it is difficult to ascertain what a term's stability can be. But even supposing that stability (whatever it may be) is necessary for a term's having logical relations, clearly having no logical relations and referring to private object are two different concepts. Thus for one thing, he who attacks private languages by claiming that they have no logical terms is precisely *committed* to showing how from the fact that some terms refer to private objects the terms cannot be linked by logical

relations; and for another thing, inasmuch as we are reducing 'Privatish is a private *language*' to absurdity, by (1) and (2) above we are not doing anything incorrect and, *a fortiori*, we are begging no question, when we are supposing that Privatish has terms with logical relations, together with whatever this implies, either because all languages must have logical terms, or because though logical terms might not be required yet we choose to consider private languages which do have logical terms.

In Regard to (v)

Here again Chappell does not notice that what he says also applies to the case of non-private terms or languages. Yet there is another point. *If* all contingent generalisations are empirical, i.e. accepted by induction, Chappell would be justified in saying that the use of generalisations in determining the correctness of one's application of a certain word presupposes previous correct applications of the word in question. There should, then, be an independent way, *or else there need be no way in either public or private languages*, of determining the correctness of those previous applications. But here is no problem for Privatish: as remarked in my counter-comments on Chappell's criticisms (i), (iii) and (iv), either there are no independent criteria in public language any more than in private, or else Privatus may very well have definitions, entailments and paradigms, just as the speaker of a public language has. Clearly, once Privatus holds a generalisation in whose acquisition those other means of deciding correctness have been employed, he is in a position to use his generalisation in *future* uses of the words entering in its formulation.

But, as Wittgenstein suggested, perhaps not all contingent generalisations are accepted by induction. Perhaps, as he suggested, certain contingent beliefs are required for the possession of a language about certain kinds of objects. Then, if this Kantian-flavoured suggestion about language is true, on (1) and (2) above we must allow Privatus the possession of some contingent generalisations without his having come to hold them by induction. This is a very intricate topic, but whatever may ultimately be found to be the case, Chappell has not shown that I err in allowing Privatus the use of some contingent generalisations.

For Chappell's commentary, however, I am grateful. He has provided a kind of criticism which has made it possible for me to clarify the point of my arguments more than I could otherwise have hoped to do.

II

Concerning Mr Thomson's Reply
I am pleased to find that Professor J. F. Thomson agrees with my
major contentions. For my part I am ready to concede that the
obscurities of the private language argument are much greater
than I have allowed for.

1. *My counter-example claim.* Thomson represents me as claiming, *simpliciter*, that private languages exist, that, e.g., our ordinary
language of pains is private. My claim, however, is slightly different:
that the idea of private language is so obscure that there are many
senses of 'privacy' and that in *some* of these senses we find counter-
examples.

2. *Thomson's challenge.* Next Thomson formulates the condition
which in his view is required by *Inv.* 243 to make the language of
pains a counter-example:

> (T) If a man has a pain it is *possible* for him to know something
> about his pain which it is impossible that anyone else should
> know.

Then Thomson argues: 'That pains are private in this stronger
sense is certainly not obvious, nor would Wittgenstein have admitted
that it was true (see *Inv.* 246). *So* I cannot see that Castañeda's
counter-example is anything more than an *ignoratio elenchi*' (p. 170
above, my italics in 'so'). Thomson has, of course, no right to assume
that Wittgenstein's refusal to accept that pains are private objects
in the relevant sense would be consistent. This is part and parcel of
the whole issue. But I want to show that the example of pains is not
an *ignoratio*, even in the presence of Thomson's condition (T).

3. *The challenge met.* There are several senses of 'know' and of
'private object' in which pains have properties that satisfy Thomson's condition (T). Indeed, there is a trivial, obvious property, regardless of the sense of 'know', which satisfies (T); it is ϕ_1: being a
pain had by a person who alone knows that he has the pain. Clearly,
it is possible for a man, X, having a pain, to know that he alone
knows that he has it; but it is impossible that there is a person different from X who both knows that X has the pain and knows that

X alone knows that X has the pain. (Actually, even physical objects may have properties like ϕ_1 – e.g. the property of being a rock which X alone knows to be a rock. It is logically impossible that there exist a person Y, different from X, who knows that something is a rock which X alone knows to be a rock. Obviously Wittgenstein did not mean to consider rocks as private objects. Since Thomson's principle (T) is a very natural exegesis of *Inv.* 243, this shows that the allegation that private languages are impossible is groundless, and perhaps also that the idea of a private language is so obscure that it defies precise statement.)

Thomson apparently concedes that one knows about one's pains in a way impossible to others. He only contends that this is not enough to yield a counter-example since it does not amount to (T). Let us write 'X KNOWS that P' to indicate that X has knowledge in the unique, first-person way, that P. Consider now the property ϕ_2: being X's pain such that whoever knows that X has it KNOWS that X has it. Here ϕ_2 satisfies (T). Clearly, it is possible for X to know about his pain p that he has p and that every man who knows this KNOWS it – for instance, in one possible case, because he knows that he is the only man in the universe. But if a man Z, different from X, knows that X has p then he knows this in the third-person or second-person way; thus, it is not the case that Z KNOWS that X has p. But then Z cannot know that every man, including himself, who knows that X has p KNOWS that X has p. Therefore, for every man X and every pain p that X has, it is possible for X to know that p has ϕ_2 while it is impossible that anyone else knows that p has ϕ_2. (The proof requires the obvious principles that 'X knows that P' entails P and that 'X knows that P and Q' entails 'X knows that P and X knows that Q'.)

4. *Thomson's challenge strengthened.* Thomson may rejoin that it is only a contingent matter whether a certain pain has either the property ϕ_1 or the property ϕ_2. Hence, it is not necessary that all pains be private objects in the sense of having ϕ_1 or ϕ_2. This is all true, provided that we read *Inv.* 243, not as requiring merely Thomson's (T), but also the following:

(T'). If a man has a pain, then *there is something about the pain* which it is possible for him to know and which it is impossible for anybody else to know.

5. *The private language argument checked.* I agree that not all

pains have ϕ_1 or ϕ_2. Furthermore, wherever a pain has ϕ_1 or ϕ_2, it does not have it necessarily. Thus, it is *possible* that no pain is in fact a private object in the sense of meeting condition (T'), so far as ϕ_1 or ϕ^2 is concerned. *But this is enough.* Wittgenstein's thesis is supposed to be that private languages are impossible; hence that our language of pains is necessarily not about private objects. But if pains *may* be private objects, even if in fact they are not, then it is certainly false that our language of pains is necessarily not private, even if in fact it is not.

Note, incidentally, that neither (T) nor (T') requires that one knows that one's own pains are private objects, i.e. that one knows that one alone knows that they have (or may have) the property which nobody else can know that they have (or may have). Thus, for all we know many of our pains, in particular our unexpressed and unmentioned pains, may (as is quite likely) have had property ϕ_2, namely, of being known only by those who have KNOWN them, even though we have failed to know this in turn. Thus, it is likely that our language of pains is in fact at least a mixed lauguage, since at least *some* pains are probably private as required by the strong principle (T'), even though we are unable to tell which ones are private.

6. *A private language established.* Matters are not so clear as Thomson suggests. There are senses of 'know' in which one knows only what one has *conclusively* verified. And in such senses, all pains are private objects even in the sense indicated by (T'). And there are yet weaker senses of 'know' in which others may know that one is in pain, but not that one's pains present *to one* a certain quale with a certain degree of intensity. Thus, either the following property ϕ_3 or its negation will make pains private objects in the sense indicated by (T'): being a pain felt by X and having the same quale and intensity as a previous or later pain felt by X. Doubtless, X himself may fail to know that a given pain of his has (or lacks) ϕ_3. But this is irrelevant. Neither (T) nor (T') requires that X knows that his pains are private objects.

7. *Understanding.* Thomson reinforces his charge of *ignoratio* by asking whether I accept that a dentist cannot understand his patient's 'I have a toothache'. But Thomson does not mention that 'understand' is as unclear as 'know'. Here the dentist does not understand fully the patient's utterance of 'toothache' to the extent that he fails to know the thing the patient is referring to. Once

again, if knowing the thing referred to requires acquaintance with or experience of it, then if the postulate of privacy is a necessary truth, the dentist does not understand the utterance fully. If knowing the thing referred to requires complete personal verification that the patient has it, then even if the privacy postulate is false, the dentist does not understand fully. And so on through my list of senses of 'private object'.

8. *The opposition defended.* Thomson is somewhat unfair to the defenders of the private language argument. I do find in their writings arguments which do more than beg the question. Some of the arguments do prove that certain kinds of language are impossible, e.g. a language with only words referring to private objects or with no logical terms. Unfortunately some of their arguments also prove too much: they require conditions which are not met by ordinary languages, or even that part of existing languages which is just about material objects.

9. *Conclusion.* In conclusion, I am content with claiming simply that I have refuted the private language argument, so that concerning the private language issue there is simply an impasse. I have some doubts about the possibility of settling the matter conclusively either way. But I think that further careful examination of the issue and arguments is required, in spite of there being a 'mare's nest'. In philosophy we ought to work carefully to erect impasses, to build philosophical views on each side of the impasse, and examine the views on their over-all merits; then we may find a solution for the impasse. Thus, while I find valuable the efforts of Malcolm and other Wittgensteinians at building views on the assumption that private languages are impossible, I feel that, with Thomson's support, I have earned a right to philosophise on the assumption that private languages *are* possible. I am glad that Thomson has helped me to make this clearer.

VI The Verification Principle and the private language argument

(i) *Judith Jarvis Thomson*

There is a thesis which has been argued for by certain Wittgenstein-ians, namely the thesis that there can be no such thing as a private language. This thesis is often referred to as, and we are given to understand that it is, both important and original. I hope to show that it is, properly understood, something very familiar and rather trite. But the philosophers who argue for it are no more to be confused with Wittgenstein than the Platonists are to be confused with Plato; so to show this is not to cast discredit on Wittgenstein himself. On the contrary, the disservice was done by those who credited the thesis to him. If nothing else, they failed utterly to take seriously his claim that he held no opinions and put forward no theses in philosophy.

I

Norman Malcolm (p. 41 above) says 'By a "private" language is meant one that not merely is not but *cannot* be understood by anyone other than the speaker.' This characterisation is presumably suggested by *Inv.* 243, where Wittgenstein asks if we can imagine a language of which he says, 'Another person cannot understand the language.' And a little later on, Malcolm tells us that the 'cannot' here is to be a logical 'cannot': A private language is one of which it is not merely the case that it is not understood by anyone other than the speaker, but more that it is logically impossible that it should be understood by anyone other than the speaker. The thesis then – and I'll call it Malcolm's form of the thesis, or more briefly Malcolm's thesis – is that there can be no such thing as a language which is private in this sense.

Now what is remarkable is that some philosophers[1] who have understood the thesis in this way nevertheless take it to be relevant to discuss the question whether or not a man who grew up alone on a deserted island could have invented a language for his own use. But why should a man's growing up alone make the language he invents (if he can invent a language) of necessity unintelligible to the anthropologists who discover him? And if what is in question is the possibility of a language which is of necessity unintelligible to anyone but its speaker, then having shown that a man who grew up alone couldn't have such a language you would still have to do the job of showing that a man who grew up in company couldn't have such a language. Were one to look at the nature of the arguments which have actually been produced *for* Malcolm's thesis, they would do exactly the same thing in both cases, i.e. the supposed proof of Malcolm's thesis calls for no assumptions whatever about how the supposed speaker of the private language grew up.

It may be objected that Malcolm doesn't *own* the private language thesis, and that there is this or that other thesis (turning on this or that other definition of the expression 'private language') which is th*e real* private language thesis, and that I should have been dealing with them instead. I'm not going to take time to canvass these other possible theses, for (though I shall not defend this) it seems to me so plain that either they would rule out that English is a language or they rest on the (so far as I can see) utterly unjustified assumption that a man who grew up alone couldn't exhibit behaviour which would justify us in saying of him: 'Now he is following this rule.' So I shall be dealing in what follows strictly with Malcolm's thesis – i.e. the thesis that there can be no private language, where a private language would be one which it was logically impossible for anyone but its speaker to understand.

II

But in fact not much has yet been made clear about what the denial of the possibility of a private language amounts to. For the question arises: What could there be about or in a language in virtue of which it would be logically impossible for anyone but its speaker to understand it?

Wittgenstein says (*Inv.* 258): 'Let us imagine the following case. I want to keep a diary about the recurrence of a certain sensation.

To this end I associate it with the sign "E" and write this sign in a calendar for every day on which I have the sensation.' Now what would make 'E' such that it was logically impossible for anyone but L.W. to know what it meant? For suppose that we were to watch L.W. very carefully every day for several years, and suppose we were to notice the following regularities in his use of the word 'E': Generally when he does write 'E' in his diary he has held his cheek and furrowed his brow, he has gingerly touched his tongue to a tooth (and then winced), he has looked into his mouth in a mirror, ... and he has phoned the dentist. Why are we not entitled to say that by 'E' L.W. means 'toothache' or 'I have a toothache today'?

Malcolm cites a passage from *Inv.* 243: 'E' would be a word in (or itself a small self-contained) private language if it referred to 'what can only be known to' L.W., to an 'immediate private sensation' of his. Now as we described L.W.'s use of the sign 'E' it certainly looks as if we do know what the sensation is which he uses 'E' to report on; so what we must take to be meant here is this: If in using 'E' to report on the having of a sensation L.W. is referring to that sensation, *and* if it is the case that no matter how much cheek-clutching and dentist-phoning L.W. does it is logically impossible that we should know what sensation it is that he refers to by 'E', then it is logically impossible that we should know what he means by 'E'. L.W.'s use of the sign 'E' would then be a small self-contained private language.

Who says that when we use sensation-terms (such as 'pain', 'toothache', etc.), we are referring to our sensations, and that it is impossible that you should know what sensation it is that I refer to when I use these terms of myself? The sceptic about other minds does. Smith alone (he says) can *know* what it is he's feeling when he thrashes about like that, or even if he's feeling anything at all.

So the point, then, is this: If the sceptic about other minds is right, then no matter what we observe of L.W.'s behaviour, it is logically impossible that we should know what sensation it is that he is feeling, and in particular, what sensation it is that he is referring to by the use of 'E'. So then it is logically impossible that we should know what he means by 'E'.

It is worth remarking that if the sceptic about other minds were right, then not only would 'E' be a word in (or the whole of) a private language, but so also would *all* the sensation terms. We would each of us be speaking private languages in using the words 'toothache', 'pain', 'hunger', and the rest. And this is as it should be. For one thing which is plain is that the point of raising these questions in this part of the *Investigations* is not to discredit the possibility that you or I should invent a special kind of language, but rather to bring out what queer things would have to be said about our ordinary language if the sceptic about other minds were right.

III

One last point remains to be cleared up. As I said, the sceptic says that it is logically impossible that anyone but Smith should *know* what Smith is feeling, and it may be argued that this still leaves open the possibility that the rest of us should be entitled on occasion to claim that it is *probable* that he is (say) in pain, or hungry. We should distinguish, then, between Weak Scepticism about other minds, which is the view that we can never know what is in the mind of another, but that we may have good reason for thinking that he is feeling this or that; and Strong Scepticism about other minds, which is the view that we can never know what is in the mind of another, and more, that we are never in a position even to have good reason for thinking he is feeling this or that – that any claim we make about what Smith is feeling can at best be a mere guess. Now it is certainly arguable that Weak Scepticism is not a consistent doctrine – there are very familiar arguments which purport to show that where there can be no knowledge there can be no probability either – and thus that a Weak Sceptic must, to avoid self-contradiction, grow into a Strong Sceptic. I am not going to consider these arguments. I want only to point out that with each degree of Scepticism goes a different strength of 'private' in the expression 'private language'. With Weak Scepticism goes the view that we can never know what L.W. means by 'E' but that it is conceivable we should have good reason for thinking he means (say) 'toothache', and with Strong Scepticism goes the view that we can never know what L.W. means by 'E' and that it is not conceivable that we should have any good reason for thinking he means 'toothache' or anything else – any view we have as to what 'E' means can at best be a mere guess.

Now I think that what Malcolm means to be denying is the possibility of any strongly private language – i.e. any language in which it is logically impossible we should have any ground at all for supposing we understand. (In fact I think that he would not regard

Weak Scepticism as even a consistent view to take, and thus as not interestingly to be distinguished from Strong Scepticism.) I shall not cite the passages which make me think this. It is not necessary, for it would plainly be *harder* to show that there can be no weakly private language than it would be to show that there can be no strongly private language. For by my definitions, if you have proved that there can be no strongly private language, then you would have still to do something more to prove that there can be no weakly private language, whereas proving that there can be no weakly private language calls for proving that which would already make a strongly private language impossible. And this can in any case be seen independently. If I can and could have no reason to think I knew what was meant by 'E', then this would surely be a better ground for doubting that 'E' was a word in a language than if, while I could never know that I was right, I could at all events form a reasonable conjecture to the effect that it means 'toothache'. So in attributing to Malcolm the thesis that there can be no strongly private language I do him no injustice: I give him the easier rather than the harder task.

IV

The thesis, then, is this: There can be no such thing as a language in which it is logically impossible that anyone else but its speaker should have any good reason at all for thinking he understands. And now why should we suppose that this is true?

There seem to me to be three steps in the argument. The first is this: If a sign which a man uses[2] is to be a word in a language, his use of it must be governed by a rule or set of rules; and this means that it must be possible for him to use the sign correctly or incorrectly – i.e. on the one hand to follow the rule or act in accordance with it, or on the other hand, to violate or disobey or break it. For R is not a rule unless it is possible either to follow or to violate it.

Straightaway, however, the difficulties rush in. What could *the* or *a* rule governing the use of the words 'table' or 'pain' or 'revolution' be? Indeed it is not only the Wittgensteinians who rely heavily on the notion of a linguistic rule which one could follow or violate, and it is worth bringing out that thus far at all events nothing whatever has been done in the way of making this notion clear. For let us notice that something familiar from Carnap's writings, what he called Semantical Rules, will not do what is wanted here. For example, there is the Semantical Rule that says the sentence 'The moon is round' means that or is true if and only if the moon is round; but this isn't anything you could follow or violate because it doesn't say anything about your doing anything. The rules of inference in the more familiar logical systems do at all events say 'You may do thus and so' – e.g. the *modus ponens* rule. But what would count as a violation of a rule which says only 'You may do thus and so?' What would even count as an instance of following such a rule? Not just doing the thing, for the rule didn't enjoin it on me to do it, but said only that I might do it. It would be a joke to say 'I'm only following the rules' as I sit smoking in a carriage marked 'Smoking Permitted'.

I gather that there are some systems of logic which do contain rules which prohibit – rules which say 'You may not do thus and so'. These rules could of course be both followed and violated, but it can scarcely be supposed that the linguistic rules meant by the philosophers I have in mind could *all* be of this sort. It would follow that a sign could be a word in a language so long as there was a prohibition against its use.

Malcolm gives an example of a purported linguistic rule: 'I will call this feeling "pain" and will thereafter call the *same* thing "pain" whenever it occurs.' As this sounds more like the adoption of a policy than a rule which I hereby subscribe to, let us rewrite it in the form of a rule – and also replace 'table' for 'pain' so as not to prejudge any issues about private languages: Call this object 'table' and thereafter call the same sort of thing 'table' whenever – but now whenever what? Whenever you see one? It sounds mad; who would subscribe to a rule which enjoined it on him that every time he sees a table he make some remark about it? But then what should be filled in here? Even 'whenever you want to refer to one' would be mad, for why shouldn't I allow myself just to use the word 'that' and point to the thing when I want to refer to it? And very much worse still, *what* would I be accepting if that were what I should always do? I am to *call* things 'tables', and just what is it to do this? I might say to you 'Call Henry', and then if you are obliging you'll call out 'Henry!'; but I suppose I point to myself and say 'Call me Ishmael' – is it so clear what it is I am requesting you to do? Must you ever actually *say* the word 'Ishmael'? I'm not saying we don't say this sort of thing, but just that the notion of a linguistic rule is at least as much in need of an explanation as any of the things philosophers make use of it *to* explain.

But these difficulties may be set aside here, for they are not difficulties peculiar to the private languages thesis. Let us set out the form of a linguistic rule for a name 'K' of a kind of thing – leaving it open that words which play a different role should be governed by linguistic rules of different forms – as follows: You may call anything of kind X 'K' and you may not call 'K' anything which is not of kind X. And let us, for the sake of bringing out the rest of the argument, just *pretend* that there are no difficulties with it – we shall pretend that 'call' is transparent, and that we need not worry about the fact that one couldn't either follow or violate the first conjunct of the rule. At all events, to subscribe to it is not to commit oneself to always doing something, or to always doing something in this or that kind of situation.

It is to be remarked about rules of this form (and this is an important fact about them from the point of view of the private language argument) that they involve mention of a sign, 'K', *and* of a kind of thing, the X's. What the rule says is that X's and only X's are to be called 'K's' and 'X' of course can be any expression whatever that stands for a kind of thing.

The first step of the argument, then, can be restated in this way: If a sign 'K' which a man uses is to be a name of a kind of thing in a language, his use of it must be governed by a rule of the form, X's and only X's are to be called 'K's'.

V

The second step of the private language argument has been thought to be self-evident (so it seems to me) by everyone who has written on this subject at all; and the fact that it is not self-evident is worth bringing out because what it says *is* peculiar to this argument. What it says is this: A man's use of a sign is not governed by a rule unless it is not merely possible that he should violate the rule but more, that he should violate it unwittingly. That is, it must be possible that he should think he is following the rule, it need not follow that he really is following it. And it is said that this is essential to the concept of a rule (cf. Malcolm, p. 43 above). Wittgenstein's *Inv.* 202 is generally appealed to here: 'to *think* one is obeying a rule is not to obey a rule'.

At first sight this second step does look to be self-evident. It seems so clear: After all, if from the fact that I think x-ing is following rule R it follows that it is following rule R, I am then free to do anything or nothing. That 'rule' doesn't point in any direction. No restriction is imposed on what I do. R is not a rule but a mere 'impression of a rule' (cf. Malcolm, pp. 47–8 above). Now indeed, a 'rule' which rules out nothing isn't a rule. But *does* it follow from the fact that if I think that x-ing is following rule R it is following rule R, that rule R rules out nothing? For why should it not be the case that I think of some activities that if I were to perform them, I would be violating rule R? And then it would certainly seem that if, thinking this of an activity, y-ing, I then y, I *am* violating rule R. The adoption of rule R does seem to impose this restriction on me: I must not y, thinking that to y is to violate rule R.

All this is too abstract. So consider the rule 'Always decide to do what you think at the time it would be most fun to do'. Note, not 'Always *do* what etc., etc.', for I might think I was following this rule, and not really be following it – e.g. all unknown to me I am paralysed, and so I am not doing what I think I am doing. Rather, 'Always *decide* to do etc., etc.' Is there anything in the concept 'rule' which rules it out that this should be a rule? Indeed, it even appears that this rule satisfies the first condition on rules, namely that a thing isn't a rule unless I can either follow or violate it. For I could surely, out of some moral compunction, say, decide not to do what I think at the time it would be most fun to do.

It might be objected that it is not at all plain how a man could adopt this rule while not adopting the rule 'Always *do* what etc., etc.' 'All I resolve on is to decide in that way. What I actually do is another matter entirely; I adopt no rule to govern that.' This is very odd indeed. 'I just do the deciding – which has nothing whatever to do with what I actually *do*.' But a man might not have anything nearly so strong as this in mind. One can almost hear a philosopher say to himself, 'Now it is not possible to know for certain whether or not one really will be able to bring off what one decides to do. At some times it seems very likely indeed, at other times not. But still, I shouldn't commit myself to anything unless I am absolutely certain I can bring it off. Hence I should adopt "Always decide", and not "Always do".' (It is reported of Prichard that he would never say 'I promise', but only 'I fully intend'.) Now one might argue that if this is what's behind it, then this man's rule 'Always decide' is the same as another man's 'Always do'; these are not distinct rules. (Prichard's 'I fully intend' was as good as a promise, and was taken for that by his friends.) At all events this calls for an argument – that this is so (*if* it is) is not something that follows from the concept 'rule'.

Or again, Mummy writes 'Whenever you feel the least bit gloomy, think of your Mummy. (It will cheer you up.)' Could I think I was following this rule and not be? (Of course it may be said that it is not possible – knowingly at all events – to violate this rule, so that it does not satisfy the first condition on rules which was set out in step one of the argument. But then surely the possibility of something like this should rather show either that step one of the argument is not true for all rules, *or* that, while one must be able to violate a rule if it is to be a rule, it is not required that one be able to violate it knowingly. And in fact things are really even worse than this. For notice that one can't even violate this rule unwittingly unless one has, in a sense, forgotten the rule. And now what rules – however private – can't be 'violated' in that way? How much help *is* all this abstract talk about rules anyway?)

To say S is not a rule unless I can think I am following S and not in fact be, is to set out a condition on rules which would rule it out that rules of the sort I mention here – rules which could in a perfectly ordinary, garden-variety sense be called private rules – are rules. But that they should be ruled out as not really rules is surely by no means self-evident.

But let us turn to linguistic rules in particular. The form of a linguistic rule for a kind-name. 'K' was to be this: You may call anything of kind X 'K' and you may not call 'K' anything which is not of kind X. So the requirement is this: If the sign 'K' which a man uses is to be a kind-name in a language, it must be possible for him to think he is following a rule of this form and not in fact be. Now I think it would plainly not satisfy that he might make a slip of the tongue: to be confronted with something which is not X, and to mean to say 'It's L' or 'It's M', and for 'It's K' to come out instead. For one thing, one might wish to say that if his utterance of 'It's K' was a slip of th tongue, then he did not *call* the thing of which he said it a K, for this is not what he meant to say of it. For another, it is not plain that following a rule of this kind requires that a man should actually say anything. But more important, since it is always possible that a man should make a slip of the tongue or pen, there would be no sign which a man might use which would be such that his use of it would fail to meet this condition. However private you imagine his use of it, he could not think he was saying or writing it and not in fact be. (And moreover, looking ahead to the third step of the argument, that he had made a slip of the tongue or pen could be independently established.³) But then if the mistake is not to lie in his thinking he is calling a thing by some other name than 'K' and its being 'K' that in fact comes out, it must be that the mistake is to lie in his belief that the thing in question is an X when in fact it is not (or vice versa): he calls it 'K' thinking it is an X when it is not an X, thus unwittingly violating the prohibition against calling anything which is not of kind X 'K'. And so the requirement in the case of linguistic rules for kind-names is the following: If a sign 'K' which a man uses is to be a kind-name in a language, then it must be possible that he should call a thing a 'K' thinking it is an X when it is not an X, where it is the X's and only the X's which (in his use) are to be called 'K's'.

This certainly *sounds* a reasonable thing to say. But in the first place it is not so far as I can see a consequence of the concept 'rule' itself, and in the second place I do not see how it should even be examined for correctness or incorrectness until the notion 'call' is made clearer to us than has anywhere been done.

But before turning to the third step of the argument there are three further points which should be made:

(1) The Wittgensteinians I refer to – and many other philosophers besides – are in agreement on this, that it is *not* possible that a man should think he is in pain and not be in pain. And it might appear that one who says the following three things contradicts himself – namely (*a*) I can't think I'm in pain and not be in pain, (*b*) if a sign 'K' which a man uses is to be a kind-name in a language, then it must be possible for him to call a thing a 'K' thinking it is of the kind to be called 'K' and that it nevertheless not be one, and (*c*) that 'pain' is in fact a word in the English language. In defence of the Wittgensteinians, who do say all these three things, we should bring out that one may say them all without being guilty of an inconsistency. For one thing, it could be said that 'pain' just isn't a kind-name – and the Wittgensteinians of course do say this. 'Pain' is not the name of a kind of thing (a kind of sensation) but rather something that 'replaces pain-behaviour'. But more important, it could be said that it is not required for 'pain' to be a kind-name that a man should be able to think he is in pain and not be, as one can think this is alcohol (from its being a colourless liquid) and it not be (cf. Malcolm, pp. 37–8 above). It is only required that he should be able to think that the sensation he now has is of the kind of which he, years ago, thought that sensations of that kind and only sensations of that kind are to be called 'pains', and yet that it should not be. (Here 'X' in the rule is replaced by 'sensation of

the same kind as that one'.) And this, it might be said, is, for all that
has so far been argued at any rate, surely possible – for he might
have forgotten just which sensation it was of which he had said to
himself (or been told): Sensations of the same kind as this one are
to be called 'pains'. And also the Wittgensteinians could (though
they don't) insist that though 'pain' is not a kind-name it is all the
same a word in the language in virtue of (among other things) its
meeting conditions analogous to that which we set out for kind-
names – perhaps that a man's use of, e.g., the sentence 'I'm in pain'
is only a use of a *sentence* in a language if it is possible that he
should say 'I'm in pain' thinking he is in (roughly) a *situation*
(which includes his behaviour as well as what is happening to him)
of the kind in which he may say 'I'm in pain' and only in which he
may say 'I'm in pain', and he is not. And a man could make a mistake in this way if he had forgotten just which situation it was of
which he had said to himself (or been told): In situations of this
kind you may say 'I'm in pain'. (Malcolm does say [*Philosophical
Review*, LXIII (1954) p. 541] that the verbal utterance 'I'm in pain',
like crying, is in some sense 'incorrigible', which if I understand it at
all would mean that this condition is not met for the statement 'I'm
in pain'. And it is no wonder Malcolm does this, for he is here trying
to derive yet another thesis from the *Investigations* – this one from
Wittgenstein's suggestion as to *one* possible answer to the question,
how do human beings learn the meaning of the names of sensations
(cf. *Inv.* 244). [And it should be noticed that Wittgenstein nowhere
else says anything about 'pain' or 'I'm in pain' replacing pain-
behaviour – he says only such things as that these are 'tied to' the
natural expressions of pain.] But then of course it is equally no
wonder that Malcolm has trouble making out how the sentence 'I'm
in pain' can all the same be used to report on a matter of fact, i.e.
be true or false.) [Cf. pp. 257–8 below. Ed.]

(2) The second point which should be made comes directly out of
the first. We said that (for all that has so far been said) one can
think something is of the kind to be called a 'pain' and it not be;
and in exactly the same way it is (for all that has so far been said)
possible to think a thing to be of the kind to be called a 'decision to
do what one thinks at the time it would be most fun to do', or a
'gloomy feeling' or 'thought of Mummy', and that it not actually
be one. But this does not show that it is possible to think one is following the two non-linguistic rules I mentioned above and not be; it
does not show the two rules do after all satisfy this second condition
on rules. For the two rules did not enjoin it on me that I should or

should not, may or may not, *call* anything anything, but only that I form a certain kind of decision, think a certain thought. And it is not to be understood that one who grants 'It is not possible to think one is in pain and not be' should also insist 'But it is possible to think one is making a certain decision, feeling gloomy, thinking of Mummy, and not be.'

And lastly, (3), it may be thought that this condition which a man's use of a sign 'K' must satisfy if it is to be a kind-name in a language *already* rules it out that a private language should be a language, and we should bring out that it does not. Let us go back to L.W. who invented the sign 'E' to report on the recurrence of a certain kind of sensation. Wittgenstein said (*Inv.* 258): 'Let us imagine the following case. I want to keep a diary about the recurrence of a certain sensation. To this end I associate it with the sign "E" and write this sign in a calendar for every day on which I have the sensation.' And it may be asked: How does the sign *get* associated with a kind of sensation? Presumably L.W. gives himself a 'private ostensive definition'. He fixes his attention on a sensation, and says to himself: You may call this sensation and any others of the same kind as this one 'E'. Same kind? *What* kind? Supposedly 'sensation of the same kind as *this* one' is to stand for a kind of sensation, but how do I get it to do that? Just by fixing my attention on this sensation? For there to be a kind of sensation (kind of thing in general) there must be limits as to what is or isn't of that kind; and how should I get limits to the kind marked out by simply fixing my attention on one given sensation? But if I don't identify a kind of sensation, then the rule I recite to myself is mere words – my future conduct is not directed in any way.

The question, 'How do I identify a kind of sensation?' is a very respectable philosophical question. But of course it is only a special case of the very respectable philosophical question, 'How do I identify a kind of *thing*?' And we may ask: Just why is there supposed to be any more difficulty about a private ostensive definition of a newly invented sensation-word than there is about a public ostensive definition of a newly invented thing word? *Why* any more trouble about identifying a kind of *thing*? Suppose I were to set about introducing by an ostensive definition a new name for a shade of red or blue I would like to identify or (for a particularly relevant example) for a kind of squiggle I would like to identify. I write a capital letter E on a bit of paper, and I say, that and any others of the same kind are to be called 'E's'. Have I identified a kind of squiggle? Well, what other marks would also be of the same kind?

Would an italicised capital E be of the same kind? Or one with a long middle bar? Suppose when asked I said, 'Yes they are of the same kind', or, 'No, they are not of the same kind.' Need I have had them specifically in my mind when I introduced the kind-name 'E' in order for it to be the case that I was indeed picking out a kind of squiggle? Surely not.[4] Or better, if anything of this sort *were* necessary if I were to have identified a kind of thing, then it could have been present when I identifed a kind of sensation – i.e. if I could have had other squiggles in mind as also of the same kind, then I could have had other sensations in mind as also of the same kind.

Indeed, private ostensive definition of a newly invented sensation-word *is* supposed to be in a worse position than public ostensive definition of a newly invented thing-word. But then something else will be required to show that it is worse than just this; that it is a matter of fixing one's attention on a sensation and saying of it: Any sensation of this kind is to be called 'E' or 'K' or 'pain'. It would have to be shown why its having been a *sensation* (an 'immediate private sensation') that I fastened my attention on made it impossible that I should in this way identify a kind, whereas its having been a thing that I fastened my attention on did not make it impossible that I should in this way identify a kind. And in fact the third step of the argument can be regarded as an attempt to make just this very point.

VI

Now this is where we have come so far. The thesis that there can be no private language is the thesis that there can be no language which it is logically impossible that anyone but the speaker should understand. And the argument for this thesis has so far proceeded in the following way: (1) It was said that if a sign which a man uses is to count as a word in a language, his use of it must be governed by a rule – here specifically, if a sign which a man uses is to count as a kind-name in a language, his use of it must be governed by a rule of the following sort: You may call anything of a kind X 'K', and you may not call anything 'K' which is not of kind X. (2) If a sign which a man uses is to be governed by a rule of this sort it must be possible that he should call a thing a 'K' thinking it is of the kind to be called a 'K' and it not be.

The third step of the argument is this: There is no such thing as a man's thinking a thing is of the kind to be called 'K' and it not being so unless it is logically possible that it be *found out* that it is not so. And in the positive: There is no such thing as a man's thinking a thing is not of the kind to be called 'K' and it being so unless it is logically possible that it be *found out* that it is so.

Since it is so plain when this third step is set out baldly like this what it is all going to amount to, it is worth stressing that this third step of the argument is required if the desired conclusion is to come out of it. That it is involved in the argument as actually set out might be denied, for it is nowhere set out explicitly. (Though I think it would be difficult to deny this. Consider, for example, Malcolm's queries: 'Now how is it to be decided whether I have used the word consistently? What will be the difference between my having used it consistently and its *seeming* to me that I have? Or has this distinction vanished?' Of course one doesn't know for certain what a philosopher is appealing to when his argument for a thesis proceeds by the method of rhetorical questions, but it seems to me that unless Malcolm is taking it that, where it is not possible to 'decide' whether I have used the word consistently the distinction between my having used it consistently and its seeming to me that I have *has* vanished, then this passage is simply incomprehensible. But we may in fact appeal to a more explicit passage, which follows shortly after: 'My impression that I follow a rule does not confirm that I follow the rule, unless there can be something that will prove my impression correct.' And then follows Wittgenstein's ironic comparison with the man who assures himself that what was said in his copy of the morning paper was true by buying several more copies of the same paper.[5]) But whether or not it could be denied that this claim was in fact being made by those who have argued against the possibility of a private language, we should stress this: That *without* this claim, the argument simply stops dead in its tracks, since nothing that has so far been said rules out the possibility of a private language. L.W. might say: 'Indeed, there must *be* a difference between my sensations' being of the kind I had decided to call "E" and its seeming so to me if "E" is to be a kind-name of a sensation; but why should it follow from the fact that my sensations are strongly private that there is no such difference?' It might be said. 'Well, how is it to be established that the sensation is or is not of the required kind?' And now if the argument is to proceed, there must be something which rules it out that L.W. should quite acceptably reply: Perhaps it can't be found out that my sensation is or is not of the required kind, but all the same it may be that it is.

And what rules this out is what I have called the third step, which simply amounts to the denial that there is any such thing as a thing's being or not being of the kind to be called 'K' or 'E' over and above its seeming to a man that it is unless it *is* logically possible that it be found out that it is or is not of that kind. I say, 'Logically possible that it be found out' – for I think it cannot be supposed that what used to be called the 'technical' possibility of finding out is required. (Remember how careful the Positivists were in regard to all these distinctions?) For if more than the mere logical possibility is required, then far more is going to be ruled out than just private languages – e.g. it would be ruled out that 'ace' was a kind-name in English on the ground that I have just destroyed a playing card without looking at it, and so it is not any longer as a matter of fact possible to find out whether or not it was an ace. But of course you would always need a stronger premise than just that something *is* the case, e.g. 'I destroyed a playing card without looking at it', in order to get as a conclusion that it is not logically possible that something should be the case, e.g. 'It is not logically possible that we should find out whether or not the card was an ace.' (Or rather, to be more precise, there is no familiar rule of inference which will take you from a contingent premise to the conclusion 'It is logically impossible that . . .' – except the rule of inference which allows you to derive a necessary truth from *any* proposition whatever. And then of course you would have already to know independently that the conclusion 'It is logically impossible that . . .' *is* a necessary truth.) As far as the playing card is concerned, it is surely logically possible that, e.g., someone else had looked at it before I destroyed it.

In fact I think (though I shall not try to show this here) that only a private language will fail to meet this condition. Any kind-name 'P' such that there is one occasion on which it is not logically possible to find out whether or not 'P' applies to a thing must necessarily be a private kind-name – i.e. one such that it is not logically possible to find out on any occasion of its use whether or not 'P' does apply to a thing.

But what we should show is that this *is* true of private kind-names; what we should show is that if 'E' is a word in or the whole of a private language, then it is not anywhere at any time for any person logically possible to find out that 'E' applies or is true. And thus that, whether or not anything else does, at all events every sign in a private language *does* fail to meet the condition for being a kind-name in a language laid down in this third step of the argument.

To bring this out we have to fill in a certain vagueness in the statement of the condition. I put the condition in the words 'unless it is logically possible that it be found out that a given thing is or is not of the relevant kind', and the question arises what 'finding out' is to mean here. Must it be logically possible to establish conclusively that the thing is or is not of the relevant kind? Or would it be enough that it was logically possible that one should have or obtain good reason for thinking the thing was or was not of the relevant kind? (Malcolm does use the word 'prove' here – I quoted the passage above – but in fact the Wittgensteinians use the word 'prove' and the related word 'criterion' in so relaxed a manner that it is not really fair that we should take the appearance of this word as proof that it is 'proof' that is meant.) It seems to me that it is very likely that it is the former that is required – as we might call it, strong finding out. For one thing it appears to me that the two possibilities would not be regarded as distinct – we have already mentioned the familiar arguments purporting to show that there can be no probabilities where there can be no knowledge. (Cf. above on the distinction between Weak and Strong Scepticism.) But more important, it is not plain how a private language would be ruled out if it were not strong finding out what is required. For consider L.W. again: Could it not happen that he should think his present sensation was of the kind to be called 'E' – and then later think 'Oh what a fool I am. Now I remember what the sensation was which struck me that afternoon last May. And I was wrong just now in thinking the one I just had was of that kind – it wasn't like it at all.' It could of course be said: This appealing to further impressions shows nothing unless it produces an impression 'which is actually correct' (cf. Malcolm, p. 44 above, on memories). But to take this line suggests that it *is* conclusive or strong finding-out which is required – either because good reasons are not enough, or because where there can be no strong finding-out there can be no good reasons either. A case could *perhaps* be made for saying: This that happens later is not a reason for thinking that his former impression was false, but just itself the impression that his former impression was false. A good reason for thinking the former impression was false would be enough – strong finding-out is not necessary – but the impression that you were or were not mistaken cannot amount to a reason for thinking it so. However, this is not at all clear; and it may in fact be absurd.

I am inclined to think that the finding-out which is mentioned in the third step must be a conclusive or strong finding-out if private languages are to be ruled out. But let us leave all this open. At all events, the possibility L.W. may later have the impression he was mistaken is not to count as the possibility that he should find out he was mistaken.

People have raised the question in connection with the denial of the possibility of a private language just why 'corrigibility by others' should be required if the sign a man uses is to be a word in a language. So far as I can see it is not specially corrigibility by others that is being required, but rather just corrigibility. Corrigibility by others comes in in this way. The Strong Sceptic about other minds says that no amount of observation of L.W.'s behaviour could give us any reason whatever for thinking we knew what sensations he was having at any time – thus we are not in a position to find out whether or not he makes a mistake in thinking the sensation he now has is of a kind which he formerly had. But then similarly no amount of observation of L.W.'s behaviour by L.W. himself could give *him* any reason for thinking he knew what sensations he was having at any time – and in particular, no behavioural traces (such as a photograph of himself he had taken the day he was first struck by the sensation he wished to record) could give him any more reason for thinking he knows what he then felt than it could give us reason for thinking we know what he then felt. So what makes it impossible for us to correct his use of the sign 'E' goes half-way to making it impossible for him to correct his use of the sign 'E' – and if there were that which would make his use corrigible by us, it would also make his use corrigible by him. But it is supposed by hypothesis that there isn't that which would do this. Now add to the strong privacy of the sensations whatever it is that you need to make out in addition that L.W.'s later impressions that he was or wasn't mistaken can't count as L.W.'s finding out that he was, and you now have it that no one can find out whether or not he is now mistaken.

A private language, then, will fail to meet this condition, so long as we are given either an appropriate account of 'finding out' (i.e. strong finding out) or an appropriate account of 'later memory impressions' (i.e. that they could not count as finding out).

Well, is this third step of the argument true? I shall not bother to bring out the things that can be said in defence of it, or the things that can be said against it, for it will be plain what sorts of things they are the moment we conjoin the three steps of the argument to form one general principle, which is what I want to say the denial of the possibility of private languages amounts to. The general principle is this: A sign 'K' which a man uses is not a kind-name in a language unless (by 1) he has identified a kind of thing to be called 'K', which will only be the case (by 2) if it is possible for him to call a thing a 'K' thinking it is of that kind when it is not, which will only be the case (by 3) if it is possible to find out whether the thing is or is not of that kind. Or in sum: A sign 'K' is not a kind-name in a man's language unless it is possible to find out whether or not a thing is of the kind associated with 'K' (over and above its seeming or not seeming to him to be so) – or more simply still, a sign 'K' is not a kind-name in a man's language unless it is possible to find out whether or not a thing is a K.

And it is plain that this is nothing more than a revised formulation of something very familiar indeed, namely the Principle of Verification.[6] We are no longer to say that what purports to be a kind-name 'K' has meaning if and only if it is possible to find out whether or not a thing is a K. But we are instead to say that what purports to be a kind-name 'K' is a kind-name in a man's language only if it is possible to find out whether or not a thing is a K. Strong finding-out goes with what used to be called Strong Verificationism; weak finding-out goes with what used to be called Weak Verificationism. And the change, then, amounts to this: from 'if and only if' to 'only if'; and from 'is meaningless' to 'is not a kind-name in a man's language'. Perhaps the reasons why this might not be thought to be much of an improvement will not need to be set forth.

Since the denial of the possibility of a private language is surely a denial of the possibility of a pure sense-datum language – since the thesis we are concerned with is often appealed to in order to discredit phenomenalism – it may seem strange to suggest that the private language thesis is really a mere restatement of verificationism. After all, in recent philosophical history, verificationism has been taken to lead directly *to* phenomenalism. But we have only to reflect that there were physicalists as well as phenomenalists who rested their case on verificationism. Verificationism does not lead by itself either to one or to the other; your choice between them rested not on the question whether or not you adopted the Principle of Verification, but rather on the question what kinds of ascriptions you took it to be possible to verify. And on this matter, our Wittgensteinians are at one with physicalists.

VII

It may be asked, how can it be that the thesis we are considering really amounts to something quite general, like a revised formulation of the Principle of Verification, when all that was at stake was a private language – a language which a man invents to report on his own sensations, or the language which we would be using in reporting on our sensations if the sceptic about other minds were right.

In fact, if we take seriously Malcolm's definition of the expression 'private language', then it is not merely our use of sensation-terms which (if the sceptic about other minds were right) would count as private languages, but many other things as well. Malcolm said that a private language would be (if there could be such a thing) 'one that not merely is not but [of necessity] *cannot* be understood by anyone other than the speaker'. I now give a recipe for constructing hypothetical languages which would be private in Malcolm's sense. Take any classical metaphysical problem on which there is such a thing as a Sceptical View. Now take the range of statements of which it is the relevant Sceptical View that we can never know whether or not any statement in that range is true. And now *if* the sceptic's view were correct, then what we might call the relevant term or kind of term or form of term will be such that if a man uses that term or kind of term or form of term, he speaks a (at least partly) private language. Consider the metaphysical problem about the existence of material objects. And now suppose that the sceptic about material objects were right – i.e. that it is not possible that any of us should know of any term purporting to stand for a material object whether or not it really applies to anything. So, in particular, we are supposing that it is not possible that anyone should know of the word 'table' whether or not it really applies to anything. We are supposing that although it can *seem* to us as if this really is a table, it is not possible that anyone should *know* that it is one (Weak Scepticism), nor even possible that anyone should have good reason for thinking it is one (Strong Scepticism). Now suppose some man – let us arbitrarily call him Moore – insists that *he does* know of many things that they are (and not merely appear to be) tables. 'Here's one, for example', he says, pointing. But now what shall we take Moore to be saying here? That it looks as if he's pointing to a table, that generally when he uses these words there appears to be a table in the vicinity, is no proof (Weak Scepticism), or even good reason (Strong Scepticism), for thinking that he *is* pointing to a table, that generally when he uses these words there *is* a table in the vicinity. So how should we know – suppose ourselves to have good reason for thinking we know – what he means to be saying is here when he says 'Here's a table'?

All that is needed for turning a class of sentences 'S' into sentences of a private language is that whatever it is which is a way of finding out whether or not sentences of kind S are true should be made logically irrelevant to the truth of sentences of kind S. *Instantly* it is not possible that we should know whether or not any sentences of kind S are true; and *instantly* if any man uses sentences of kind S it is not possible that we should know what he means by them.

Indeed it is surprising that those who have tried to derive the thesis we have been considering from the *Investigations* have failed to notice this possibility of generalising the notion 'private language'.[7] Particularly in view of the fact that, as Malcolm notes, Wittgenstein explicitly suggests (cf., e.g., *Inv.* II, p. 180) that the relation between reports about the behaviour of another and reports about the contents of the mind of another is analogous to the relation between reports about one's sense-impressions and reports about physical objects.

VIII

So the thesis we have been considering amounts to no more than a restatement of the Principle of Verification. But of course it then amounts to no less than this. Whatever can be said both for and against the one can be said both for and against the other. The only trouble is: The arguments on both sides are excessively familiar.

But it is worth bringing out explicitly that two objections in particular which were made to the Principle of Verification can also be made against Malcolm's restatement of it.

(1) Is this principle really of any use to us? How is it to be decided if an expression *does* satisfy the principle? Suppose a man were to claim to be able to see a new colour – for want of a word he calls it 'K'. He says: 'I can't explain to you what it is any more than I can explain to a man who is colourblind what redness is. You just have to be able to see which things are K and which are not. And if you can't, you're just colour-blind to K-ness.' Well, in fact

we don't see any difference between the things he calls 'K' and the things he says are not K; the things he calls 'K' all look black to us, but many black things, he says, are not K. Is his word 'K' a kind-name in a language, or are his utterances in which 'K' appears mere noises? The principle tells us 'K' is a kind-name in his language only if it is possible to find out whether or not a thing is K. Only if it is possible that *we* should find this out, for *his* memory impressions aren't going to count here. *Is* it possible that we should find out, i.e. come to be able to see which things are K and which are not? One is inclined to say: It is possible only if 'K' *is* a kind-name in his language, and not a mere noise. So we come full circle.

(2) Connected with this is a second objection. The principle, it will be remembered, was this: A sign 'K' is not a kind-name in a man's language unless it is possible to find out whether or not a thing is K; and let us call this condition on a man's use of a sign 'C'. What we might then ask is: Is 'C' a kind-name in a language? Well, it is a kind-name in a man's language if it is possible to find out whether or not a sign in a given use does satisfy this condition. Does 'K' in the preceding example satisfy it – over and above its perhaps seeming to its user that it does? Do 'table' and 'chair' satisfy it – over and above its seeming to some non-sceptic that they do? (And this difficulty becomes especially acute if it is strong finding-out that is required.) How should I find out whether or not they do – which is not merely to be a matter of my asking myself whether or not it seems to me that they do? And it should be stressed that unless this is possible for some man, then if the new principle is true, 'C' is not a kind-name in anyone's language. In which case, what should we take the principle to be saying? One is always inclined to suspect that this kind of question – what happens when we apply the principle to itself? – is something of a game, for can we not learn something important from the principle anyway? All the same, if a thesis is to be defended, then embarrassing difficulties have to be faced.

IX

In conclusion, I would just like to say this about the new form of the Principle of Verification, that it seems to me very clear that Wittgenstein himself would never for one moment have subscribed to it. It is astonishing that a man who repeatedly insists that he put forward no thesis in philosophy should constantly be credited with having proved this or that thesis, from the private language thesis to the sorts of things that get called 'Wittgenstein's Theory of Meaning', or 'Wittgenstein's Theory of Meaning As Use'.

There is a vast difference between proposing that we ask a certain question in order to get clearer about the nature of a certain kind of claim, and declaring that if this question does not receive the sort of answer one might have expected, or has no answer at all, then claims of the kind in question are spurious, or meaningless, or not really in the language.

Wittgenstein does say to the Solipsist: You have made a *grammatical* movement, which you interpret as a quasi-scientific discovery. And yet he adds (*Inv.* 401): 'But there is an objection to my saying that you have made a "grammatical" movement. What you have primarily discovered is a new way of looking at things. As if you had invented a new way of painting; or, again, a new metre, or a new kind of song.' No doubt hints of this sort are obscure; no doubt it is not clear what it is that we are to do with them. But that is no reason for thinking that we are free to disregard them, or for thinking that they are (perhaps mere poetic embellishments on what is really a quite straightforward theory about the necessary conditions for meaningfulness or for being-in-a-language.

(ii) *Anthony Kenny*[8]

In his *Philosophical Investigations*, Wittgenstein argued that a private language is impossible. What is a private language, we may wonder, and why does its possibility matter? A private language, in the sense discussed by Wittgenstein, is a language whose words 'refer to what can only be known to the person speaking: to his immediate private sensations' (*Inv.* 243). Whether such a language is possible has philosophical importance not so much as a question in its own right as because of its consequences for epistemology and philosophy of mind. It is entailed by several traditional and influential philosophical theories that a private language is possible; consequently, if private languages are impossible, those theories are false. For instance, some empiricist philosophers have thought that the only matters of fact we really know are our own experiences: what we claim to know about the world or about other people is based on our knowledge of our own mental states and processes. The same philosophers have commonly taken for granted that our knowledge of our experiences can be expressed in language, at least to ourselves, and that the possibility of this expression does not presuppose any acquaintance with the external world or other minds. Anyone who accepts this much must believe in the possibility of a private language whose words acquire meaning simply by being linked to private experience. Indeed, he must believe that our actual language is a private language, not in the sense that it is peculiar to a single user, but in the sense that its words have acquired their meaning for each of us by an essentially private process: an internal ostensive definition in which an appropriate sample of experience was attended to and associated with a word. Of course, if words are thought of as acquiring meaning in this way, a doubt may arise whether the samples from which one person has acquired his vocabulary are really like the samples from which another person has done so. Thus this form of empiricism carries with it a version of scepticism which finds expression in such thoughts as the following: 'For all we know, what I call "red" you call "green" and vice versa' (cf. BB 60; *Inv.* 272). One point of the private language argument is to refute this version of empiricism with its attendant scepticism; to show that the thought just expressed is a nonsensical one, and that the doubts it conjures up are spurious. The programme of the private language argument can be well summed up in a quotation from the *Tractatus*. 'Scepticism it *not* irrefutable, but obviously nonsensical, when it tries to raise doubts where no questions can be asked. For doubt can exist only where a question exists, a question only where an answer exists, and an answer only where something *can be said*' (TLP 6.51). The *Investigations* shows that the empiricist sceptic must use a private language in order to formulate his question; but in a private language nothing can be said and so no questions can be asked.

Wittgenstein considered that the notion of a private language rested on two fundamental mistakes, one about the nature of experience, and one about the nature of language. The mistake about experience was the belief that experience is private; the mistake about language was the belief that words can acquire meaning by bare ostensive definition. I will discuss the latter mistake first, postponing the former until later (p. 213 below).

THE INSUFFICIENCY OF BARE OSTENSIVE DEFINITION

The mistake about language is attacked in the *Investigations* long before the topic of private language is introduced in section 244. It is very natural to think that one can learn the meaning of a word simply by becoming acquainted with what the word stands for. We learn language, it may seem, by giving names to objects, to human beings, say, and shapes, colours, pains, moods and so on (*Inv.* 26). The essential part of the learning process appears to be the encounter with the object: others may teach us what words mean, but they must do so by putting us in a position where we ourselves can become acquainted with the object which is the meaning of the word to be learnt (*Inv.* 362). Once such acquaintance is secured, it seems the learner has only to fix his attention on the appropriate object and associate the word with it and henceforth he knows its meaning. Once you know what the word stands for, we feel, you understand it, you know its whole use (*Inv.* 264).

Wittgenstein criticised this view of the operation of ostensive definition in the first part of the *Investigations* (see esp. *Inv.* 27–35). There he insists that acquaintance with the object for which a word stands is not the same thing as knowledge of the word's meaning: the meaning of a word is not the thing that 'corresponds' to the word. We must beware of confusing the bearer of a name with the meaning of a name. 'When Mr N. N. dies, one says that the bearer of the name dies, not that the meaning dies' (*Inv.* 40). Though bearer and meaning are distinct, the meaning of a name is sometimes explained by pointing to its bearer: that is what an ostensive explanation is (*Inv.* 40). But if such explanation is to be successful, the learner must not only be acquainted with the bearer, but also grasp the role in language of the word to be defined. Thus, if I know that someone means to explain a colour-word to me, the ostensive definition 'That is called "sepia"' will help me to understand the word (*Inv.* 30). But the ostensive definition will not suffice by itself, because it can always be variously interpreted. For instance, suppose that I explain the word 'tove' by pointing to a pencil and saying 'This is called "Tove"'. I may be taken to mean 'This is a pencil' or 'This is round' or 'This is wood' or 'This is one' or 'This is hard' and so on (BB 2). So in the acquisition of the understanding of a word, acquaintance with the word's bearer is not so important as mastery of the word's general use. Knowing that what I am now seeing is called 'tove' does not by itself enable me to answer the question 'And what else am I to call "tove"?' Wittgenstein illustrates the point by an analogy with chess. 'When one shews someone the king in chess and says "this is the king", this does not tell him the use of this piece – unless he already knows the rules of the game up to this last point: the shape of the king' (*Inv.* 31).

Thus, in the first part of the *Investigations*, Wittgenstein argued against the primacy of ostensive definition, against the idea that bare ostension without training in the use of words could constitute the teaching of a language. His arguments concern public ostensive definition as well as private ostensive definition: they apply to the naming of shapes and colours and men as well as to the naming of pains and moods. But if the arguments are accepted, then the private language theory is refuted before it is stated: at least if it supposes the meanings of names for sensations could be learnt simply by acquaintance with the names' bearers, i.e. simply by having and attending to the sensations. However, a defender of private languages might suggest the possibility of a language which was private in that its words *referred to* private sensations without necessarily being private in that its words were *learnt from* private sensations by bare ostension. A private language, he might maintain, might be learnt from private sensations not by bare ostension but by some private analogue of training in the use of words. This suggestion shows that the critique of the primacy of ostensive definition does not render superfluous the later explicit discussion of private languages. What that later discussion does, in effect, is to show that in the case of the private ostensive definition there *cannot* be any analogue of the background which is necessary if public ostensive definition is to convey meaning.

Is 'Pain' the Name of a Sensation?

After these prolegomena we may consider section 243 in which Wittgenstein introduces the private language. Could we, he asks,

imagine a language in which a person could write down or give vocal expression to his inner experiences – his feelings, moods, and the rest – for his private use? – Well, can't we do so in our ordinary language? – But that is not what I mean. The individual words of this language are to refer to what can only be known to the person speaking; to his immediate private sensations. So another person cannot understand the language. (*Inv.* 243).

Having defined a private language as a language whose words refer to the speaker's immediate private sensations, Wittgenstein goes on to comment on the expressions occurring in this definition, and first of all on the expression 'refer to'. In section 244 he asks 'How do words *refer* to sensations?' From this passage it would appear that Wittgenstein has no objection to calling 'pain' the name of a sensation, or to calling 'I am in pain' a proposition (*Satz*). 'We talk about sensations every day', he says, 'and give them *names*', and he asks, 'How does a human being learn the meaning of the *names* of sensations?' As a possible answer to this question he suggests that words replace the natural pre-verbal expression of sensation. 'A child has hurt himself and he cries; and then adults talk to him and teach him exclamations and, later *sentences* (*Sätze*)' (*Inv.* 244; italics added).

Elsewhere, however, Wittgenstein has been taken to deny that a word such as 'pain' names a sensation. He says, for instance, 'If we construe the grammar of the expression of sensation on the model of "object and name" the object drops out of consideration as irrelevant' (*Inv.* 293). This seems to suggest that we should not so construe the grammar, i.e. should not consider a sensation-word like 'pain' as the name of an object. In the *Zettel*, Wittgenstein's wayward self says ' "joy" surely designates an inward thing' and his sterner self replies 'No. "Joy" designates nothing. Neither any inward nor any outward thing' (Z 487).

These passages can be reconciled in the light of the attack on the primacy of ostensive definition. The model of 'object and name' which we are to reject is the idea that a speaker understands a name by being acquainted with its bearer. This is clear from the context: at *Inv.* 293, Wittgenstein is criticising the theory that one knows what pain is only from one's own case. That theory is one formulation of the idea that it is acquaintance which conveys meaning: it is only one's own pain that one is acquainted with, so it is only from one's own case that one knows what pain is. If this were true, and each man knew what pain was only from his own case, then no one could teach anyone else the meaning of the word 'pain'; each speaker would have to name the sensation for himself by a private ostensive definition.

Wittgenstein considers this suggestion at *Inv.* 257, and brings the critique of ostensive definition to bear:

What does it mean to say that he has 'named his pain'?! – How has he done this naming of pain?! And whatever he did, what was its purpose? – When one says 'He gave a name to his sensation' one forgets that a great deal of stage-setting in the language is presupposed if the mere act of naming is to make sense. And when we speak of someone's having given a name to pain, what is presupposed is the existence of the grammar of the word 'pain'; it shews the post where the new word is stationed.

This echoes the remarks about public ostensive definition: 'the ostensive definition explains the use – the meaning – of the word when the overall role of the word in language is clear' (*Inv.* 30). Wittgenstein is not denying that one can give a name to a sensation; he is merely affirming that giving a name presupposes stage-setting. Such stage-setting, he will go on to argue, is possible in a public language, but not in a private language. Given the stage-setting, the word for a sensation may be ostensively defined no less than the name of a colour or a piece of furniture (BB 69; *Inv.* 288).

To sum up: if by 'name' one means 'word whose meaning is learnt by bare ostensive definition', then 'pain' is not the name of sensation; but if by 'name' one means what is ordinarily meant by that word, then of course 'pain' is the name of a sensation.

A passage in the *Brown Book* throws light on Wittgenstein's apparent inconsistency:

> Our use of expressions like 'names of numbers', 'names of colours', 'names of materials', 'names of nations' may spring from two different sources. One is that we might imagine the functions of proper names, numerals, words for colours, etc., to be much more alike than they actually are. If we do so we are tempted to think that the function of every word is more or less like the function of a proper name of a person, or such generic terms as 'table', 'chair', 'door', etc. The second source is this, that if we see how fundamentally different the functions of such words as 'table', 'chair', etc., are from those of proper names, and how different from either the functions of, say, the names of colours, we see no reason why we shouldn't speak of names of numbers or names of directions either, not by way of saying some such thing as 'numbers' and directions are just different forms of objects', but rather by way of stressing the analogy which lies in the lack of analogy between the functions of the words 'chair' and 'Jack' on the one hand, and 'east' and 'Jack' on the other hand. (BB 82.)

When Wittgenstein speaks of names of sensations, he does so in the spirit in which he here says we might speak of names of directions;

when he says that we must not construe sensation-expressions on the model of object and name, he is discouraging the thought 'tables, colours, and sensations are just different forms of object'.

THE CONNECTION BETWEEN 'PAIN' AND PAIN

If the word 'pain' does not refer to a sensation by being attached to it by bare ostensive definition, how does it refer? In what way is it connected with the sensation? One possibility, Wittgenstein says, is that it is a learned, articulate replacement of unlearned, inarticulate expressions of sensation such as moans and winces (*Inv.* 244; cf. pp. 253 and 257–8 below). The word 'pain' cannot, as it were, hook on to pain directly; it must be attached to pain through its connections with the natural expressions of pain (cf. *Inv.* 256, 257, 271). To try to connect 'pain' with pain in isolation from unlearned pain-behaviour would be to try to insert language between pain and its expression. This, Wittgenstein thinks, is absurd: presumably because the verbal manifestation of pain is itself an expression of pain.[9]

Few people are immediately convinced by Wittgenstein's suggestion that it is only via the expression of pain that the word 'pain' can mean pain. Surely, we want to say, we can have a pain without ever saying or showing that we do; and on the other hand we can say that we have a pain without really having one; the only connection between pain and the expression of pain is that they sometimes coincide. Pain and its expression seem no more essentially connected than redness and sweetness: sometimes what is red is sweet, and sometimes not.

In the face of this objection Wittgenstein immediately agrees that in our language we use the words 'being in pain' in such a way that we can say 'A is in pain but he does not show it'. But he insists that we should have no use for the expression if its application was severed from behavioural criteria. So the relation of pain to pain-behaviour is not the same as the relation of redness to sweetness. It is essential to the language-game with the word 'pain' that the people who play it both behave in the particular way we call expressing pain, and sometimes more or less entirely conceal their pains.[10]

Thus Wittgenstein's position differs from behaviourism. If pain is identified with pain-behaviour, then 'A is in pain' means 'A is behaving in such and such a way'. But Wittgenstein rejects this interpretation of his theory that pain-language is connected with pain-behaviour. 'Pain' does not mean crying: the verbal expression of pain does not describe the natural expression of pain, but takes its place (*Inv.* 244).

If pain and pain-behaviour are separable, how are our words for sensations 'tied up with' our natural expressions of sensations? One way suggested by Wittgenstein is that they are *learnt in connection with* the natural expression (*Inv.* 244; pp. 250, 252 below). Is this the only possible connection? If so, then an innate knowledge of the meaning of 'pain' would be inconceivable: if only learning connects word and sensation, an unlearned connection would be impossible. I think that Wittgenstein did not mean to rule out the possibility of innate knowledge.[11] But even an innate knowledge of the meaning of 'pain' would have to connect with the natural expression of pain in a certain way. Knowledge of the meaning would have to be exercised in use of the word, and the use of the word would have to fit in with the usual symptoms and circumstances of pain – with symptoms such as wincing and circumstances such as injury (cf. *Inv.* 270). Knowledge of the meaning of 'pain', whether inborn, or conferred by a drug, or a sudden gift of the gods, must always be capable of investigation by such criteria. If some humanoid creatures used a word which had no such connection with the symptoms and circumstances of pain, it would be difficult to see why the word should be translated as 'pain'.[12]

Two Sorts of Privacy

The private language was to consist of words 'to refer to private sensations'. Having discussed, in *Inv.* 244–5, the expression 'refer to', Wittgenstein turns in 246–55 to the word 'private'. He asks: 'To what extent are my sensations *private*?' and he distinguishes two senses of the word 'private'. The first sense of privacy has to do with knowledge and the second sense has to do with possession: in the first sense, something is private to me if only I can know about it, and in the second sense something is private to me if only I can have it. To claim that pains are private in the first sense is to say 'Only I can know whether I am really in pain; another person can only surmise it' (*Inv.* 246); to claim that pains are private in the second sense is to say 'Another person can't have my pains' (*Inv.* 253). Using words that are not used by Wittgenstein, we may use for

the first sense of 'private' the abbreviation 'incommunicable', and
for the second sense of 'private' the abbreviation 'inalienable'.[13]
The question 'Are sensations private?' breaks up into two questions:
(i) 'Are sensations incommunicable?' (ii) 'Are sensations inalienable?' Crudely, Wittgenstein's answer is: (i) no; (ii) not in any way
peculiar to sensations.

Are Pains Incommunicable?

The thesis that pains are incommunicable is a conjunction of two
separable theses: (i) I can know that I am in pain; (ii) other people
cannot know that I am in pain. Wittgenstein rejects both theses. Let
us consider the second first (*Inv.* 246 ff.). 'In one way', he says, 'this
is false, and in another nonsense.' If we take the word 'know' as it is
normally used, then the claim is false: other people often know when
I am in pain: for instance, if they see me falling into flames and
crying out (p. 273 below). On the other hand, if we take the word
'know' to mean 'know in such a way that doubt is logically excluded', then the thesis is senseless, for there can only be knowledge
where doubt is possible (cf. *Inv.* II, p. 221).

One reason why people believe that one man can never know if
another man is in pain is the possibility of pretence: may not a man
who appears to be in pain be merely pretending? To this Wittgenstein replies that there are cases in which the supposition of pretence
is senseless: for instance, the case of infants (*Inv.* 249) and animals
(*Inv.* 250). In order to be able to pretend or lie one needs to master
certain skills which infants and animals lack (cf. also II, pp. 227–9).

Sometimes people claim that one man can never really know of
another's pain because they fail to distinguish between incommunicability and inalienability. They assume that to know pain is to
have pain, and because they believe that one person cannot have
another's pain, they conclude that one person cannot know another's
pains. But the impossibility they have in mind is not a mere matter-
of-fact impossibility: they mean that it makes no sense to say that
A knows B's pain. If so, Wittgenstein replies, then it makes no sense
to say that A *doesn't* know B's pain: the negation of a senseless
sentence is itself senseless. 'You did not state that knowing was a
goal which you could not reach, and that you have to be content
with conjecturing; rather there is no goal in this game'. The statement 'You can't know when A has pain' is analogous to a statement
like 'There is no goal in an endurance race' (BB 54).

Wittgenstein rejects also the second part of the incommunicability thesis: 'I can know when I am in pain.' 'It can't,' he says, 'be said of me at all (except perhaps as a joke) that I *know* I am in pain.' 'Other people cannot be said to learn of my sensations *only* from my behaviour – for *I* cannot be said to learn of them. I *have* them' (*Inv.* 246).

Many people are disconcerted by this. It is true, they say, that there is no such thing as *learning* that one is in pain, but that only shows that there are some things we know without having learnt them. If I cannot know of my own sensations, how can I know of anything else? One cannot doubt that one is in pain (as Wittgenstein himself agrees, *Inv.* 288), and surely one knows what one cannot doubt! Wittgenstein may be right when he says that doubt here is not just impossible, but actually senseless: but isn't that so much the better? If doubt is not merely psychologically, but logically impossible, then the corresponding knowledge must be so much the more secure.

To a first approximation, Wittgenstein's answer runs as follows. 'I know when I am in pain' can be taken in two ways: as an empirical proposition or as a grammatical one. As a grammatical proposition (a proposition to explain the meaning of a word) it means: it is senseless to say 'I doubt whether I am in pain'. So taken, the proposition is correct (*Inv.* 247). But those who argue that because we cannot doubt our sensations we must know of them are misled by the form of the proposition into taking it as an empirical proposition (*Inv.* 251). Where it is senseless to say 'I doubt whether...' it is not always true to say 'I know that...'. This can be seen if we complete the expressions not with 'I am in pain' but with 'Good morning!' or 'Shut the door'. 'I doubt whether good morning' and 'I know that good morning' are equally senseless, as are 'I doubt whether shut the door' and 'I know that shut the door'. Of course, 'I am in pain', unlike the other two completions, has the form of a declarative sentence; but Wittgenstein may fairly insist that this is insufficient to show that it *is* a declarative sentence. The words 'I am in pain' may look like a description of a mental state; but they may in fact be more like a cry of complaint (cf. *Inv.* II, 189). If they are, then 'I doubt whether I am in pain' may be senseless in the same way as 'I doubt whether ouch'. If so, then it is clearly out of place to talk of knowledge and certainty. It would be foolish to say 'Since it is not just psychologically but logically impossible to doubt whether good morning, the knowledge that good morning must be so much the more secure.'

Whether Wittgenstein is right about 'I know I am in pain'
depends, therefore, on whether 'I am in pain' is, as it appears to be,
a declarative sentence, a description of a mental state. This question
will have to be pursued later: it can be waived for the moment since
the rejection of 'when I am in pain I know that I am in pain'
does not function as a premise in the argument against private language.

Are Pains Inalienable?

In *Inv.* 253 Wittgenstein passes from the incommunicability thesis
to the claim that pains are inalienable: 'Only I can have my pains'.
Is this claim true? 'If they are *my* pains then *I* have them' is a
straightforwardly grammatical statement, drawing attention to the
connection between the pronoun 'I' and the possessive 'my'; but
it tells us nothing particular about pain, since the sentence remains
correct no matter what plural noun is substituted for 'pains'. But
two questions arise: what is *having* here? and granted that if they
are my pains I must have them, can anyone else have them in
addition to me? (Cf. 'Since it is *my* bank account, *I* have it; but
my wife shares it too.')

' Which are *my* pains? What counts as a criterion of identity
here?' asks Wittgenstein (*Inv.* 253). The two questions are distinct.
One asks for the criterion for the possessor of a pain, the other for
the criterion of identity for a pain. The first question is answered in
section 302: the possessor of pain (*die leidende Person*) is the person
who gives it expression. *My* pains, then, are the pains which I
express.[14]

This may seem a strange criterion. Surely my pains are the pains
felt in my body? Against this Wittgenstein argued repeatedly that
one could quite conceivably feel pain in someone else's body. (Cf.
WWK 49; PB sec. 60 f.; BB 49–55.)

> In order to see that it is conceivable that one person should have
> pain in another person's body, one must examine what sort of
> facts we call criteria for a pain being in a certain place.... Sup-
> pose I feel a pain which on the evidence of the pain alone, e.g.
> with closed eyes, I should call a pain in my left hand. Someone
> asks me to touch the painful spot with my right hand. I do so and
> looking round perceive that I am touching my neighbour's hand.
> (BB 49.)

This would be pain *felt in* another's body, and not just pain *caused by injury to* another's body (which would also be conceivable – e.g. if I feel pain in my head whenever you expose yours to cold air; cf. BB 54). So my pain is not necessarily pain felt in my body. My pains are the pains to which I give expression; and the expression of my pain (e.g. pointing to places, singling them out for solicitude) may determine a place outside my own body.

Now what of the criteria of identity for pains? How, Wittgenstein asks, are pains such as toothache distinguished from each other? (PB sec. 61.) By intensity, and similar characteristics, and by localisation. Suppose that these are the same – suppose that you and I both feel a sharp pain in the upper abdomen – then it is perfectly natural to say that we both feel the same pain. But, it might be thought, this is not strictly correct, since the pains are not felt literally in the same place, but only in corresponding places in two different bodies. Well, Wittgenstein points out, Siamese twins might feel pain in exactly the same place, namely, the place where they are joined together. Even so, it might be said, the pains are only specifically the same, but numerically distinct; because one pain is Tweedledum's pain and the other is Tweedledee's pain. But this, Wittgenstein says, is to make the possessor a characteristic of the pain itself; in the terminology I used above, it is to make the identity of the possessor part of the criterion of identity for the pain: if there are two possessors then there are two pains. This makes '*Only* I can have my pains' a grammatical statement like 'If they are my pains I have them'. It also makes it comparatively uninformative about pain. 'Only I can have my X' is true, not indeed of bank accounts, but of many things besides sensations: for instance, blushes and sneezes. If you blush, then that is your blush, and nobody else's; and if you sneeze, it is not my sneeze or the President's sneeze. But there is nothing specially occult about blushes and sneezes; their inalienability is a very tenuous sort of privacy. We may allow, then, that pains are inalienable; but this will not make sensations any more private than behaviour.

SECRECY *v.* PRIVACY

There is, of course, *one* sense in which experiences are more private than behaviour: experiences such as pain *can be* kept secret without being publicly manifested in any way. If one wants to call an ex-

perience thus kept to oneself a private experience, then clearly there
are such things as private experiences, as Wittgenstein expressly
admits.[15] But if a private experience is one that is kept secret, there
is no reason to call an experience that is *not* kept secret a private
experience. If a man itches, but does not scratch or report his itch,
we may call that a private experience; but if he itches and does
scratch, why should we call the itch private? If we take 'private' in
this sense, and ask 'Are pains private experiences?', the only possible answer is 'Some are, and some are not'. And from the fact that
some experiences are, in this sense, private experiencs, it does not
follow that all experiences could be private experiences. 'What sometimes happens could always happen' is a fallacy. Some money is
forged, but it could not be the case that all money was forged.[16]

THE SENSATION S

In the *Investigations*, then, from 246 to 252 Wittgenstein has
argued that pain is not incommunicable; from 253 to 255 he has
argued that pain has no special inalienability. At 256 he restates
the private language hypothesis. From what has been said up to
this point it follows that *our* word 'pain' does not belong to a private
language: from 258 onwards Wittgenstein is going to consider not
pain, but pseudo-pain, i.e. a sensation supposed to be like pain but
different from pain in being incommunicable. The name of pseudo-
pain must be learnt by private ostensive definition. It would be
cheating to call this process 'the naming of pain', Wittgenstein
argues in 257, since naming is part of a language-game (and the
private ceremony is not) and since the language-game with pain
presupposes the outward signs of pain (whereas pseudo-pain has no
outward expression). In 257 Wittgenstein argues that it is futile to
start from pain and attempt to subtract its ntaural expression; in
258 he discusses the attempt to start from pseudo-pain and add to
it a linguistic correlate. This section is the kernel of the private language argument.

We are to suppose that I want to keep a diary about the occurrence of a certain sensation, and that I associate the sensation with
the sign 'S'. It is essential to the supposition that no definition of
the sign can be expressed (*sich aussprechen lässt*): that is to say,
that no definition can be given in terms of our public language. If
this condition were not fulfilled, then the language to which the

sign belonged would not be a private one. The sign must be defined for me alone, and this must be a private ostensive definition, by my attending to the sensation and producing the sign:

> I speak, or write the sign down, and at the same time I concentrate my attention on the sensation ... in this way I impress on myself the connection between the sign and the sensation.

Wittgenstein argues that no such ceremony could establish an appropriate connection:

> 'I impress it on myself' can only mean: this process brings it about that I remember the connection right in future. But in the present case I have no criterion of correctness. One would like to say: whatever is going to seem right to me is right. And that only means that here we can't talk about 'right'. (*Inv.* 258.)

This crucial passage is often misinterpreted. What would it be to remember the connection right? Many philosophers have taken 'I remember the connection right' to mean 'I use "S" when and only when I really have S'. They then take Wittgenstein's argument to be based on scepticism about memory: how can you be sure that you have remembered aright when next you call a sensation 'S'? In support of this interpretation they may quote Wittgenstein's advice 'Always get rid of the private object in this way: assume that it constantly changes, but that you do not notice the change because your memory constantly deceives you' (*Inv.* II, p. 207).

Critics of Wittgenstein have found the argument, so interpreted, quite unconvincing. Surely, they say, the untrustworthiness of memory presents no more and no less a problem for the user of a private language than for the user of a public one. No, Wittgenstein's defenders have said, for memory-mistakes about public objects may be corrected, memory-mistakes about private sensations cannot; and where correction is impossible, talk of 'correctness' is out of place. At this point critics of Wittgenstein have either denied that truth demands corrigibility, or have sought to show that checking is possible in the private case too.[17]

Both criticism and defence rest on a misunderstanding of the argument. Wittgenstein is not arguing 'When next I call something "S" how will I know it really is S?' He is arguing 'When next I call something "S" how will I know what I mean by "S"?' Even to think *falsely* that something is S I must know the meaning of

'S'; and this is what Wittgenstein argues is impossible in the private language.

This is best shown by a consideration of section 265:

> Let us imagine a table (something like a dictionary) that exists only in our imagination. A dictionary can be used to justify the translation of a word X into a word Y. But are we also to call it a justification if such a table is to be looked up only in the imagination? – 'Well, yes; then it is a subjective justification'. – But justification consists in appealing to something independent. – 'But surely I can appeal from one memory to another. For example, I don't know if I have remembered the time of departure of a train right and to check it I call to mind how a page of the time-table looked. Isn't it the same here?' – No; for this process has got to produce a memory which is actually *correct*. If the mental image of the time-table could not itself be tested for correctness, how could it confirm the correctness of the first memory? (As if someone were to buy several copies of the morning paper to assure himself that what it said was true.)

On the common interpretation, Wittgenstein is here propounding and rejecting the suggestion that the memory of one private experience might confirm the memory of another, as the visual memory of a time-table might confirm the audio memory of an announced departure. Two things are puzzling about the passage on this interpretation. First, why does Wittgenstein say that the memory produced has to be *correct*, rather than *corrigible*? Secondly, surely he ought to compare the process not to the purchase of two copies of one newspaper, but to the purchase of two newspapers owned by the same magnate. For the memories of two private objects would be two distinct memories, even if produced by the same untrustworthy faculty.

The first puzzle arises partly from a mistranslation. '*Dieser Vorgang muss nun wirklich die richtige Erinnerung hervorrufen*' appears to mean not 'This process has got to produce a memory which is actually *correct*' but 'This process has got to call up the right memory'.[18] We are supposing that I wish to justify my calling a private sensation 'S' by appealing to a mental table in which memory-samples of private objects of various kinds are listed in correlation with symbols.[19] To make use of such a table one must call up the right memory-sample: e.g. I must make sure to call up the memory-sample that belongs alongside 'S' and not the one which belongs to 'T'.

But as this table exists only in the imagination, there can be no real looking up to see which sample goes with 'S', i.e. remembering what 'S' means. But this is precisely what the table was supposed to confirm. In other words, the memory of the meaning of 'S' is being used to confirm itself. Once we realise this, we have the solution of our second puzzle of interpretation. Since the process involves making use twice over of a single memory – the memory of which sample corresponds to 'S' – it is fairly compared to purchasing two copies of the same newspaper.

'Remembering the connection between sign and sensation', then, does not mean always identifying the sensation correctly but simply remembering which sensation the sign means. This is, of course, what should have been expected: attaching meaning to a name does not mean acquiring infallibility in its use – knowing what 'woman' means does not guarantee that one will never mistake a woman for a man.

With this established, we may return to the key section 258. Wittgenstein wishes to show that the private ostensive definition 'This is called "S"' cannot confer meaning on 'S'. Suppose that at some time after the would-be definition, the private language speaker says of a later sensation 'This is S again'. We may ask him 'What do you mean by "S"?' Three types of answer are open to him: he may say "I mean *this*'; he may appeal to a private memory sample of S; he may mention a correlate of S. All three types of reply are countered by Wittgenstein.

If the private language speaker says 'By "S" I mean *this*', gesturing, as it were, to his current sensation, then it is clear that 'This is S' is not a genuine proposition capable of being true or false; for what gives it its content is the very same thing as gives it its truth: the significance of the predicate is supposed to be settled by the reference of the subject. 'Whatever is going to seem right to me is right', therefore; and 'that only means that here we can't talk about "right"' (*Inv.* 258).[20]

Suppose next that the private language speaker says 'By "S" I mean the sensation I named "S" in the past'. Since he no longer has the past sensation he must rely on memory: he must call up a memory-sample of S and compare it with his current sensation to see if the two are alike. But of course he must call up the *right* memory. Now is it possible that the wrong memory might come at his call? If not, then 'S' means whatever memory occurs to him in connection with 'S', and again whatever seems right is right. If so,

then he does not really know what he means. It is no use his saying
'Well, at least I *believe* that this is the sensation "S" again', for he
cannot even believe that without knowing what 'S' means (*Inv.*
260). This appeal to memory-samples, as we have seen, is considered
by Wittgenstein in section 265; and it is this memory-sample which
is the private object of which Wittgenstein says 'assume that it constantly changes, but you do not notice the change' (*Inv.* II, p. 207;
cf. *Inv.* 271).

The third possibility is that the private language speaker corre-
lates his use of 'S' with a public phenomenon:

> Let us now imagine a use for the entry of the sign 'S' in my diary.
> I discover that whenever I have a particular sensation a mano-
> meter shews that my blood-pressure rises. So I shall be able to say
> that my blood-pressure is rising without using any apparatus.
> This is a useful result. And now it seems quite indifferent whether
> I have recognised the sensation *right* or not. Let us suppose I
> regularly identify it wrong, it does not matter in the least. And
> that alone shews that the hypothesis that I make a mistake is
> mere show. (*Inv.* 270.)

Here 'S' has a genuine use, but not as a part of a private language:
it is tantamount to 'sensation which means my blood-pressure is
rising'. Why does Wittgenstein say no mistake is possible? Cannot I
say 'S' and then find my blood-pressure is *not* rising? Yes, but that
is not what Wittgenstein is rejecting: he is talking about a would-be
intermediate step between having the sensation and judging 'Now
my blood-pressure is rising', a step which would consist in recognising the sensation as a sensation of a particular kind, and remembering that a sensation of that kind indicated a rise in blood-pressure.
Misidentification here would not matter, provided that I both misidentified the kind of sensation *and* misremembered what kind of
sensation indicated the blood-pressure rise. It is this, according to
Wittgenstein, which shows that the hypothesis of a mistake is mere
show. Suppose that I say 'S' and the blood-pressure does not rise:
what reason have I to say that I have misidentified the sensation
rather than misremembered which kind of sensation goes with the
rise? None at all unless 'identifying the sensation' means 'identifying it as the blood-pressure-rising sensation'; but if it does, then
there is no room for the intermediate step, and 'S' is not the name
of a private object but a word in a public language.

PRIVATE LANGUAGE AND PICTURE THEORY

As we have seen, a crucial part is played in the private language argument by Wittgenstein's advice 'Always get rid of the idea of the private object in this way: assume that it constantly changes, but that you do not notice the change because your memory constantly deceives you.' This advice has a verificationist ring, and some philosophers have thought that the private language argument depends, in the last analysis, on verificationist premisses.[21] But Wittgenstein's advice is not meant to be followed by the question 'How would you ever find out?' but by the question 'What possible difference would it make?' The private language argument does indeed depend on premisses carried forward from Wittgenstein's earlier philosophy: but they derive not from the verificationism of the 1930s but from the picture theory of the proposition in the 1910s.

Wittgenstein's earliest *Notes on Logic* begin with a section "Bipolarity of Propositions' in which he says: 'We must be able to understand a proposition without knowing if it is true or false.... Every proposition is essentially true-false. Thus a proposition has two poles (corresponding to the case of its truth and the case of its falsity)' (NB, p. 94). When Wittgenstein first compared propositions to pictures he stressed the bi-polarity of pictures (NB, 29 Sept. 1914) and insisted that propositions were pictures in so far as they were articulated (NB, 3, Oct. 1914). A proposition must contain the possibility of its truth, but *no more than* its possibility: hence there are no such things as analytic propositions (NB, 21 Oct., 29 Oct., 1914). 'In order for a proposition to be capable of being true it must also be capable of being false' (NB, 5 June 1915). These ideas received their classical exposition in the *Tractatus* (2. 21–2. 225) and remained influential in the 1930s (cf. WWK 67, 88, 97).

It is clear that 'This is S' does not satisfy the conditions for propositionhood laid down in the 1910s. It is not articulate, since 'this' and 'S' are not given their meaning independently. It has no true-false poles, since what is supposed to give it its content is the same as what is supposed to give it its truth. In the *Notebooks* (24 Nov. 1914) Wittgenstein wrote 'Proposition and situation are related to one another like the yardstick and the length to be measured'. 'This is S' is related to the sensation which it purports to identify like a yardstick which grows or shrinks to the length of the object to be measured. 'Imagine', Wittgenstein says, 'someone saying: "But I know how tall I am!" and laying his hand on top of his head to prove it' (*Inv.* 279).[22] A measure must be independent of what is measured; as we have seen, there is no way of giving 'S' genuine independence of the object it purports to name short of taking it into a public language.

The Picture of Pain and the Language-game with 'Pain'

It is time to return from 'This is S' to 'I'm in pain'. It cannot be said of 'I'm in pain', as it could of 'This is S', that what gives it its content gives it its truth; for 'I'm in pain' may be a lie, and therefore meaningful but false. ('This is S', of course, being in a language which only the speaker could understand, could not be a lie.) So 'I'm in pain' has true-false poles, and passes that test for being a proposition. Why then does Wittgenstein appear to reject the idea that 'I'm in pain' is a declarative sentence, a description of a conscious state? (Cf. *Inv.* 290 f., 294; ii, p. 189.)

One might seek to give an account of what description is in the following manner: to describe a state of affairs is to read off certain features from the facts and portray them in words according to rules (*Inv.* 292). Such a description of a state of affairs would be a picture of a fact in the sense of the *Tractatus*: to see whether such a picture is true or false I compare it with what it depicts. 'His eye is black' is a picture in this sense: it is compared with the real eye to see whether it is correct. Now 'He is in pain' – let us leave aside 'I am in pain' for the moment – is not a picture in this sense. It can be compared with reality, and checked for truth and falsehood, certainly; but what it is compared with is not his pain, but the criteria of his pain, e.g. what he says and does.

The previous paragraph draws on a passage in the *Blue Book*:

> 'Surely there is quite a definite act of imagining the other person to have pain'. Of course we don't deny this, or any other statement about facts. But let us see: If we make an image of the other person's pain, do we apply it in the same way in which we apply the image, say, of a black eye when we imagine the other person having one?

He suggests that we suppose the image replaced by a literal picture:

> A very important application of this picture will be comparing it with the real eye to see if the picture is correct. When we vividly

imagine that someone suffers pain, there often enters in our image what one might call a shadow of a pain felt in the locality corresponding to that in which we say his pain is felt.

This 'shadow of a pain' corresponds to the picture of a black eye which we supposed to be substituted for the image of a black eye.

But the sense in which an image is an image is determined by the way in which it is compared with reality. This we might call the method of projection. Now think of comparing an image of A's toothache with his toothache. How would you compare them? If you say, you compare them 'indirectly' via his bodily behaviour, I answer that this means you *don't* compare them as you compare the picture of his behaviour with his behaviour.

In the *Investigations* and the *Zettel*, Wittgenstein repeats that in the language-game with 'pain' there is no comparing of pain with its picture. We are tempted, he says, to say that it is not merely the picture of pain-behaviour which enters into the game, but also the picture of the pain (*Inv.* 300). That is, we feel that in order to use 'He is in pain' we need not only a sample of pain-behaviour as a paradigm for comparison with his behaviour, but also a sample of *pain* for a comparison with his pain. This sample, of course, need not, we think, be a real pain, but only an imagined pain, a mental proxy for pain. But surely real pain will be at least as good a sample as shadow-pain: so in the *Zettel* Wittgenstein imagines someone saying 'I am not certain whether he is in pain', and pricking himself with a pin while saying it, so as to have the meaning of pain vividly before him, so that he knows *what* he is in doubt of about the other man. 'So he has real pain; and now he knows what he is to doubt in someone else's case. He has the object before him and it is *not* some piece of behaviour or the like' (Z 546–8).[23]
Of course this would not guarantee the sense of his statement, if it needed guaranteeing: what he needs is not pain but the *concept* pain, the mastery of the use of 'pain'. 'It is a misunderstanding', Wittgenstein continues (*Inv.* 300), 'to say "The picture of pain enters into the language-game with the word 'pain'." The image of pain is not a picture and this image is not replaceable in the language-game by anything we should call a picture.' When I imagine someone in pain, my image is not something which is compared with his pain, but something which is compared with his behaviour; it is not replaceable by a picture of pain, because there

is no method of projecting to enable pain to be pictured.[24] If I were to construct a table linking pictures with words, in order to help me learn the meaning of 'pain', the table would not contain pictures of pain (or even my own pain itself, as a model or paradigm: *Inv.* 302) linked with pain: the pictures would have to be pictures of pain-behaviour (cf. *Inv.* 265; Z 552).

This is summed up in a cryptic metaphor. 'If water boils in a pot, steam comes out of the pot and also pictured steam comes out of the pictured pot. But what if one insisted on saying that there must also be something boiling in the pictured pot?' (*Inv.* 297.) According to Professor Pitcher (*The Philosophy of Wittgenstein*, Englewood Cliffs, N.J., 1964) pp. 298–300) Wittgenstein is here saying that sensations do not enter into pain language-games, since they are private and cannot be talked about: they do not enter into the picture any more than the contents of that pictured pot. Since Wittgenstein did not believe that there are private sensations about which nothing can be said, Pitcher's interpretation is mistaken; Wittgenstein does in fact believe that sensations 'enter into' the language-game: the game is precisely the game of expressing sensations. What Wittgenstein is denying is not that *sensations* enter into the language-game, but that *pictures of sensations* do. In the metaphor, the water is the pain, the steam is the pain-behaviour, the pot is the sufferer's body. In the language-game with pain (the *picture* of the water boiling in the pot) there are pictures only of the sufferer and of his behaviour, not of his pain.

Is 'I am in Pain' a Description?

It is time to return from 'He is in pain' to 'I am in pain'. We have seen that 'X is in pain' is not a picture of what it says, since when it is assessed for truth-falsity it is compared not with X's pain but with X's behaviour. Considered, then, as an instance of 'X is in pain', 'I am in pain' will get compared not with my pain, but with my behaviour, that is, with the part of my behaviour concerned with the expression of pain, with the *criteria* for pain. But my utterance of 'I am in pain' is itself an expression of pain. Consequently, if it is to be a description of my state, it is a description of a special kind: for it is a description which is to be compared with – *inter alia* – itself; and this is a unique type of comparison.

This insight was expressed by Wittgenstein in ways which *prima facie* conflict with each other. In the lectures recorded by Moore he denied that 'I have toothache' was a value of the propositional function 'X has toothache' (ML 307). In the *Investigations* he denied that when I say with truth 'I am in pain' I am identifying my sensation as pain and then describing it. I do not identify the sensation by criteria, but simply make use of the expression I have learnt. This is not the *end* of the language-game, but the beginning: we must beware of thinking that the beginning of the language is the sensation, which I go on to describe (*Inv.* 290).

This does not mean that 'I am in pain' is *not* a description. Wittgenstein goes on: 'Perhaps the word "describe" tricks us here: there is a great difference between the language-game of describing a room and the language-game of describing a conscious state. It is *correct* to call 'I am in pain' a description: but the use of 'description' differs from that in 'description of my room'. It differs because my description of my room is not a criterion for what my room is like, whereas my description of my conscious states is a criterion for what they are like. The language-game of describing the room begins with observation of the room; the language-game of describing sensations begins with criteria for sensations. Hence 'I am in pain' is not the end of a language-game, but a beginning (cf. *Inv.* 291, 363).

Just as Wittgenstein thought that 'pain' was in one sense a name and in another not, so he can regard 'I am in pain' as in one sense a description and in another not. He can admit that when a doctor on a ward round asks a patient how he feels, it is perfectly natural to call the reply 'I am in pain' a description of the patient's state (cf. *Inv.* II, p. 188). But he will deny that 'I am in pain' is a description that means that it is something read off from an internal state of affairs. To treat the expression of pain in this way as a description of pain is to make it seem too distant from pain. It is 'as when travelling in a car and feeling in a hurry I instinctively push against something in front of me as though I could push the car from inside'. Or it is as if 'I constructed a clock with all its wheels etc. and in the end fastened the dial to the pointer and made it go round with it' (BB 71[25]). A description must be independent of what it is to be compared with if it is to be assessed as a correct or incorrect description: just as in order to tell the time the hands of a clock must be unfastened from the dial. 'I'm in pain', since it is an utterance which is a criterion for my conscious state, is not independent of it, and so cannot be a description of it in the same way as 'There is a chair in the corner' may be a description of my room cf. p. 275 below).

Clearly, this point has nothing to do with verificationism. The trouble with a clock whose hands are attached to its dial is not that we can never know whether it is telling the right time, but that it is not telling the time at all. Moreover, the point has nothing to do with the nature of the speech-act which 'I'm in pain' may be used to perform. 'We surely do not always say that someone is *complaining* because he says he is in pain. So the words "I am in pain" may be a cry of complaint, and may be something else' (*Inv.* II, p. 189). They might, for instance, be uttered in order to give information to a doctor. But this would not make them, in the full sense, a description; for the doctor might acquire the same information from a wordless cry. A cry, which cannot be called a description, for all that may perform the same service as a description of one's inner life (*Inv.* II, p. 189; cf. pp. 274–5 below).

When I am in Pain, do I Know that I am in Pain?

Just as 'I am in pain' is only a description in a special sense, so it is only true or false in a special sense (cf. pp. 249–50 below). For its truth coincides with its truthfulness. One might adapt to the case of the avowal of pain what Wittgenstein says about the confession of a past thought (*Inv.* II, p. 222). The criteria for the truth of the avowal that I am in pain are not the criteria for the true description of a process. The importance of the true avowal does not reside in its being a correct and certain report of a process. It resides rather in the special conclusions which can be drawn from an avowal whose truth is guaranteed by the special criteria of truthfulness. In this case, there is no comparison of a proposition to reality (pp. 251–2 below; cf. p. 258 below).

We can now see why Wittgenstein rejected the idea that when I am in pain I know that I am in pain. Throughout his life he thought of knowledge as involving the possession of a true description of a state of affairs. That was why, in the *Tractatus*, he declared knowledge of tautologies impossible, since tautologies were not pictures of states of affairs (4.462, 5.51362; cf. 5.542). That is why, since 'I am in pain' is not, when I am in pain, a true description in the normal sense, 'I know that I am in pain' cannot be in order if 'know' is being used in the normal sense. Since the truth of 'I am in pain' coincides with its truthfulness, and there is no such thing as making a mistake here, Wittgenstein does not want to call it an assertion, or the expression of a piece of knowledge.

But once again, his position is nuanced, and expressed in dicta which *prima facie* conflict. Consider the following passages:

It can't be said of me at all (except perhaps as a joke) that I *know* I am in pain. What is it supposed to mean – except perhaps that I am in pain? ... The truth is: it makes sense to say about other people that they doubt whether I am in pain; but not to say it about myself. (*Inv.* 246.)

'I know what I want, wish, believe, feel ...' (and so on through all the psychological verbs) is either philosophers' nonsense, or alternatively *not* a judgement *a priori*.

'I know' may mean 'I do not doubt' but does not mean that the words 'I doubt ...' are *senseless*, that doubt is logically excluded (*Inv.* II, p. 221).
[If I say I wish so-and-so to happen, and am asked 'Are you sure that it is this you wish?' I should say 'Surely I must know what I wish.'] Now compare this answer with the one which most of us would give to the question: 'Do you know the ABC?' Has the emphatic assertion that you know it a sense analogous to that of the former assertion? Both assertions in a way brush aside the question. But the former doesn't wish to say 'Surely I know such a simple thing as this' but rather: 'The question which you asked me makes no sense' .... In this way the answer 'of course I know what I wish' can be interpreted to be a grammatical statement. (BB, 30.)

When in a metaphysical sense I say 'I *must* always know when I have pain', this simply makes the word 'know' redundant; and instead of 'I know that I have pain' I can simply say 'I have pain'. The matter is different of course if we give the phrase 'unconscious pain' sense by fixing experimental criteria for the case in which a man has pain and doesn't know it. (BB, 55.)

Altogether it seems that Wittgenstein recognises the following senses, or would-be senses, of 'I know I'm in pain'.

1. Non-philosophical, empirical use (to rule out unconscious pain: BB 55).
2. Non-philosophical, non-empirical use (as a joke, or as in 'I know I'm in pain but we can't afford the doctor'[26]): in these cases 'I'm in pain', with some nuance, is substitutable.

3. Correct philosophical use (of 'when I'm in pain I know I'm in pain'): the expression of doubt is senseless.
4. Philosophers' nonsense: doubt is both logically possible (to make its expression sensible) and logically impossible (I can't, *a priori*, be wrong about pain).

The philosophers' nonsense is once again a sin against the *Tractatus* principle that a proposition must be independent of what it records as a measure must be independent of what it measures. Against this background, the philosophers' nonsense can be seen as treating expressions of mental states as if they were measurements of mental states (and therefore independent) but infallible measurements (the infallibility, however, being purchased by non-independence). From this point of view, the epistemologists' complaint 'If I can't know my own sensations, how can I know anything' appears like the lament 'If I can't place a winning bet after I've seen the race run, how can I ever place a winning bet at all?'

VII 'Private Experience' and 'Sense Data'

(i) *Rush Rhees*

I. NOTE ON THE TEXT

Wittgenstein wrote these notes in pencil in three paper-covered notebooks. They are not dated, but the first of them seems to have been written in the latter part of 1934 or the beginning of 1935 and the last of them in March 1936.

When he was making notes for his own writing, Wittgenstein almost always wrote in German. But he wrote these notes in English, changing to German occasionally for a single remark or perhaps two or three together. The reason, I think, is that he wrote the first of the notebooks while he was still working on the material of his dictations to Francis Skinner and Alice Ambrose (which became *The Brown Book*) and the rest in thinking of lectures he was giving in Cambridge. There is a similar notebook written before these three and running over into the first of them, with more than half of it in English notes for *The Brown Book*. A still earlier notebook contains English drafts for passages towards the end of *The Blue Book*. I say 'drafts'; but Wittgenstein revised and changed them when he dictated, both in *The Blue Book* and in *The Brown Book*. Some sentences stand as in the notebooks; but more often they are changed, and the arrangement is generally very different. Some of the suggestions in the notes are discarded, and the dictated versions have things not in the notes at all. (He wrote his last German version of *The Brown Book* in August 1936. This is unfinished, but it contains important changes and it will be published.)

The first notes printed here come after discussions developed in *The Brown Book*: the impressions one gets from words in reading; the sense in which the colour pattern of a pansy 'says something'; understanding a facial expression; whether a feeling of pastness distinguishes memory images from others. 'Take as example the feeling of "long, long ago", because this is a strong and clearly circumscribed experience. And yet in a sense it seems just as elusive as any other feeling of memory. ("Far away look in his eyes.")' (This is from the notebook. Compare *The Brown Book*, p. 184.)

While he was still making notes for *The Brown Book* (though he never called it that) Wittgenstein began writing notes for the criticism of Russell's theory of numbers which he developed in lectures on the foundations of mathematics during the Lent and summer terms (from January to early June) of 1935. But the main body of notes for those lectures comes in the same notebook with remarks printed here: between ' "I know what I mean by 'toothache' ..." ' and 'When one says "I talk to myself" . . .', given here on p. 234. I call them 'notes for those lectures' because there are parallels between what he has written in them and what he said, and especially because so many of the diagrams drawn in the notes were used in the lectures. On the other hand, the notes do not contain or even suggest all that he talked about. And when he did make the same point as he had written, his statement was probably no nearer to the notebook than the dictated *Brown Book* is to the notes for that.

The notes which come after those on the foundations of mathematics are related to what he was saying in lectures during 1935–6. But in these lectures he also spoke of many things that are not mentioned in the notebooks, and what he wrote here was not always something he was going to say. What is printed here from p. 239 onward is generally connected with his lectures from January to early June 1936. Some notes are clearly drafts or versions of what he said, and they are often phrased as though he were addressing a class. But we cannot say, 'These are the lectures he gave.' Only in the final passage printed here – from p. 271 to the end – does he seem to be writing a lecture. The first part of this is pretty much what he did say, I think; and if he did not give the rest (which is not complete) he gave something close to it. But he did not lecture from notes, and what he said was both a revision and a discussion of what he had thought and written in preparing.

Between the remark on p. 268 which ends 'Isn't this due to a misunderstanding?' and the remark 'I wish to say . . .' which I have placed just after it, he had begun what looks like the draft of another lecture on the philosophy of mathematics: this time about existence proofs – 'Are there an infinite number of primes or not?', 'Are there 777 in the development of π?' – and what a question is in mathematics. He did lecture on questions which he treats here, in four or five lectures at the end of January and the beginning of

February 1936, but none of them was just the lecture he has written
in the notebook.

For special reasons, I have not included the sections on mathematics. In the longest of them the diagrams are so inseparable from
what he says that a reproduction of the notes would have to be a
photograph. Anyway, it would have made the whole selection too
long. Yet without them the selection is misleading: it leaves out
something of the way Wittgenstein thought about questions of 'personal experience'. Of course he never thought that personal experience provided a foundation for mathematics. But again and again
we find the same sort of difficulties here, in our thinking about
private experience and in our thinking about mathematics. (This
may be important in considering what he means in speaking of 'a
deep-seated disease of language or of thought'.)

For example, Russell once expressed his axiom of infinity as:
'If n be any inductive cardinal number, there is at least one class
of individuals having n terms'; and he added that 'without this
axiom we should be left with the possibility that n and $n + 1$ might
both be the null-class.... Suppose there were exactly nine individuals in the world.... Then the inductive cardinals from 0 up
to 9 would be such as we expect, but 10 (defined as $9 + 1$) would
be the null-class.... Thus 10 and all subsequent cardinals will all
be identical, since they will all be the null-class' (*Introduction to
Mathematical Philosophy* (1919) pp. 131, 132). In explaining his
notation for identity in the *Tractatus*, Wittgenstein said that 'what
the axiom of infinity is intended to say would express itself in language through the existence of infinitely many names with different
meanings' (5.535). In such 'expressing' there would be nothing like
'there is a class of individuals having n terms', which would be
meaningless. Russell needs this phrase because he gives an analysis
of the cardinal number 10 in terms of a function satisfied by
exactly ten different arguments; and he thinks we can ask whether
there *is* any function. Now we might show that 10 and 11 were signs
with different meanings by constructing each of them in a formal
series of cardinal numbers. But although this 'expresses itself in our
symbolism', we still cannot say that our symbolism shows the existence of a function satisfied by ten individuals as arguments. Or sup-
pose I did write $(\exists\varphi): (E\ 10x).\varphi x$; I could not add: 'If I *say* there
is such a function – if I write this down – then there must *be* such
a function, for I have written it as a paradigm in my expression.'
The paradigm shows what I am saying. But here I seem to be treating
it both as a paradigm and as something *for which* it is a paradigm.

It is like saying that the presence of the standard metre rod in Paris shows that there *is* something which is exactly one metre long. It is the same with confusions about the grammar of ostensive definition when we speak of private experiences and sense data. Here we confuse *giving* a sample (to explain what colour 'indigo' is) and *using* a sample (to show what colour my neighbour's curtain is). If I tell myself, 'I now have a visual impression of *this* colour' (concentrating on it), I am trying to use the impression to show me what colour it is.

In both cases Wittgenstein would say: 'Nothing has been said so far to show us how this paradigm is *used* – in what sense it is a paradigm.'

This is one of many parallels which anyone can find.

All that is printed here is a collection of rough notes or memoranda which Wittgenstein made for his own use. He would never have published them – he would not even have had them typed – without revising and rearranging them. Certainly he would have revised the language. I have left the Germanisms even when I felt sure he would have corrected them, as one reminder that these are rough notes. The notes are in the order in which they come in the manuscript, except for two passages given in square brackets after other remarks. I have left out certain remarks, particularly in the first part. These are: (*a*) earlier versions of what is much better said later on in these notes; (*b*) jottings which are too sketchy to be intelligible; and (*c*) some remarks which do not seem closely connected with the main discussions. Wittgenstein kept returning to questions he had treated earlier. This was not a fault, and repetition of this sort can stand.

(ii) *L. Wittgenstein*

II. Notes for Lectures on 'Private Experience' and 'Sense Data'*

The experience of fright appears to us (when we philosophise) to be an amorphous experience behind the experience of starting.

All I want to say is that it is misleading to say that the word 'fright' signifies something which goes along with the experience of expressing fright.

The 'far away' look, the dreamy voice seem to be only means for conveying the real inner feeling.

The philosophical problem is: 'What is it that puzzles me in this matter?'

Es läßt sich über die bestimmte Erfahrung einiges sagen und außerdem scheint es etwas, und zwar das Wesentlichste, zu geben was sich nicht beschreiben läßt. [Some things can be said about the particular experience and besides this there seems to be something, the most essential part of it, which cannot be described.]

Man sagt hier, daß ein bestimmter Eindruck benannt wird. Und darin liegt etwas seltsames und problematisches. Denn es ist als wäre der Eindruck etwas zu ätherisches um ihn zu benennen. (Den Reichtum einer Frau heiraten.) [We say here that a name is given to a particular impression. And this is strange and puzzling. For it seems as though the impression were too ethereal to be named. (Marrying a woman's wealth.)]

Du sagst, Du hast einen ungreifbaren Eindruck. Ich bezweifle nicht, was Du sagst. Aber ich frage ob Du damit etwas gesagt hast. D.h., wozu hast Du diese Worte geäußert, in welchem Spiel? [You say you have an intangible impression. I am not doubting what you say. But I question whether you have said anything by it. I.e. what was the point of uttering these words, in what game?]

It is as though, although you can't tell me exactly what happens inside you, you can nevertheless tell me something general about it. By saying e.g. that you are having an impression which can't be described.

As it were: There is something further about it, only you *can't say* it; you can only make the general statement.

It is this idea which plays hell with us.

---

* Editor's note: All Rhees's footnotes in this work as originally printed, including translations of the German, have here been incorporated into the main text within square brackets.

'There is not only the gesture but a particular feeling which I can't describe': instead of that you ought to have said: 'I am trying to point out a feeling to you' – this would be a grammatical remark showing how my information is meant to be used. This is almost similar as though I said: 'This I call "A" and I am pointing out a *colour* to you and not a shape.'

How can we point to the colour and not to the shape? Or to the feeling of toothache and not to the tooth, etc.?

What does one call 'describing a feeling to someone'?

'I'm giving the feeling which I'm having now a name.' – I don't quite know what you are doing.

'This pain I call "toothache" and I can never make him understand what it means.'

But we are under the impression that we can point to the pain, as it were unseen by the other person, and name it.

For what does it mean that this feeling is the meaning of this name?

Or, that the pain is the bearer of the name?

'I know what I mean by "toothache" but the other person can't *know* it.'

When one says 'I talk to myself' one generally means just that one speaks and is the only person listening.

If I look at something red and say to myself, this is red, am I giving myself information? Am I communicating a personal experience to myself? Some people philosophising might be inclined to say that this is the only real case of communication of personal experience because only I know what I really mean by 'red'.

Remember in which special cases only it has sense to inform another person that the colour which he sees now is red.

The difficulty is that we feel we have said something about the nature of pain when we say that one person can't have another person's pain. Perhaps we shouldn't be inclined to say that we had said anything physiological or even psychological, but something metapsychological, metaphysical. Something about the essence, nature, of pain as opposed to its causal connections with other phenomena.

Es scheint etwa als wäre es zwar nicht falsch sondern unsinnig zu sagen 'ich fühle seine Schmerzen', aber als wäre dies so infolge der Natur des Schmerzes, der Person etc. Als wäre also jene Aussage letzten Endes doch eine Aussage über die Natur der Dinge.

Wir sprechen also etwa von einer Asymmetrie unserer Ausdrucksweise und fassen diese auf als ein Spiegelbild des Wesens der Dinge. [It seems as though it would be not false but meaningless to say 'I feel his pains', and as though this were because of the nature of the pain, of the person, etc. So that the assertion would after all be an assertion about the nature of things.

So we speak perhaps of an asymmetry in our mode of expression and we look on this as a mirror image of the nature of the things.]

Kann man sagen: 'In das was ich über die Erfahrung des Andern sage, spielt solche Erfahrung selbst nicht hinein. In das was ich über meine Erfahrung sage, spielt diese Erfahrung selbst hinein?'

'*Ich spreche über meine Erfahrung, sozusagen, in ihrer Anwesenheit.*' [Can one say: 'In what I say of someone else's experience, the experience itself does not play any part. But in what I say of my experience the experience itself does play a part?'

'I speak about my experience, so to say, in its presence.']

Aber die Erfahrung, die ich habe, scheint eine Beschreibung dieser Erfahrung, in gewissem Sinne, zu ersetzen. 'Sie ist ihre eigene Beschreibung.' [But the experience which I have seems, in a certain sense, to take the place of a description of this experience. 'It is its own description.']

(I can't know whether he sees anything at all or only behaves as I do when I see something.) There seems to be an undoubted asymmetry in the use of the word 'to see' (and all words relating to personal experience). One is inclined to state this in the way that 'I know when I see something by just seeing it, without hearing what I say or observing the rest of my behaviour, whereas I know *that* he sees and *what* he sees only by observing his behaviour, i.e. indirectly.'

(*a*) There is a mistake in this, viz.: 'I know what I see because I see it.' What does it mean to know that?

(*b*) It is true to say that my reason for saying that I see is not the observation of my behaviour. But this is a grammatical proposition.

(*c*) It seems to be an imperfection that I can only know — — — — [indirectly that he sees]. But this is just the way we use the word — — — — ['see']. Could we then — — — — [say I know directly that he sees] if we would? Certainly. [The manuscript contains only the dashes, not the words suggested in brackets.]

Should we say that the person who has not learned the language knows that he sees red but can't express it? – Or should we say: 'He knows what he sees but can't express it'? – So, besides seeing it, he also knows what he sees?

Now suppose I asked: 'How do I know that I see, and that I see red? I.e. how do I know that I do what you call seeing and seeing red?' For we use the words 'seeing' and 'red' in a game we play with one another.

Use of: 'He knows what colour he sees', 'I know what colour I saw', etc.

How do we know what colour a person sees? By the sample he points to? And how do we know what relation the sample is meant to have to the original? Now are we to say 'We never know ...'? Or had we better cut these 'We never know' out of our language and consider how as a matter of fact we are wont to use the word 'to know'?

What if someone asked: 'How do I know that what I call seeing red isn't an *entirely* different experience every time? and that I am not deluded into thinking that it is the same or nearly the same?' Here again the answer 'I can't know' and the subsequent removal of the question.

'He's in a better position to say what he sees than we are.' – That depends.

If we say 'he'll tell us what he saw', it is as though he would make use of language which we had never taught him.

It is as if now we have got an *insight* into something which before we had only seen from the outside.

Inside and outside!

'Our teaching connects the word "red" (or is meant to connect it) with a particular impression of his (a private impression, an impression in him). He then communicates this impression – indirectly, of course – through the medium of speech.'

As long as you use the picture direct-indirect you can't trust yourself about the grammatical situation otherwise [in other ways].

Is telling what one sees something like turning one's inside out? And learning to say what one sees learning to let others see inside us?

'We teach him to make us see what he sees.' He seems in an indirect way to show us *the object* which he sees, the object which is before his mind's eye. 'We can't look at it, it is in him.'

The idea of the private *object* of vision. Appearance, sense datum.

Whence the idea of the privacy of sense data?

'But do you really wish to say that they are not private? That one person can see the picture before the other person's eye?'

Surely you wouldn't think that *telling* someone what one sees could be a more direct way of communicating than by pointing to a sample!

If I say what it is I see, how do I compare what I say with what I see in order to know whether I say the truth?
Lying about what I see, you might say, is knowing what I see and saying something else. Supposing I said it just consists of saying to myself 'this is red' and aloud 'this is green' [see below, pp. 250–1].

Compare lying and telling the truth in the case of telling what colour you see, with the case of describing a picture which you saw, or telling the right number of things you had to count.
Collating what you say and what you see.
Is there always a collating?

Or could one call it giving a picture of the colour I see if I say the word red? Unless it be a picture by its connections with a sample.

But isn't it giving a picture if I point to a sample?

'What I show *reveals* what I see' – in what sense does it do that? The idea is that now you can so to speak look inside me. Whereas I only reveal to you what I see in a game of revealing and hiding which is entirely played with signs of one category. 'Direct-indirect.'

We are thinking of a game in which there is an inside in the normal sense.

We must get clear about how the metaphor of revealing (outside and inside) is actually applied by us; otherwise we shall be tempted to look for an inside behind that which in our metaphor is the inside.

'If he had learned to show me (or tell me) what he sees, he could now show me.' Certainly – but what is it like to show me what he sees? It is pointing to something under particular circumstances. Or is it something else (don't be misled by the idea of indirectness)?
You compare it with such a statement as: 'If he had learned to open up, I could now see what's inside.' I say yes, but remember what opening up in this case is like.

But what about the criterion whether there is anything inside or not? Here we say 'I know there's something inside in *my* case. This is how I know about an inside and am led to suppose it in the other person too.'
Further, we are not inclined to say that only hitherto we have not known the inside of another person, but that the idea of this knowledge is bound up with the idea of myself.

'So if I say "he has toothache" I am supposing that he has what I have when I have toothache.' Suppose I said: 'If I say "I *suppose* he has toothache" I am supposing that he has what I have if I have toothache' – this would be like saying 'If I say "this cushion is red" I mean that it has the same colour which the sofa has if it is red.' But this isn't what I intended to say with the first sentence. I wished to say that talking about his toothache at all was based upon a supposition, a supposition which by its very essence could not be verified.

But if you look closer you will see that this is an entire misrepresentation of the use of the word 'toothache'.

Can two people have the same after-image?

Language game: 'Description of the picture before one's mind's eye'.

Can two persons have the same picture before their mind's eye?

In which case would we say that they had two images exactly alike but not identical?

It seems as though I wished to say that to me L.W. something applied which does not apply to other people. That is, there seems to be an asymmetry.

I *express* things asymmetrically and could express them symmetrically; only then one would see what facts prompt us to the asymmetrical expression.

I do this by spreading the use of the word 'I' over all human bodies as opposed to L.W. alone.

I want to describe a situation in which I should not be tempted to say that I assumed or believed that the other had what I have. Or, in other words, a situation in which we would not speak of *my consciousness* and *his consciousness*. And in which the idea would not occur to us that we could only be conscious of our own consciousness.

The idea of the ego inhabiting a body to be abolished.

If whatever consciousness (there is) spreads over all human bodies, then there won't be any temptation to use the word 'ego'.

If it is absurd to say that I only know that *I* see but not that the others do – isn't this at any rate less absurd than to say the opposite?

Ist eine Philosophie undenkbar, die das diametrale Gegenteil des

Solopsismus ist?   [Is it impossible to imagine a philosophy that would be the diametrical opposite of solipsism?]

The idea of the constituent of a fact: 'Is my person (or a person) a constituent of the fact that I see or not?' This expresses a question concerning the symbolism just as if it were a question about nature.

Language game: I paint, for myself, what I see. The picture doesn't contain *me*.

What if the other person always correctly described what I saw and imagined, would I not say he knows what I see? – 'But what if he describes it wrongly on some occasion? Mustn't I say he was mistaken?' Why should I say this and not, rather, he has forgotten the meanings of his words?

'But after all, only I can finally decide whether what he said is right. We can't assume that *he* knows what I see and *I don't*!' We can also do this!

Can a man doubt whether what he sees is red or green? (Elaborate this.)

'Surely if he knows anything he must know what he sees!' – It is true that the game of 'showing or telling what one sees' is one of the most fundamental language games; which means that what we in ordinary life call using language mostly presupposes this game.

I can for what I see use the impersonal form of description, and the fact that I say 'for what I see' doesn't say at all that after all this is only a disguised personal description! For I just expressed myself in *our* ordinary form of expression, in English.

Does the solipsist also say that only he can play chess?

But he will say that behind the sentence 'I see . . .' when he says it and it's true, there stands something which does not stand behind 'he sees' or 'I see' when the other man says it.

'Surely,' I want to say, 'if I'm to be frank I must say that I have something which nobody has.' – But who's I? – Hell! I don't express myself properly, but there's *something*! You can't deny that there is my personal experience and that this in a most important sense *has no neighbour*. – But you don't mean that it *happens* to be alone but that its grammatical position is that of having no neighbour.

'But somehow our language doesn't bring it out that there is something unique, namely real present experience, and do you just wish me to resign myself to that?'

(Funny that in ordinary life we never feel that we have to resign ourselves to something by using ordinary language.)

The normal use of the expression 'he sees red where...' is this: We take it as the criterion for meaning the same by 'red' as we do, that as a rule he agrees with us in giving the same names to the colours of objects as we do. If then in a particular instance he says something is red where we should say it's green, we say he sees it different from us.

Notice how in such cases we would behave. We should look for a cause of his different judgement, and if we had found one we should certainly be inclined to say that he saw red where we saw green. It is further clear that even before ever finding such a cause we might under circumstances be inclined to say this. But also that we can't give a strict rule for....

Consider this case: someone says 'I can't understand it, I see everything red blue today and vice versa.' We answer 'it must look queer!' He says it does and, e.g., goes on to say how cold the glowing coal looks and how warm the clear (blue) sky. I think we should under these or similar circumstances be inclined to say that he saw red what we saw blue. And again we should say that we know that he means by the words 'blue' and 'red' what we do as he has always used them as we do.

On the other hand: someone tells us today that yesterday he always saw everything red blue, and so on. We say: But you called the glowing coal red, you know, and the sky blue. He answers: That was because I had also changed the names. We say: But didn't it feel very queer? and he says: No, it seemed all perfectly natural. Would we in this case too say:....?

The case of contradictory memory images: tomorrow he remembers this, the day after tomorrow something else.

The whole trend, to show that the expression 'letting one look into his soul', is often misleading.

Now I ask what are our criteria for there being or having been a personal experience besides the expression? And the answer seems to be that for the other man the criteria are indeed mere outside expressions, but that I myself know whether I have an experience or not; in particular, whether I see red or not.

But let me ask: What is knowing that I see red like? I mean: look at something red, 'know that it is red', and ask yourself what you are doing. Don't you mean seeing red and impressing it on your mind that you are doing so? But there are, I suppose, several things that you are doing: You probably *say* to yourself the word 'red' or 'this is red' or something of the sort, or perhaps glance from the red object to another red one which you're taking to be the paradigm of red, and suchlike. On the other hand you just silently stare at the red thing.

In part of their uses the expression 'visual image' and 'picture' run parallel; but where they don't, the analogy which does exist tends to delude us.

(Tautology.) [A few pages later in the same manuscript:

'But it seems to me that I either see red or don't see red. Whether I express it or not.

'Picture we use here.

'This picture is not questioned, but its application.

'Other cases of tautologies.']

The grammar of 'seeing red' is connected to the expression of seeing red closer than one thinks.

We may say a blind man doesn't see anything. But not only do we say so but he too says that he does not see. I don't mean 'he agrees with us that he does not see – he doesn't dispute it', but rather: he too describes the facts in this way, having learned the same language as we have. Now whom shall we call blind? What is our criterion for blindness? A certain kind of behaviour. And if the person behaves in that particular way, we not only call him blind but teach him to call himself blind. And in *this* sense his behaviour also determines the meaning of blindness for *him*. But now you will say: 'Surely blindness isn't a behaviour; it's clear that a man can behave like a blind man and not be blind. Therefore "blindness" means something different; his behaviour only helps him to understand what we mean by "blindness". The outward circumstances are what both he and we know. Whenever he behaves in a certain way, we say that he sees nothing; but he notices that a certain private experience of his coincides with all these cases and so concludes that we mean this experience of his by saying that he sees nothing.'

The idea is that we teach a person the meaning of expressions relating to personal experiences *indirectly*. Such an indirect mode of teaching we could imagine as follows. I teach a child the names of colours and a game, say, of bringing objects of a certain colour when 'the name of the colour' is called out. I don't however teach him the colour names by pointing to a sample which I and he see and saying, e.g., the word 'red'. Instead I have various spectacles each of which, when I look through it, makes me see the white paper in a different colour. These spectacles are also distinguished by their outside appearance: the one that makes me see red has circular lenses, another one elliptical ones, etc. I now teach the child in this way: that when I see him putting the circular ones on his nose I say the word 'red', when the elliptical ones 'green', and so forth. This one might call teaching the child the meanings of the colour names in an indirect way, because one could in this case say that I led the child to correlate the word 'red' with something that I didn't see but hoped the child would see if he looked through the circular glasses. And this way is indirect as opposed to the direct way of pointing to a red object etc.

(Mind-reading)

From this it should follow that we sometimes rightly, sometimes wrongly, teach a man to say that he is blind: for what if he saw all the time but nevertheless behaved exactly like a blind man? – Or should we say: 'Nature wouldn't play such a trick on us!'

We can see here that we don't quite understand the real use of the expression 'to see something' or 'to see nothing'.

And what is so misleading to us when we consider this use is the following. We say, 'Surely we can see something without ever saying or showing that we do, and on the other hand we can say that we see so-and-so without ever seeing it; therefore seeing is *one* process and expressing what we see another, and all that they have to do with another is that they sometimes coincide – they have the same connections as being red and being sweet. Sometimes what is red is sweet – etc.' Now this is obviously not quite true and not

quite false. It seems somehow that we look at the use of these words
with some prejudice. It is clear that we in our language use the
words 'seeing red' in such a way that we can say '*A* sees red but
doesn't show it'; on the other hand it is easy to see that we should
have no use for these words if their application was severed from the
criteria of behaviour. That is to say: to the language game which
we play with these words it is both essential that the people who
play it behave in the particular way we call expressing (saying,
showing) what they see, and also that sometimes they more or less
entirely conceal what they see.

Balance. [Weighing. Later in the notebook: Sometimes these
bodies change their weight, and then we look for the cause of the
change and find, say, that something's come off the body. Sometimes
however the weight of the body changes and we can't account for
the change at all. But we nevertheless don't say that weighing it had
lost its point 'because now the body really doesn't have any weight'.
Rather we say that the body had changed somehow – that this was
the cause of the change of weight – but that so far we have not
found this cause. That is, we shall go on playing the game of
weighing, and we try to find an explanation for the exceptional
behaviour.

We use the form of expression 'the weight of this body' to desig-
nate something inherent in the body, something which could only
be diminished by destroying part of the body. The same body – the
same weight.

Grocer.

Supposing what in fact is the rule became the exception. Under
certain peculiar circumstances indeed a body kept on weighing the
same; say, iron in the presence of mercury. A piece of cheese, on the
other hand, though keeping its size, calories, etc., weighed different
weights at different times unaccountably. Would we still. . . .] The
point of the game depends on what *usually* happens.

But doesn't the word 'seeing red' mean to me a particular experience, a *fact* in the realm of primary experience – which surely is
utterly different from saying certain words?

The words ' "seeing red" means a particular experience' are
useless unless we can follow them up by: 'namely this – (pointing)'.
Or else they may say experience as opposed to physical object; but
then this is grammar.

How does he know that he sees red (or has the visual image), i.e. how does he connect the word 'red' with 'a particular colour'? In fact what does the expression 'a particular colour' here mean? What is the criterion for his connecting the word always to the same experience? Is it not often just that he calls it red?

In fact, if he is to play a language game, the possibility of this will depend upon his own and other people's reactions. The game depends upon the agreement of these reactions; i.e. they must *call* the same thing 'red'.

'But if he speaks to himself, surely this is different. For then he needn't consult other people's reactions and he just gives the name "red" now to *the same colour* to which he gave it on a previous occasion.' But how does he know that it is *the same colour*? Does he also recognise the sameness of colour as what he used to call sameness of colour, and so on ad infinitum?

'Surely seeing is one thing, and showing that I see is another thing' – This certainly is like saying 'skipping is one thing and jumping another'. But there is a supplement to this statement – 'skipping is this (showing it) and jumping is this (showing it).' Now how about this supplement in the first case? 'Seeing red is this (showing it) and showing that we see red is this (showing it).' The point is that there just isn't a 'showing that I see' except showing that I see. 'But can't I say "seeing red is what I'm doing now" (looking at something red)? And although in a sense the other man can't directly see what I'm talking about (be aware of the activity), I certainly know what it is that I'm talking about. That is, although for him I can't point directly to my seeing red, for myself I point to it; and in this sense I can give an ostensive definition of the expression to myself.' But an ostensive definition is not a magic act.

So what does giving myself the ostensive definition of red consist in? – Now how am I to describe it? shall I say: seeing red and saying to myself 'I see red' – or is it 'seeing a certain colour sensation and saying "I see red"'? The first version I don't like. It assumes that the other knows the very same private impression which I am having. So I would rather leave it open what colour I am concentrating my attention on. But then how can I call it a colour? Isn't it just as uncertain that I mean by 'colour' what they mean as that I mean by 'red' what they mean? And the same applies of course to 'seeing' (for what here I mean by this word is not an activity of the inner eye).

'But it's a blatant error to mix up "seeing red" with showing that you see red! I know what seeing red is and I know what showing ... is.' Couldn't we say that knowing what showing ... is is seeing showing? Now what is knowing what seeing is?

In knowing what seeing red is you seem to say to yourself 'seeing red is this' – you seem to give yourself a sample but you don't because the usual criteria for the sameness of the sample don't apply. I can say I call 'red' always the same colour, or whenever I explain 'red' I point to a sample of the same colour.

Consider the proposition: He makes sure what it means *to him* by.... Would you say the word had meaning to him if it meant something else every time? And what is the criterion of the same colour coming twice?

If we describe a game which he plays with himself, is it relevant that he should use the word 'red' for the same colour in our sense, or would we also call it a language game if he used it anyhow? Then what is the criterion for using it in the same way? Not merely the connection between 'same', 'colour', and 'red'.

'Let me see if I still know which of these colours is red? – (Looking about.) Yes I know.' (Here I could have said 'is called red'.)

Making sure that you know what 'seeing red' means, is good only if you can make use of this knowledge in a further case. Now what if I see a colour again, can I say I made sure I knew what 'red' was so now I shall know that I recognise it correctly? In what sense is having said the words 'this is red' before a guarantee that I now see the same colour when I say again I see red?

The grammar of 'private sense data'.

' "Toothache" is a word which I use in a game which I play with other people, but it has a private meaning to me.'

In the use of the word 'meaning' it is essential that the same meaning is kept throughout a game.

'Are you sure that you call "toothache" always the same private experience?'

What's the use here of being sure, if it doesn't follow that it is so and if your being sure is the only criterion there is for its being so? This means: This isn't at all a case of being sure, of conviction.

'So-and·so has excellent health, he never had to go to the dentist, never complained about toothache; but as toothache is a private experience, we can't know whether he hasn't had terrible toothache all his life.'

How does one assume such and such to be the case? What is an assumption that, e.g., '*A* has toothache'? Is it saying the words "*A* has toothache"? Or doesn't it consist in doing something with these words?

'A game of assumption.' –

Assuming: a state of mind. Assuming: a gesture.

Certain behaviour under certain circumstances we call showing our toothache, and other behaviour hiding our toothache. Now would we talk about this behaviour in this way if people didn't ordinarily behave in the way they do? Suppose I and they described my behaviour without such a word as pain, would the description be incomplete? The question is: do *I* consider it incomplete? If so, I will distinguish between two cases of my behaviour, and the others will say that I use two words alternately for my behaviour and thereby they will acknowledge that I have toothache.

'But can't he have toothache without in any way showing it? And this shows that the word "toothache" has a meaning entirely independent of a behaviour connected with toothache.'

The game we play with the word 'toothache' entirely depends upon there being a behaviour which we call the expression of toothache.

'We use "toothache" as the name of a personal experience.' – Well, let's see how we *use* the word!

'But you know the sensation of toothache! So you can give it a name, say "*t*".'

But what is it like to give a sensation a name? Say it is pronoun-
cing the name while one has the sensation and possibly concentrating on the sensation – but what of it? Does this name thereby get
magic powers? And why on earth do I call these sounds the 'name'
of the sensation? I know what I do with the name of a man or of a
number, but have I by this act of 'definition' given the name a use?

'To give a sensation a name' means nothing unless I know already
in what sort of a game this name is to be used.

––––––––––––––

We describe a certain behaviour by 'it is obvious that he was
hiding his pain', or: 'I think he was hiding his pain', or: 'I don't
know at all whether he was hiding his pain.'

But can't I just assume with some degree of certainty that he has
pain although I have no reason whatever for it? I can say 'I
assume . . .', but if I sent them all to the doctor although they
showed no sign of pain (illness), I should just be called mad.

––––––––––––––

In our private language we had, it seemed, given a name to an
impression – in order, of course, to use the name for this impression
in the future. The definition, that is, should have determined on
future occasions for what impression to use the name and for which
not to use it. Now we said that on certain occasions after having
given the definition we did use the word and on others we didn't;
but we described these occasions only by saying that we had 'a
certain impression' – that is, we didn't describe them at all. The
only thing that characterised them was that we used such and such
words. What seemed to be a definition didn't play the role of a
definition at all. It did not justify one subsequent use of the word;
and all that remains of our private language game is therefore that
I sometimes without any particular reason write the word 'red' in
my diary.

'But surely I feel justified when normally I use the word "red"
although I don't think of a definition while doing so.' Do you mean
that whenever normally you use the word "red" you have a particular feeling which you call a feeling of justification? I wonder
if that is true. But anyhow by "justification" I didn't mean a feeling.
But I think I know what makes you say that on saying, e.g., 'this

book is red' you have a feeling of being justified in using the word.
For you might ask: isn't there an obvious difference between the
case in which I use a word in its well-known meaning – as when
I say to someone 'the sky is blue today' – and the case in which I
say any arbitrary word on such an occasion, e.g. 'the sky is moo'.
In this case, you will say, I either know that I am just *giving* a
meaning to the word 'moo', or else I shall feel that there is no justification whatever for using the word. The word is just *any* word and
not the appropriate word. I quite agree that there is a difference
between the cases of 'using the name of the colour', 'giving a new
name to the colour', and 'using some arbitrary word in place of the
name of the colour'. But that doesn't mean that it is correct to say
that I have a feeling of appropriateness in the first case which is
absent in the third. 'But "red" somehow seems to us to fit this
colour.' We certainly may be inclined to say this sentence on certain
occasions, but it would be wrong to say that therefore we had a feeling of fitting when ordinarily we said that something was red.

'But do you mean that one man couldn't play a game of chess
with himself and without anyone else knowing that he did?' – What
would you say he should do to be playing a private game of chess?
Just anything?

I suppose you would say, e.g., that he imagines a chessboard with
chessmen on it, that he imagines certain moves, etc. And if you were
asked what it means to imagine a *chessboard*, you would explain it
by pointing to a real chessboard, or say to a picture of one, and
analogously if you were asked what does it mean to imagine the
king of chess, a pawn, a knight's move, etc. Or should you have
said: he must go through certain . . . ? But what private experiences
are there? and would any of them do in this case? For instance, feeling hot? 'No! The private experiences I am talking of must have
the multiplicity of the game of chess.' But again, does he recognise two private experiences to be different by a further private
experience and this to be the same in different cases? (Private
experience in fiction.) Mustn't we say in this case that we can't say
anything whatever about private experiences and are in fact not
entitled to use the word 'experiences' at all? What makes us believe
that we are is that we really think of the cases in which we can
describe his private experiences, describing different ways of playing chess in one's imagination.

What is it that happens when in the one case I say 'I see red/have toothache/' and mean it, and am not lying, and on the other hand I say the words but know that they are not true; or say them not knowing what they mean, etc.?

The criteria for it being the truth are laid down in *language*, in rules, charts, etc. 'But how am I to know how in the particular case to apply them? For in so far as they are laid down in common language, they join the rest of the rules of common language; i.e. they do not help me in my particular case. Is there such a thing as justifying what I do in the particular case, merely by what then is the case and not by a rule? Can I say I am now justified in using the sentence . . . just by what is now the case?' No!

Nor does it help me to say 'I am justified – when I *feel* justified'. For about feeling justified the same thing can be said as about feeling toothache.

But showing toothache can never be lying.
I must assume an expression which is *not* lying.

When I say that moaning is the expression of toothache, then under certain circumstances the possibility of its being the expression without the feeling behind it mustn't enter my game.

Es ist Unsinn zu sagen: der Ausdruck kann immer lügen. [It is senseless to say: the expression may always lie.]

The language games with expressions of feelings are based on games with expressions of which we don't say that they may lie.

'But was I when a baby taught that "toothache" meant my expression of toothache?' – I was taught that a certain behaviour was called expression of toothache.

'But surely there's a case in which I'm justified in saying "I see red", where I'm not lying, and one where I'm not justified in saying so!' Of course I can be justified by the ostensive definition or by asking the others 'now isn't this red?' and they answer that it is. But you didn't mean this by justification, but one which justifies me privately, whatever the others may say.

If I say 'I see red' without reason, how can I distinguish between saying it with truth and saying it as a lie?

It is important here that I exclude the case of saying the untruth by mistake.

Wir haben hier keinen Vergleich des Satzes mit der Wirklichkeit! *(Kollationieren.)* [Here there is no comparing of propositions and reality. (Collating.)]

Imagine a Robinson Crusoe lying to himself. – Why is this difficult to imagine?

But one might call it lying to oneself if one, e.g., turns one's watch forward to make oneself get up earlier.

Falsifying an account. I add up numbers, arrive at 273 shillings, then rub out 3 and put a 5 instead.

When in this discussion we talk of lying, it ought always to mean *subjective*ly lying, and subjectively lying to the other person and not to oneself.

One could imagine someone constantly lying *subjectively* but not objectively.
He always lies calling red 'green' and green 'red', but as a matter of fact what he says agrees with the usage of other people and so his lying is never taken notice of.

'Der lügt, der sagt "ich sehe rot" und sieht die Farbe, die er selbst mit dem Worte "grün" bezeichnen würde.' Aber das heißt doch, warheitsgemäß *so bezeichnen würde. Oder können wir sagen*, 'für sich *so bezeichnen würde'?*

Daher ist die Idee, daß man lügen kann indem man laut das eine und leise das andere sagt – und was man laut sagt ist hier die Lüge. ['He is lying if he says "I see red" when he sees the colour that he himself *would call* "green".' But this means: he would call it that if he were speaking *truthfully*. Or can we say, 'would call it that *to himself*'? Hence the idea that one may lie by saying one thing softly and something else out loud – and what one says out loud is the lie.]

Was soll es dann heißen: einen Farbeneindruck wahrheitsgemäß mit 'rot' bezeichnen? Paßt das Wort denn einem Eindruck besser als dem andern? [What could be meant by: truthfully calling a colour impression 'red'? Does the word fit one impression better than another?]

Man könnte hier auch sagen: man solle gar nicht von subjektiver Wahrheit des Satzes sprechen. Die Wahrheit des Satzes 'ich habe Zahnschmerz' habe nur objektiv beurteilt zu werden. [We might even say here: one ought not to talk of the subjective truth of the sentence. The truth of the sentence 'I have a toothache' can be judged only objectively.]

The word 'lying' was taught us in a particular way in which it was fastened to a certain behaviour, to the use of certain expressions under certain circumstances. Then we use it, saying that we have been lying, when our behaviour was not like the one which first constituted the meaning.

'Expressions can always be lying.' How can we say this of the expressions to which we fasten our words?

Suppose a child learned the word 'toothache' as an equivalent for its moaning, and noticed that whenever it said the word or moaned the grown-ups treated it particularly well. The child then uses moaning or the word 'toothache' as a means to bring about the desired effect: is the child lying?

You say: 'Surely I can moan with toothache and I can moan without toothache; so why shouldn't it be so with the child? Of course I only see and hear the child's behaviour but from my own experience I know what toothache is (I know toothache apart from behaviour) and I am led to believe that the others sometimes have the pains I have.' – the first sentence already is misleading. It isn't the question whether I *can* moan with or without toothache, the point is that I distinguish 'moaning with toothache' and 'moaning without toothache' and now we can't go on to say that of course in the child we make the same distinction. In fact we don't. We teach the child to use the words 'I have toothache' to replace its moans, and this was how I too was taught the expression. How do I know that I've learned the word 'toothache' to mean what they wanted me to express? I ought to say I *believe* I have!

Now one can moan because one has pain, or, e.g., one can moan on the stage. How do I know that the child, small as it is, doesn't

already act, and in this case I teach it to mean by 'toothache' something I don't intend it to mean.

I have taught the child to use the expression 'I have toothache'
under certain circumstances. And now it uses the words under these
circumstances. – But what are these circumstances? Shall I say 'the
circumstances under which it moaned', and what are these?

But now I also teach the child to moan on the stage! That is to
say, I *teach* it to use this expression in a different game. I also
teach it to read out the sentence 'I have toothache' from a book,
when it hasn't toothache. In fact I could teach it to lie, as a separate
language game. (In fact we often play this kind of game with
children.)

'But doesn't what you say come to this: that it doesn't matter
what the persons feel as long as only they behave in a particular
way?'

'Do you mean that you can define pain in terms of behaviour?'
But is this what we do if we teach the child to use the expression
'I have toothache'? Did I define: 'Toothache is such and such a
behaviour'? This obviously contradicts entirely the normal use of
the word! 'But can't you, on the other hand, at least for yourself
give an *ostensive* definition of "toothache"? Pointing to the place
of your pain and saying "this is . . ."?' Can't I give a name to the
pain I've got? Queer idea to give one's pain a name! What's it to
do with a name? Or what do I do with it? What do I do with the
name of a person whom I *call* by the name? What connection is
the name to have with the pain? The only connection so far is that
you had toothache, pointed to your cheek, and pronounced the
word 'moo'. 'So what?' Remember what we said about private
ostensive definition.

'But aren't you neglecting something – the experience or whatever you might call it – ? Almost *the world* behind the mere words?'

But here solipsism teaches us a lesson: It is that thought which is
on the way to destroy this error. For if the *world* is idea it isn't any
person's idea. (Solipsism stops short of saying this and says that
it is my idea.) But then how could I say what the world is if the
realm of ideas has no neighbour? What I do comes to defining the
word 'world'.

'I neglect that which goes without saying.'

'What is seen *I* see' (pointing to my body). I point at my geometrical eye, saying this. Or I point with closed eyes and touch my
breast and feel it. In no case do I make a connection between what
is seen and a person.

Back to 'neglecting'! It seems that I neglect life. But not life
physiologically understood but life as consciousness. And consciousness not physiologically understood, or understood from the outside,
but consciousness as the very essence of experience, the appearance
of the world, the world.

Couldn't I say: If I had to add the world to my language it
would have to be one sign for the whole of language, which sign
could therefore be left out.

How am I to describe the way the child learns the word 'toothache' – like this?: The child sometimes has toothache, it moans and
holds its cheek, the grown-ups say '...', etc. Or: The child sometimes moans and holds its cheek, the grown-ups ...? Does the first
description say something superfluous or false, or does the second
leave out something essential? Both descriptions are correct.

'But it seems as if you were neglecting something.' But what more
can I do than *distinguish* the case of saying 'I have toothache' when
I really have toothache, and the case of saying the words without
having toothache. I am also (further) ready to talk of any *x* behind
my words so long as it keeps its identity.

Isn't what you reproach me of as though you said: 'In your
language you're only *speaking*!'

But why shouldn't I say '*I* have toothache in his tooth'? I would
insist on his tooth being extracted. Who is supposed to cry out if
it is?

What does it mean: distributing primary experience over all subjects? [Cf. above, p. 239] Imagine that they all have *real* toothache
in their teeth. The one which you only have. I now describe certain
facts. (Not metaphysical ones, but facts about the coincidence of
certain experiences.)

He gets a blow and cries – I think: 'no wonder for it really hurts'. But wouldn't I say to myself: Queer that *he* cries, for *I* feel the pain all right – but he?!

It seems there is a phenomenon which in general I refer to as 'my toothache', which, experience teaches me, is always connected with one particular person (not 'I' but) L.W. I now imagine facts other than they are and connect up this phenomenon to all sorts of persons so as to make it not at all tempting to call this phenomenon 'my toothache'.

'I see so-and-so' does not mean 'the person so-and-so, e.g., L.W., sees so-and-so'.

A language game in which everybody calls out what he sees but without saying 'I see...'. Could anybody say that what I call out is incomplete because I have left out to mention the person?!

A language game in which everybody (and I too) calls out what *I* see without mentioning *me*.

They always know what I see. If they don't seem to, I misunderstand what they say. [Cf. above, p. 240.]

I am tempted to say: 'It seems at least a fact of experience that at the source of *the visual field* there is mostly a small man with grey flannel trousers, in fact L.W.' – Someone might answer to this: It is true you almost always wear grey flannel trousers and often look at them.

'*Ich bin* doch *bevorzugt. Ich bin der Mittelpunkt der Welt.*' *Denken wir uns ich sähe mich in einem Spiegel das sagen und auf mich zeigen! Wäre es noch richtig?* ['But I *am* in a favoured position. I am the centre of the world.' Suppose I saw myself in the mirror saying this and pointing to myself. Would it still be all right?]

When I say I play a unique role I really mean the geometrical eye.

On the other hand, if I describe the visual appearance of my body around the geometrical eye, this is on the same level as saying that in the middle of the visual field there is in general a brown table and at the edges a white wall (as I generally sit in my room).

Now suppose I described this in the form: The visual world in general is like this: (follows the description). Would this be wrong? – Why should it be wrong?! But the question is, what game I intend to be played with this sentence; e.g. who is allowed to say it and in what way are those to whom it is said to react to it? I should like to say that it's I who say it – not L.W., but the person at the source of the visual field. But this I seem not to be able to explain to anyone. (Queer state of affairs.) The game played might be the one which is in general played with 'I see so-and-so'.

What if I see before me a picture of the room as I am seeing the room? Is this a language game?

Can't I say something to nobody, neither to anybody else *nor* to myself? What is the criterion of saying it to myself?

I want to say: 'the visual world is like that . . .' – but why *say* anything?

But the point is that I don't establish a relation between a person and what is seen. All I do is that alternately I point in front of me and to myself.

But what I now see, this view of my room, plays a unique role, it is the visual world!

(*Der Solipsist flattert und flattert in der Fliegenglocke, stößt sich an den Wänden, flattert weiter. Wie ist er zur Ruhe zu bringen?* [(The solipsist flutters and flutters in the flyglass, strikes against the walls, flutters further. How can he be brought to rest?)]

But the real question for me here is: How am *I* defined? Who is it that is favoured? *I.* But may I lift up my hand to indicate who it is? – Supposing I constantly change and my surrounding does: is there still some continuity, namely, by it being *me* and *my surrounding* that change?

(Isn't this similar to thinking that when things in space have changed entirely there's still one thing that remains the same, namely space.) (Space confused with room.)

Suppose someone asked me, 'What does it mean to play a private game of chess with oneself?' and I answered: 'Anything, because if I said I was playing a game of chess I would to be so sure that I was that I would stick to what I said, whatever anyone else might say.'

Suppose someone painted pictures of the landscape which surrounds him. He sometimes paints the leaves of trees orange, sometimes blue, sometimes the clear sky red, etc. Under what circumstances would we agree with him that he was portraying the landscape?

Under what circumstances would we say that he did what we call portraying, and under what circumstances that he called something portraying which we didn't call that? Suppose here we said: 'Well I can never know what he does inwardly' – would this be anything more than resignation?

We call something a calculation if, for instance, it leads to a house being built.

We call something a language game if it plays a particular role in our human life.

'But can't he play a game with colour names, against whatever anybody else says?' But why call it a game with colour names? 'But if *I* played it I would stick to saying that I was playing a game with colour names.' But is that all I can say about it; is all that I can say for its being this kind of game that I stick to calling it so?

Under what circumstances do I say that I'm entitled to say that I'm seeing red? The answer is showing a sample, i.e. giving the rule. But if now I came into constant contradiction with what anybody else said, should I not say that I am applying the rule in a way which prevents me from playing the game? That is: is all that is necessary that the rule I give should be the rule they give, or isn't besides this an agreement in the application necessary?

If 'having the same pain' *means* the same as 'saying that one has the same pain', then 'I have the same pain' means the same as 'I say that I have the same pain' and the exclamation 'Oh!' means 'I say "Oh!" '

Roughly speaking: The expression 'I have toothache' stands for a moan but it does not mean 'I moan'. [In lectures W. said 'is a substitute for moaning' and 'replaces moaning': 'Of course "toothache" is not *only* a substitute for moaning – but it is *also* a substitute for moaning: and to say this shows how utterly different it is from a word like "Watson".' – And again: 'Suppose you were asked "What were the phenomena which were pointed out when you learned the word 'pain' "? There were certain noises in others, and then one's own. Then one is taught to replace the moan by "I have pain.". . . . You might ask "What does the moan stand for?" Nothing at all. "But you don't just wish to say that you moan?" No; but the moan is not the statement "I moan".' Cf. above, p. 252.]

If I say we must assume an expression which can't lie, this can't be explained by saying that pain really corresponds to this expression.

We aren't lying, we are speaking the truth, if a fact corresponds to the sentence. This is no explanation at all but a mere repetition unless we can supplement it by 'namely this —>' and a demonstration; and the whole explanation lies just in this demonstration. The whole problem here only arose through the fact that the demonstration of 'I see red', 'I have toothache', seems indirect.

'But aren't you saying that all that happens is that he moans, and that there is nothing behind it?' I am saying that there is nothing *behind* the moaning.

'So you really don't have pain, you just moan?!' – There seems to be a *description* of my behaviour, and also, in the same sense, a description of my pain! The one, so to speak, the description of an external, the other of an internal fact. This corresponds to the idea that in the sense in which I can give a part of my body a name, I can give a name to a private experience (only indirectly).

And I am drawing your attention to this: that the language games are very much more different than you think.

You couldn't call moaning a description! But this shows you how far the proposition 'I have toothache' is from a description, and how far teaching the word 'toothache' is from teaching the word 'tooth'.

One could from the beginning teach the child the expression 'I think he has toothache' instead of 'he has toothache', with the corresponding uncertain tone of voice. This mode of expression could be described by saying that we can only believe that the other has toothache.

But why not in the child's own case? Because there the tone of voice is simply *determined* by nature.

In 'I have toothache' the expression of pain is brought to the same form as a description 'I have 5 shillings'.

We teach the child to say 'I have been lying' when it has behaved in a certain way. (Imagine here a typical case of a lie.) Also this expression goes along with a particular situation, facial expressions, say of shame, tones of reproach, etc.
'But doesn't the child know that it is lying before ever I teach him the word?' Is this meant to be a metaphysical question or a question of facts? The child doesn't know it in words. And why should it know it at all? – 'But do you assume that it has only the facial expression of shame, e.g. without the feeling of shame? Mustn't you describe the inside situation as well as the outside one?' – But what if I said that by facial expression of shame I meant what you mean by 'the facial expression + the feeling', unless I explicitly distinguish between genuine and simulated facial expressions? It is, I think, misleading to describe the genuine expression as a *sum* of the expression and something else, though it is just as misleading – we get the function of our expressions wrong – if we say that the genuine expression is a particular behaviour and nothing besides.

We teach the child the use of the word 'to speak'. – Later it uses the expression 'I spoke to myself'. – We then say 'We never know whether and what a person speaks to himself.'

Surely the description of the facial expression can be meant as a description of feelings and can be meant otherwise. We constantly use such expressions as 'when he heard that, he pulled a long face' and don't add that the expression was genuine. In other cases we describe the acting [on the stage] of a person in the same words, or again we wish to leave it open whether the expression was genuine or not. To say that we describe the feeling indirectly by the description of expressions is wrong!

Imagine a language in which toothache is called 'moaning' and the difference between just moaning and moaning with pain is expressed by the moaning or dry tone in which the word is pronounced. People would not say in this language that it became clear later on that *A* didn't really have pain, but they would perhaps in an angry tone say that at first he moaned and then he suddenly laughed.

Suppose he says to himself 'I lie', what is to show that he means it? But we would any day describe this lying by saying: 'He said ..., and told himself at the same time that he was lying.' Is this too an indirect description of lying?

But couldn't one say that if I speak of a man's angry voice, meaning that he was angry, and again of his angry voice, not meaning that he was angry, in the first case the meaning of the description of his voice was much further reaching than in the second case? I will admit that our description in the first case doesn't *omit* anything and is as complete as though we had said that he really was angry – but somehow the meaning of the expression then reaches below the surface.

But how does it do that? The answer to this would be an explanation of the two uses of the expression. But how could this explanation reach *under the surface*? It is an explanation about symbols and it states in which cases these symbols are used. But how does it characterise these cases? Can it in the end do more than distinguish two expressions? i.e. describe a game with two expressions?

'Then is there nothing under the surface?!' But I said that I was going to distinguish two expressions, one for the 'surface' and one for 'what is below the surface' – only remember that these expressions themselves correspond to just a *picture*, not to its usage. It is just as misleading to say that there is just the surface and nothing underneath it, as that there is something below the surface and that there isn't just the surface. Because we naturally use this picture to express the distinction between 'on the surface' and 'below the surface'. Because once we make use of the picture of the 'surface' it is most natural to express with it the distinction as on and below the surface. But we misapply the picture if we ask whether both cases are or aren't on the surface.

Now in order that with its normal meaning we should teach a child the expression 'I have lied' the child must behave in the normal way. E.g. it must under certain circumstances 'admit' that it lied, it must do so with a certain facial expression, etc., etc., etc. We may not always find out whether he lied or not, but if we never found out, the word would have a different meaning. 'But once he has learned the word he can't be in doubt whether he is lying or not!'

This of course is like saying that he can't be in doubt whether he has toothache or whether he sees red, etc. On the one hand: doubting whether I have the experience *E* is not like doubting whether someone else has it. On the other hand, one can't say 'surely I must know what it is I see' unless 'to know what I see' is to mean 'to see whatever I see'. The question is what we are to call 'knowing what it is I see', 'not being in doubt about what it is I see'. Under what circumstances are we to say that a person is in no doubt (or is in doubt) about this? (Such cases as being in no doubt about whether this looks red to the normal eye, and analogous ones, of course, don't interest us here.) I suppose that the knowledge of what it is I see must be the knowledge that it is so-and-so I see; 'so-and-so' standing for some expressions, verbal or otherwise. (But remember that I don't give myself information by pointing to something I see with my finger and saying to myself I see this.) 'So-and-so' in fact stands for a word of a language game. And doubting what it is I see is doubting, e.g., what to call what I see. Doubting, for instance, whether to say 'I see red' or 'I see green'. 'But this is a simple doubt about the appellation of a colour, and it can be settled by asking someone what this colour (pointing) is called.' But are all such doubts removable by this question (or which comes to the same, by giving a definition: 'I shall call this colour so-and-so')?

'What colour do you see?' – 'I don't know, is it red or isn't it red; I don't know what colour it is I see.' – 'What do you mean? Is the colour constantly changing, or do you see it so very faintly, practically black?' Could I say here: 'don't you see what you see?'? This obviously would make no sense.

It seems as though, however the outward circumstances change, once the word is fastened to a particular personal experience it now retains its meaning; and that therefore I can now use it with sense whatever may happen.

To say that I can't doubt whether I see red is in a sense absurd, as the game I play with the expression 'I see red' doesn't contain a doubt in this form.

It seems, whatever the circumstances I always know whether to apply the word or not. It seems, at first it was a move in a special game but then it becomes independent of this game.

(This reminds one of the way the idea of length seems to become emancipated from any particular method of measuring it.) [Wittgenstein marked this whole passage as unsatisfactory and wrote 'vague' in the margin.]

We are tempted to say: 'Damn it all, a rod has a particular length however I express it.' And one could go on to say that if I see a rod I always see (know) how long it is, although I can't say how many feet, metres, etc. – But suppose I just say: I always know whether it looks tiny or big!

But can't the old game lose its point when the circumstances change, so that the expression ceases to have a meaning, although of course I can still pronounce it.

He sticks to saying that he has been lying although none of the usual consequences follow. What is there left of the language game except that he says the expression?

We learn the word 'red' under particular circumstances. Certain objects are usually red, and keep their colours; most people agree with us in our colour judgments. Suppose all this changes: I see blood, unaccountably sometimes one sometimes another colour, and the people around me make different statements. But couldn't I in all this chaos retain my meaning of 'red', 'blue', etc., although I couldn't now make myself understood to anyone? Samples, e.g., would all constantly change their colour – 'or does it only seem so to me?' 'Now am I mad or did I really call this "red" yesterday?'

The situations in which we are inclined to say 'I must have gone mad!'

'But we could always call a colour-impression "red" and stick to this appellation!'

Die Atmosphäre, die dieses Problem umgibt, ist schrecklich. Dichte Nebel der Sprache sind um den problematischen Punkt gelagert. Es ist beinahe unmöglich, zu ihm vorzudringen. [The atmosphere surrounding this problem is terrible. Dense mists of (our) language are situated about the crucial point. It is almost impossible to get through to it.]

Do I by painting what I see tell myself what I see?

'This picture is unique, for it represents what is really seen.' What is my *justification* for saying this?

I see two spots on this wall and lift two fingers. Do I tell myself that I see two spots? But on the other hand couldn't this be the sign for my seeing two spots?

Ist das Bild ausgezeichnet oder zeichne ich es aus? [Is it a special picture or do I give it special attention?]

'Today he points at *me*; and yesterday he pointed at *me* also.'

The meaning of: 'He points at me.'

'I see that he points at *A*.'
'I see that he points at me.'

Imagine a game: One person tells the other what he (the other) sees; if he has guessed it rightly he is rewarded. If *A* hasn't guessed correctly what *B* sees, *B* corrects him and says what it is he sees. This game is more instructive if we imagine the persons not to say what is seen but to paint or make models of it. Now let me imagine that I am one of the players.

Wouldn't I be tempted to say: 'The game is asymmetrical, for only what I say I see corresponds to a visual image.'

The problem lies thus: This ↗ is what's seen; and this is also what I see.

Frage Dich: Kann das ↗ *nur ich sehen, oder kann es auch ein Andrer sehen? Warum nur ich?* [Ask yourself: Can only *I* see this ↗, or can someone else see it too? Why only I?]

Für mich existiert kein Unterschied zwischen ich *und das* ↗ ; *und das Wort 'ich' is für mich kein Signal, das einen Ort oder eine Person hervorhebt.* [There is no difference, for me, between *I* and *this* ↗ ; and for me the word 'I' is not a signal calling attention to a place or a person.]

Ich versuche das ganze Problem auf das nicht-Verstehen der Funktion des Wortes 'Ich' (und 'das ↗ *') zu reduzieren.* [I am trying to bring the whole problem down to our not understanding the funtion of the word 'I' (and 'this' ↗ ').

When I stare at a coloured object and say 'this is red', I seem to know exactly to what I give the name 'red'. As it were, to that which I am drinking in.

It is as though there was a magic power in the words '*this is . . .*'.

I can bring myself to say: There is no toothache there ↗ (in the man's cheek who says he has toothache). And what would be the expression for this in ordinary language? Wouldn't it be *my* saying that *I* have no toothache there?

'But who says this?' – 'I!' And who says *this*? – 'I!' –

Suppose I give this rule: 'Whenever I said "I have toothache" I shall from now on say "there is toothache".'

I tell the waiter. Bring me always clear soup, and thick soup to all the others. He tries to remember my face.
Suppose I change my face (body) every day entirely, how is he to know which is me? But it's a question of the *existence* of the game. 'If all chessmen were alike, how should one know which is the king?'
Now it seems that, although *he* couldn't know which is me, I would still know it.
Suppose now I said: 'it wasn't so-and-so, it was I who asked for clear soup' – couldn't I be wrong? Certainly. I.e. I may think that I *asked* him, but didn't. Now are there *two* mistakes I can make: one, thinking that I *asked* him, the other, thinking that *I* asked him? I say: 'I remember having asked you yesterday', he replies: 'You weren't there at all yesterday.' Now I could say either: 'well then I suppose I remember wrongly', or: 'I was here only I looked like him yesterday.'

It seems that I can *trace* my identity, quite independent of the identity of my body. And the idea is suggested that I trace the identity of something dwelling in a body, the identity of my mind.

'If anybody asks me to describe *what I see*, I describe *what's seen*.'

What we call a description of my sense datum, of what's seen, independent of what is the case in the physical world, is still a description for the other person.

If I speak of a description of *my* sense datum, I don't *mean* to give a particular person as its possessor.

(No more do I want to speak about a particular person when I moan with pain.)

It must be a serious and deep-seated disease of language (one might also say 'of thought') which makes me say: 'Of course this ↗ is what's really seen.'

I can tell you the fact p because I know that p is the case. It has sense to say 'it rained and I knew it', but not 'I had toothache and knew that I had'. 'I know that I have toothache' means nothing, or the same as 'I have toothache'.

This, however, is a remark about the use of the word 'I', whoever uses it.

Examine the sentence: 'There is something there', referring to the visual sensation I'm now having.

Aren't we inclined to think that this is a statement making sense and being true? And on the other hand, isn't it a pseudo-statement?

But what (what entity) do you refer to when you say that sentence? – Aren't we here up against the old difficulty, that it seems to us that meaning something was a special state or activity of mind? For it is true that in saying these words I am in a special state of mind, I stare at something – but this just doesn't constitute meaning.

Compare with this such a statement as: 'Of course I know what I am referring to by the word "toothache".'

Think of the frame of mind in which you say to yourself that $p \cdot \sim p$ does make sense and by repeating a statement of this form you are, as it were by introspection, trying to find out what it means.

The phenomenon of *staring* is closely bound up with the whole puzzle of solipsism.

'If I am asked "what do you see?", I describe the visual world,' – Couldn't I say instead of this '... I am describing what is there ↗ ' (pointing before me)?

But now consider the case of someone having a picture before him of the part of his room he is seeing, and he says: 'This in the picture is like *this* (a part of his visual field as he is looking at his room).'

Supposing I said 'there is something there'; and being asked 'What do you mean", I painted a picture of what I see. Would this justify making that statement? – wouldn't this picture have to be understood 'in a system'? And mustn't *I* understand it as an expression within a system?

[Reference to a geometrical diagram of two perpendiculars drawn to a given point on a line:] 'Look at the geometrical proposition as a member of the whole system of geometrical propositions, then you will see whether you really want to accept this proposition!'

'It's no use saying that the other person knows what he sees and not what I see and that therefore all is symmetrical, because there is just nothing else corresponding to my visual image, my visual image is unique!' [In the margin: '*sehr wichtig, wenn auch schlecht gesagt*'. (Very important, although badly expressed.)]

'But I can persuade myself that nobody else has pains even if they say they have, but not that I haven't.'
It makes no sense to say 'I persuade myself that I have no pain', whoever says this. I don't say anything about myself when I say that I can't persuade myself that I haven't pain, etc.

'If I say '*I* see this ↗ ' I am likely to tap my chest to show which person I am. Now suppose I had no head and pointing to my geo-metrical eye I would point to an empty place above my neck: wouldn't I still feel that I pointed to the person who sees, tapping my chest? Now I might ask 'how do you know in this case who sees this?' But what is *this*? It's no use just pointing ahead of me, and if, instead, I point to a description and tap both my chest and the description and say '*I* see *this*' – it has no sense to ask 'How do you

know it's *you* who sees it?', for I don't *know* that it's this person and
not another one which sees before I point. – This is what I meant
by saying that I don't choose the mouth which says 'I have toothache'.

Isn't it queer that if I look in front of me and point in front of me
and say 'this!', I should know what it is I mean. 'I mean just these
shades of colour and shapes, the *appearance*.'

If I say 'I mean the appearance', it seems I am telling you what
it is I am pointing to or looking at, e.g. the chair as opposed to the
bed, etc. It is as though by the word 'appearance' I had actually
directed your attention to something else than, e.g., the physical
objects you are looking at. And indeed there corresponds a particular stare to this 'taking in the appearance'. Remember here what
philosophers of a certain school used to say so often: '*I believe* I
mean something, if I say "...."'

It seems that the visual image which I'm having is something
which I can point to and talk about; that I can say of it, it is
unique. That I am pointing to the physical objects in my field of
vision, but not meaning them by the *appearance*. This object I am
talking about, if not to others then to myself. (It is almost like
something painted on a screen which surrounds me.)
This object is inadequately described as 'that which I see', 'my
visual image', since it has nothing to do with any particular human
being. Rather I should like to call it 'what's seen'. And so far it's all
right, only now I've got to say what can be said about this object,
in what sort of language game 'what's seen' is to be used. For at first
sight I should feel inclined to use this expression as one uses a word
designating a physical object, and only on second thought I see that
I can't do that. – When I said that here there seems to be an
object I can point to and talk about, it was just that I was comparing it to a physical object. For only on second thought it appears
that the idea of 'talking about' isn't applicable here. (I could have
compared the 'object' to a theatre decoration.)

Now when could I be said to speak about this object? When
would I say I did speak about it? – *Obviously* when I describe –
as we should say – my visual image. And perhaps only if *I* describe
it, and only if I describe it to myself.

But what is the point, in this case, of saying that when I describe to myself what I see, I describe an object called 'what's seen'? Why talk of a particular object here? Isn't this due to a misunderstanding?

I wish to say that we can't adduce the 'private experience' as a justification for expressing it.

We can't say 'he is justified in moaning because he has pains' if we call pain *the* justification for moaning. – We can't say 'he is justified in expressing pain, because he has pain' unless we wish to distinguish this case of being justified in expressing pain from another way of justification, e.g. that he is on the stage and has to act as a sick man.

If I am tempted to say 'my justification for moaning is having pain', it seems I point – at least for myself – to something to which I give expression by moaning.

The idea is here that there is an 'expression' for everything, that we know what it means 'to express something', 'to describe something'. Here is a feeling, an experience, and now I could say to someone 'express it!' But what is to be the relation of the expression to what it expresses? In what way is this expression the expression of this feeling rather than another?! One is inclined to say 'we *mean* this feeling by its expression', but what is meaning a feeling by a word like? Is this quite clear if, e.g., I have explained what 'meaning this person by the name "*N*"' is like?

'We have two expressions, one for moaning without pain, and one for moaning with pain.' To what states of affairs am I pointing as explanations of these two expressions?
'But these "expressions" can't be mere words, noises, which you make; they get their importance only from what's *behind* them (the state you're in when you use them)!' – But how can this state give importance to noises which I produce?
Suppose I said: The expressions get their importance from the fact that they are not used coolly but that we can't help using them. This is as though I said: laughter gets its importance only through being a *natural* expression, a natural phenomenon, not an artificial code.
Now what makes a 'natural form of expression' natural? Should

we say 'An experience which stands behind it'?

If I use the expression 'I have toothache' I may think of it as 'being used naturally' or otherwise, but it would be wrong to say that I had a *reason* for thinking either. – It is very queer that *all* the importance of our expressions seems to come from that *X*, *Y*, *Z*, the private experiences, which forever remain in the *background* and can't be drawn into the foreground.

But is a cry when it is a cry of pain not a mere cry?

Why should I say the 'expression' derives its meaning from the feeling behind it – and not from the circumstances of the language game in which it is used? For imagine a person crying out with pain alone in the desert: is he using a language? Should we say that this cry had *meaning*?

We labour under the queer temptation to describe our language and its use, introducing into our descriptions an element of which we ourselves say that it is not part of the language. It is a peculiar phenomenon of iridescence which seems to fool us.

'But can't you imagine people behaving just as we do, showing pain, etc., etc., and then if you imagine that *they don't feel pain* all their behaviour is, as it were, dead. You can imagine all this behaviour *with* or *without* pain. – '

The pain seems to be the atmosphere in which the expression exists. (The pain seems to be a *circumstance*.)

Suppose we say that the image I use in the one case is different from the image I use in the other. But I can't point to the two images. So what does it come to, to say this, except just to saying it, using *this* expression.

We are, as I have said, tempted to describe our language by saying that we use certain elements, images, which however in the last moment we again withdraw.

Isn't the expression *in its use* an image – why do I refer back to an image which I can't show?

'But don't you talk as though (the) pain weren't something terribly real?' – Am I to understand this as a proposition about pain?

I suppose it is a proposition about the use of the word 'pain', and it is one more utterance, and essential part of the surrounding in which we use the word 'pain'.

Feeling justified in having expressed pain.
I may *concentrate on the memory of pain.*

Now what's the difference between using my expressions as I do but yet not using 'toothache' to mean real pain, and the proper use of the word? –

The private experience is to serve as a paradigm, and at the same time admittedly it can't be a paradigm.

The 'private experience' is a degenerate construction of our grammar (comparable in a sense to tautology and contradiction). And this grammatical monster now fools us; when we wish to do away with it, it seems as though we denied the existence of an experience, say, toothache.

What would it mean to deny the existence of pain?!

'But when we say we have toothache we don't just talk of express- ing toothache in this or that way!' – Certainly not – we express toothache! 'But you admit that the same behaviour may be the expression of pain or may not be that.' – If you imagine a man cheating – cheating is done secretly but this secrecy is not that of the 'private experience'. Why shouldn't it be considered wrong in him to use language in this way?

We say 'only he knows whether he says the truth or lies'. 'Only you can know if what you say is true.'
Now compare secrecy with the 'privateness' of personal experi- ence! In what sense is a thought of mine secret? If I think aloud it can be heard. – 'I have said this to myself a thousand times but not to anyone else.'

'Only you can know what colour you see.' But if it is true that only you can know, you can't even impart this knowledge nor can you express it.

Why shouldn't we say that I know better than you what colour you see if you say the wrong word and I can make you agree to my word, or if you point to the wrong sample, etc.?

'I didn't know that I was lying.' – 'You *must* have known!'

Examine: 'If you don't know that you're having a toothache, you aren't having a toothache.'

'I don't just *say* "I've got toothache", but *toothache makes me say this.*' (I deliberately didn't write 'the feeling of toothache', or 'a certain feeling'.)

This sentence distinguishes between, say, saying it as an example of a sentence, or on the stage, etc., and saying it as an assertion. But it is no explanation of the expression 'I have toothache', of the use of the word 'toothache'.

'I know what the word "toothache" means, it makes me concentrate my attention on one particular thing.' But on what? You're now inclined to give criteria of behaviour. Ask yourself: 'what does the word "feeling", or still better "experience", make you concentrate on?' What is it like to concentrate on experience? If *I* try to do this, e.g., open my eyes particularly wide and stare.

'I know what the word "toothache" means, it produces one particular image in my mind.' But *what* image? 'That can't be explained.' – But if it can't be explained what was the meaning of saying that it produced one particular image? You could say the same about the word 'image in your mind'. And all that it comes to is that you are using certain words without an explanation. 'But can't I explain them to myself? Or understand them myself without giving an explanation? Can't I give a private explanation?' But is this anything you can call an explanation? Is staring a private explanation?

But how does this queer delusion come about?!

Here is language – and now I try to embody something in language as an explanation, which is no explanation.

. . .

Privacy of sense data. I must bore you with a repetition of what I said last time. We said that one reason for introducing the idea of the sense datum was that people, as we say, sometimes see different things, colours, e.g., looking at the same object. Cases in which we say 'he sees dark red whereas I see light red'. We are inclined to talk about an object other than the physical object which the person sees who is said to see the physical object. It is further clear that we only gather from the other person's behaviour (e.g. what he tells us) what that object looks like, and so it lies near to say that he has this object before his mind's eye and that we don't see it. Though we can also say that we might have it before our mind's eye as well, without however knowing that he has it before his mind's eye. The 'sense datum' here – the way the physical object appears to him. In other cases no physical object enters.

Now I want to draw your attention to one particular difficulty about the use of the 'sense datum'. We said that there were cases in which we should say that the person sees green what I see red. Now the question suggests itself: if this can be so at all, why should it not always be the case? It seems, if once we have admitted that it can happen under peculiar circumstances, that it may always happen. But then it is clear that the very idea of seeing red loses its use if we can never know if the other does not see something utterly different. So what are we to do: Are we to say that this can only happen in a limited number of cases? This is a very serious situation. – We introduced the expression that *A* sees something else than *B* and we mustn't forget that this had use only under the circumstances under which we introduced it. Consider the proposition: 'Of course we never know whether new circumstances wouldn't show that after all he saw what we see.' Remember that this whole notion need not have been introduced. 'But can't I *imagine* all blind men to see as well as I do and only behaving differently; and on the other hand imagine them really blind? For if I can imagine these possibilities, then the question, even if never answerable makes sense.' Imagine a man, say W., now blind, now seeing, and observe what you do? How do these images give sense to the question? They don't, and you see that the expression stands and falls with its usefulness.

The idea that the other person sees something else than I, is only introduced to account for certain expressions: whereas it seems that this idea can exist without any reference to expressions. 'Surely what I have he too can have.'

'And remember that we admit that the other may have pain without showing it! So if this is conceivable, why not that he never shows pain; and why not that everybody has pain constantly without showing it; or that even things have pain?!' What strikes us is that there seem to be a few applications of the idea of the other person's having pain without showing it, and a vast number of useless applications, applications which look as though they were no applications at all. And these latter applications seem to have their justification in this, that we can imagine the other person to have what we have and in this way the proposition that he has toothache seems to make sense apart from any expression at all. 'Surely,' we say, 'I can imagine him to have pain or to see, etc.' Or, 'As I can see myself, so I can imagine him to do the same.' In other words I can imagine him to play the same role in the act of seeing which I play. But does saying this determine what I mean by 'he sees'?

We arrive at the conclusion that imagining him to have pain (etc.) does not fix the sense of the sentence 'he has pain'.

'He may all along mean something different by "green" than I mean.' Evidence (verification). But there is this consideration: 'Surely I mean something particular, a particular impression, and therefore he may have another impression; surely I know what that would be like!' 'Surely I know what it is like to have the impression I call "green"!' But what is it like? You are inclined to look at a green object and to say 'it's like *this*!' And these words, though they don't explain anything to anybody else, seem to be at any rate an explanation you give yourself. But are they?! Will this explanation justify your future use of the word 'green'? In fact seeing green doesn't allow you to make the substitutions of someone else for you and of red for green.

'The sense datum is private' is a rule of grammar, it forbids [rules out] the use of such expressions as 'they saw the same sense datum'; it may (or may not) allow such sentences as 'he guessed that the other had a sense datum of this . . . kind'. It may only allow expressions of the form: 'The other looked round, had a sense datum and said. . . .' You see that this word in such a case has no use at all. But if you like to use it, do! –

'But surely I distinguish between having toothache and expressing it, and merely expressing it; and I distinguish between these two in myself.' 'Surely this is not merely a matter of using different expressions, but there are two distinct experiences!' 'You talk as though the case of having pain and that of not having pain were only distinguished by the way in which I expressed myself!'

But do we always distinguish between 'mere behaviour' and 'experience + behaviour'? If we see someone falling into flames and crying out, do we say to ourselves: 'there are of course two cases: . . .'? Or if I see you here before me do I distinguish? Do you? You can't! That we do in certain cases, doesn't show that we do in all cases. This to some of you must sound silly and superficial; but it isn't. When you see me do you see one thing and conjecture another? (Don't talk of conjecturing subconsciously!) But supposing you expressed yourself in the form of such a supposition, wouldn't this come to adopting a '*façon de parler*'?

Can we say that 'saying that I lie is justified by a particular experience of lying'? Shall we say '...by a particular private experience'? or '...by a particular private experience of lying'? or 'by a particular private experience characterised in such and such ways'?

'But what, in your opinion, *is* the difference between the mere expression and the expression + the experience?'

'Do you know what it means that W. behaves as he does but sees nothing; and on the other hand that he sees?'

If you ask yourself this and answer 'yes' you conjure up some sort of image. This image is, it seems, derived from the fact of your seeing or not seeing (if you close your eyes), and by this derivation, it seems, it must be the picture we interpret to correspond to our sentence 'he sees', 'he doesn't see'. – As when I substitute for my body, his body, and for holding a match, holding a pen. – But substituting his body for my body might mean that my body has changed so as to be now like his, and perhaps vice versa. It seems a direct and simple thing to understand 'thinking that he has what I have', but it isn't at all. The case is simple only if we speak, e.g., of physiological processes. 'I know only indirectly what he sees, but directly what I see' embodies an absolutely misleading picture. I can't be said to know that I have toothache if I can't be said not to know that I have toothache. I can't be said to know indirectly what the other has if I can't be said to know it directly. The misleading picture is this: I see my own matchbox but I know only from hearsay what his looks like. We can't say: 'I say he has toothache because I observe his behaviour, but I say that I have because I *feel* it.' (This might lead one to say that 'toothache' has two meanings, one for me and one for the other person.)

'I say "I have toothache" because I *feel* it' contrasts this case with, say, the case of acting on the stage, but can't explain what 'having toothache' means because having toothache = feeling toothache, and the explanation would come to: 'I say I have it because I have it' = I say I have it because it is true = I say I have it because I don't lie. One wishes to say: In order to be able to say that I have toothache I don't observe my behaviour, say in the mirror. *And this is correct*, but it doesn't follow that you describe an observation of any other kind. Moaning is not the description of an observation. That is, you can't be said to *derive* your expression from what you observe. Just as you can't be said to derive the word '*green*' from your *visual impression* but only from a sample. – Now against this one is inclined to say: 'Surely if I call a colour green I don't just say that word, but the word comes in a particular way', or 'if I say "I have toothache" I don't just use this phrase but it must come in a particular way!' Now this means nothing, for, if you like, it always comes in a particular way. 'But surely seeing and saying something *can't be all*!' Here we make the confusion that there is still an object we haven't mentioned. You imagine that there is a *pure* seeing and saying, and one + something else. Therefore you imagine all distinctions to be made as between *a*, *a + b*, *a + c*, etc. The idea of this addition is mostly derived from consideration of our bodily organs. All that ought to interest you is whether I make all the distinctions that you make: whether, e.g., I distinguish between cheating and telling the truth. – 'There is something else!' – 'There is nothing else!' – 'But what else is there?' – 'Well, this ↗!'

'But surely I know that I am not a mere automaton!' – What would it be like if I were? – 'How is it that I can't imagine myself not experiencing seeing, hearing, etc.?' – We constantly confuse and change about the commonsense use and the metaphysical use.

'I know that I see.' –

'I see.' – you seem to read this off some fact; as though you said: 'There is a chair in this corner.'

'But if in an experiment, e.g., I say "I see", why do I say so? surely because I see!'

It is as though our expressions of personal experience needn't even spring from regularly recurrent inner experiences but just from *something*.

Confusion of description and samples.

The idea of the '*realm of consciousness*'.

Notes

Editor's Introduction

1. I am grateful to Professor A. G. N. Flew, the General Editor of the series to which this collection belongs, and my colleague, Mr Ian Tipton, for their constructive criticisms of an earlier draft of this introduction.

2. *Action, Emotion and Will* (London, 1963) chap. 1, and 'Cartesian Privacy', in *Wittgenstein: the Philosophical Investigations,* ed. George Pitcher (London, 1968) pp. 352–70.

3. I am grateful to Miss Cora Diamond for drawing my attention to the importance of these disclaimers in Wittgenstein's writings.

4. Kenny does not dispute the point that Wittgenstein was not trying to prove theses, but holds that there is a *reductio ad absurdum* of the notion of a private language in the *Inv.*

5. The tendency in the past has been to emphasise the difference between the earlier and later Wittgenstein. For a new interest in the unity of Wittgenstein's thought, see Winch's book mentioned in the Bibliography.

6. Don Locke makes much of this point in chapter 5 of his book, which is mentioned in the Bibliography.

Chapter I

1. Even this is not quite true as it stands. There is no place for one kind of doubt, the kind that might be expressed in 'Am I interpreting the facts of this situation aright?' But there is sometimes place for another kind, which might be expressed in 'Does this quite deserve the *name* of "pain"?'

2. The fact that there are characteristic natural expressions of pain but not (or not obviously) characteristic differences between natural expressions of different kinds of pain (I do not mean different degrees or locations) is the explanation of the fact that the descriptions of the different kinds tend to be analogical, whereas the word 'pain' is not analogical.

3. Partly reprinted above. For full reference, see Acknowledgements. [Ed.]

4. [This is an error. Apparently I fell into the trap of assuming that if two people, A and B, are in pain, the pain that A feels must be *numerically* different from the pain that B feels. Far from making this assumption, Wittgenstein attacks it when he says: 'In so far as it makes *sense* to say that my pain is the same as his, it is also possible for us both to have the same pain' (*Inv.* 253). There is not some sense of 'same pain' (*numerically* the same) in which A and B *cannot* have the same pain. 'Today I have that same backache that you had last week' is something we say. 'Same' means here, answering to the same description. We attach no meaning to the

'question' of whether the backhache you had and the one I have are or are not 'numerically' the same.

A more correct account of Wittgenstein's point in *Inv.* 302 is the following: A proponent of the privacy of sensations rejects circumstances and behaviour as a criterion of the sensations of others, this being essential to his viewpoint. He does not need (and could not have) a criterion for the existence of pain that he feels. But surely he will need a criterion for the existence of pain that *he* does *not* feel. Yet he cannot have one and still hold to the privacy of sensation. If he sticks to the latter, he ought to admit that he has not the faintest idea of what would count for or against the occurrence of sensations that he does not feel. His conclusion should be, not that it is a contradiction, but that it is unintelligible to speak of the sensations of others. (There is a short exposition of Wittgenstein's attack on the idea that we learn what sensation is *from our own case*, in 'Knowledge of Other Minds', in my *Knowledge and Certainty* (Prentice-Hall, 1963); see pp. 136–8)].

Chapter II

1. My use of a similar argument in my book *The Problem of Knowledge* (1956) has led Professor Anscombe to accuse me of committing a logical fallacy (*vide* her book *An Introduction to Wittgenstein's Tractatus*, pp. 138–9). She supposes that I argue 'from the fact that it is not possible, and *a fortiori* not necessary, that every identification or recognition should in fact be checked, to the innocuousness of the notion of an uncheckable identification'. I agree with her that this is a fallacy, but I do not think I have committed it. My argument is that since every process of checking must terminate in some act of recognition, no process of checking can establish anything unless some acts of recognition are taken as valid in themselves. This does not imply that these acts of recognition are uncheckable in the sense that their deliverances could not in their turn be subjected to further checks; but then these further checks would again have to terminate in acts of recognition which were taken as valid in themselves and so *ad infinitum*. If the inference drawn from this is that an act of recognition is worthless unless it is corroborated by other acts of recognition, the recognition of private sensations will not necessarily be excluded. For there is no reason in principle why such acts of recognition should not corroborate one another.

2. I have come to doubt this. See the following footnote to 'Privacy' (reprinted in *The Concept of a Person and Other Essays* (1963)): Having tried to construct a language of this kind [viz. a language all of whose words refer to nothing but private things], I have come to doubt whether it is feasible. I am now inclined to think that in any language which allows reference to individuals there must be criteria of identity which make it possible for different speakers to refer to the same individual. This would not prevent the language from containing private sectors, but it would mean that my idea that these private sectors could be made to absorb the public sectors was not tenable.

3. This is an over-simplification; see 'Privacy'.

4. Ayer says Crusoe may think that a bird is 'of the same type as one which he had previously named, when in fact it is of a different type, *sufficiently* different *for him to have* given it a different name if he had observed it more closely'. What do the words I have italicised mean here?

Chapter III

1. Russell's reference to the notion of a private language in the *Philosophy of Logical Atomism* (University of Minnesota publication) p. 13, might also be noted. Russell is concerned primarily with the notion of a logically perfect language. He remarks that 'A logically perfect language, if it could be constructed, would not only be intolerably prolix, but, as regards its vocabulary, would be very largely private to one speaker. That is to say, all names that it would use would be private to that speaker and could not enter into the language of another speaker'. [Editor's note: Russell's lectures on 'The Philosophy of Logical Atomism' are now more conveniently available in *Logic and Knowledge: Essays 1901 to 1950*, ed. R. C. Marsh (Allen & Unwin, 1956) pp. 177–281.]

2. Professor Ryle has pointed out that the letter 'E' is a mistranslation. 'E' is the first letter of the word *Empfindung* which means 'sensation', therefore the letter 'S' should have appeared in the English translation. Hereafter we shall use the letter 'S'.

3. In the sense of something which could not conceivably be grasped by another person, and not just in the Crusoe sense.

4. Wittgenstein emphatically rejects this echo of his philosophical past for the view that 'the meaning of a word is its use in the language' (*Inv.* 43), where by 'use' he means the usual practice of speakers of the language with the word. We cannot pursue this matter further in the present paper. Wittgenstein's elaboration and defence of his new position is to be found in *Inv.* 137–242; he makes clear in 257 that the formula 'the meaning is the use' applies to names of sensations.

5. Several debater's points which Ayer makes against Wittgenstein are a result of his failure to appreciate this point. (See pp. 54 ff. above).

6. I take Frege's explanation of what an analytic proposition is as clear and adequate, provided we follow Frege in accepting only arbitrary or stipulative definitions and only strictly formal logical laws: 'The problem becomes that of finding the proof of the proposition, and of following it up right back to primitive truths. If, in carrying out this process, we come only on general logical laws and definitions, then the truth is an analytic one.' *Foundations of Arithmetic*, trans. J. L. Austin (Blackwell, 1950) p. 4.

7. Wittgenstein's remark in *Inv.* 260 is on the grammar of making notes, not on the grammar of sensation. Ayer apparently overlooked this section, or he missed the point of it. He says: 'It is all very well for Wittgenstein to say that writing down the sign "E", at the same time as I attend to the sensation, is an idle ceremony. How is it any more idle than writing down a sign, whether it be the conventionally correct sign or not, at the same time as I observe some "public" object?' (p. 54 above). The answer, of course, is that it is not, but Ayer's suggestion that Wittgenstein would make a different answer is absurd. The object of *Inv.* 260 is to bring out just

this point.

8. Such a definition could be used to explain the use of 'E' to other people, but not to *you*. There can never be an occasion for defining for you words which you use to refer to your own sensations. For further explanation see my article 'Analyticity and Grammar', *Monist*, LI (19—).

Chapter IV

1. In *Inv.* 404, Wittgenstein accepts the corollary that the 'I' in 'I am in pain' is not used to *refer* to oneself: 'Now in saying this ["I am in pain"] I don't name any person. Just as I don't name anyone when I *groan* with pain.' He supports this claim with a bad argument: ' "I" is not the name of a person' (*Inv.* 410). (Though 'I' is not anyone's name, it *is* used to *refer* to someone, to the speaker.)

2. I owe the point made in this paragraph to Dr J. W. Tucker, to whom I am also much indebted for discussion of the problems dealt with in this paper and for criticism of the paper itself.

3. I am indebted to Professors A. J. Ayer and G. E. M. Anscombe for helpful discussion of some of the points made in this paper. But they are in no way responsible for its present form.

4. Misinterpretation of this point is a fatal flaw in Michael Stocker's attempt to show that Wittgenstein 'succumbs to a *reductio*' at this point. See his article 'Memory and the Private Language Argument', *Philosophical Quarterly* (Jan. 1966).

5. Further argumentation on this point is made superfluous by Bruce Aune's penetrating discussion in 'The Complexity of Avowals', in *Philosophy in America*, ed. Max Black (London, 1965).

6. The cases of conceptual derangement used by Aune do not seem to me to count against Wittgenstein here, given that he includes in *Inv.* 288 the condition that the subject has passed various tests which establish that he has the concept.

7. For a helpful discussion of the connection between recognising that something is the same and the existence of a language, see J. O. Urmson, 'Recognition', *Proc. Arist. Soc.* (1955–6).

Chapter VI

1. E.g. Ayer in Chapter II above. A. J. Ayer says the thesis is, there can be no language which is of necessity unintelligible to anyone but its speaker, and then, oddly enough, thinks he has refuted this thesis by proving (if he has proved even these) the quite irrelevant points (1) that there can be a language which is and always has been as a matter of fact unintelligible to anyone but its speaker, and (2) that sensation-reports are not of necessity unintelligible to anyone but their maker.

Cf. also R. Rhees in Chapter II, above.

2. Sometimes the private language argument runs: And what could be the use, the role of the words in a private language? Well, why not simply to keep a record for one's own amusement? And then it seems to me that if this is to be ruled out, the argument will have to proceed as I describe it in what follows.

3. Unless the sign is 'private' too, which is a possibility that no one has remarked on – and this because it has not been noticed that the notion 'private language' as Malcolm defines it does not require that the terms of the language be names of sensations. Cf. section VII below.

4. Does the child have to write 'dog' just exactly as you do? Anything within a certain range will do. Of course in identifying for him a class of 'dog'-inscriptions, you weren't picking out a new class of thing (you were taught what the class is just as he is now). All the same, you pick out a class for him in writing 'dog', which he may learn from one sample alone. Why should I not be able to form a new class – of squiggles – and pick it out for you in the same way?

5. Cf. Mr R. Rhees (Chapter II above): 'And if every use of the mark is also a definition – if there is no way of discovering that I am wrong, in fact no sense in suggesting that I might be wrong – then it does not matter what mark I use or when I use it.' Unless I am muddled as to syntax, the 'in fact' does a job here which might equally well have been done by 'or, which amounts to the same'.

6. That there is *a* connection between the private language argument and verificationism has already been suggested by Ayer (Chapter II above) and Strawson ('Critical Notice of Wittgenstein's *Philosophical Investigations*', partly reprinted in Chapter I above). The connection is also noticed by Carl Wellman, in 'Wittgenstein and the Egocentric Predicament', *Mind*, LXVIII (Apr. 1959) – though this article seems to me to underestimate not only Wittgenstein, but also the force of the private language argument.

7. P. F. Strawson (p. 28 above) explicitly suggests that the notion 'private *language*' may be generalised: i.e. that the terms need not stand for sensations, but may also stand 'for things like colours or material objects or animals'. But in fact he is concerned with a quite different notion of 'private language': on Strawson's view (cf. pp. 28–9 above) a private language is one which merely is not, and never has been, understood by anyone but its speaker.

8. In the preparation of this article I have been greatly assisted by discussions with Professor G. E. M. Anscombe and Dr Peter Hacker.

9. 'How can I go so far to try to use language to get between pain and its expression?' (*Inv.* 245). The passage is difficult to understand, but *pace* Hintikka (see Bibliography), Anscombe's translation seems correct. The problem is that the quoted sentence immediately follows Wittgenstein's rejection of the imputation of behaviourism; but it does not apply to the behaviourist, who does not want to come between pain and its expression, since he thinks pain and its expression are in fact identical. The solution appears to be that the rejection of behaviourism is a parenthesis, and the rhetorical question is addressed to the private-language defender who wants to build his language on an unexpressed, and indeed inexpressible, sensation.

10. The two preceding paragraphs are based on pp. 243, 247 above, which deal with vision, not pain; but the *Inv.* repeats that there can be pain-behaviour without pain (*Inv.* 304) and pain without pain-behaviour (*Inv.* 281).

11. Cf. the *Blue Book*: 'In so far as ... teaching brings about the association, feeling of recognition, etc., etc., it is the *cause* of the phenomena of understanding, obeying etc.; and it is a hypothesis that the process of teaching should be needed in order to bring about these effects. It is conceivable, in this sense, that *all* the processes of understanding, obeying, etc., should have happened without the person ever having been taught the language' (BB 12; cf. also BB 96–7).

12. In 'Brains and Behaviour' (*Analytical Philosophy,* ed. Butler (1965) II, 9 ff.), Hilary Putnam argues that it is perfectly conceivable (i) that there should be a race of super-Spartans who in adult life suppress all non-verbal pain-behaviour; (ii) that in time the children of these super-Spartans may be born acculturated, so that they never express pain at all, though they are born masters of a language including 'pain'; (iii) that the members of such a species might feel pain if and only if in the presence of a magnetic field. It is important to keep separate two questions which Putnam does not sharply distinguish: (*a*) Can one have pains which are not expressed in the usual way nor occur in the usual circumstances? (*b*) Can one know what 'pain' means without one's use of the word being connected with the usual symptoms and circumstances? If Putnam's three suppositions are genuinely conceivable, then the answer to (*a*) is affirmative; but an affirmative answer to (*b*) does not follow. If the three suppositions are fulfilled, then the only reason for saying that the super-Spartans feel pain is that they say of themselves 'We feel pain'. Clearly, there must be some reason to think that they mean by 'pain' what we mean by it; within the fiction the only such reason can be that they can apply the word correctly to normal human beings in pain; but if so then their use of the word *is* connected with the usual symptoms and circumstances of pain, though not in the case of their own pains.

13. These two terms, which are not altogether happy, are to be treated simply as abbreviations for the elucidations quoted above from Wittgenstein. Perhaps 'undisclosable *v.* unshareable' would make a better pair.

14. What of pains I have without expressing? Are unexpressed pains nobody's pains? No: my unexpressed pains are pains which, if expressed at all, would be expressed by me.

15. For instance, Wittgenstein calls playing chess in the imagination a private experience – but points out that to explain what 'imagining a chessboard with chessmen on it' meant, one would have to point to a *real* chessboard, or do something similar (p. 249 above).

16. On this section, see p. 270 above. '. . . cheating is done secretly, but this secrecy is not that of the "private experience" . . . compare secrecy with the "privateness" of personal experience! In what sense is a thought of mine secret? If I think aloud it can be heard.'

17. See, for instance, Saunders and Henze, *The Private-Language Problem,* pp. 36 ff.

18. In this I agree with Hintikka (see Bibliography) against Anscombe.

19. Support for interpreting the 'dictionary' in this way will be found in Z 546–8, 552.

20. At *Inv.* II, p. 207, Wittgenstein speaks of 'the temptation to say "I

see it like *this*", pointing to the same thing for "it" and "this". Cf. WWK 97: 'Wie verifiziere ich den Satz "dies ist gelb". Zunächst ist klar. "Dies", das gelb ist, muss ich wieder erkennen können, auch wenn es rot ist. (Würde "dies" und "gelb" eine Einheit bilden, so könnten sie durch *ein* Symbol dargestellt werden, und wir hätten keinen Satz.)'

21. See Judith Jarvis Thompson, pp. 183–204 above.) Mrs Thompson is doubtful whether the *Investigations* contain an argument against private languages. I agree with her that it does not contain the argument which she states.

22. The context here is somewhat different; but *Inv.* 279 is linked with the private 'pain' by Z 536.

23. Wittgenstein is here doing what he recommends in many analogous cases, replacing workings of the imagination with real objects – see BB 4.

24. Cf. *Inv.* 301: No image is a picture, but there are some images to which pictures can correspond. If I imagine that A is in pain, this is not an image to which a picture (of pain) can correspond; and 'A is in pain' is not a picture in the *Tractatus* sense – i.e. no method of projection links it to A's being/not being in pain.

25. The metaphors occur in the different, but analogous, context of a discussion of the solipsist's 'I see *this*' meaning his visual sense-datum.

26. Cf. John W. Cook, 'Wittgenstein on Privacy' (see Bibliography).

Bibliography

BOOKS

L. Wittgenstein, *Philosophical Investigations*, trans. G. E. M. Anscombe (Oxford: Basil Blackwell; New York: Macmillan, 1953). The starting point for most discussions of the private language argument, especially Part I, sections 143–308.

G. Pitcher (ed.), *Wittgenstein: The Philosophical Investigations* (New York: Doubleday, 1966; London: Macmillan, 1968). Contains several important articles which discuss the private language problem, including 'Wittgenstein on Privacy' by John W. Cook, 'Wittgenstein on Sensation' by Alan Donagan, and 'Cartesian Privacy' by Anthony Kenny.

John Turk Saunders and Donald F. Henze, *The Private Language Argument* (New York: Random House, 1967). A comprehensive discussion in the form of a dialogue which links the private language problem with Strawson's argument in *Individuals*, ascription of experiences to one-self presupposes the possibility of ascribing experiences to other people. Contains a very comprehensive bibliography.

Peter Winch (ed.), *Studies in the Philosophy of Wittgenstein* (London: Routledge & Kegan Paul, 1969). Contains, among other things, discussions of Cartesianism, sensations and private language in relation to Wittgenstein's remarks. Attempts to elucidate Wittgenstein's earlier views on language and to relate these views to later developments in his thinking on the subject.

Don Locke, *Myself and Others* (Oxford: Oxford University Press, 1968). Includes a chapter on the private language argument which contains a criticism of Mrs J. J. Thomson's suggestion that the private language argument is an application of the Verification Principle. Locke distinguishes senses in which he maintains that a private language is, and is not, possible.

ARTICLES

J. D. Carney, 'Private Language: The Logic of Wittgenstein's Argument', *Mind* (1960). Criticises the arguments of Wellman (see below).

James W. Cornman, 'Private Languages and Private Entities', *Australasian Journal of Philosophy* (1968). Examines the private language argument with a view to showing that sensation-sentences are reports and argues that this has implications for the Identity Thesis and for scepticism about other minds.

Carl Ginet, 'How Words Mean Kinds of Sensations', *Philosophical Review*

(1968). Argues to the conclusion that there could not be a sensation-term whose meaning could only be understood by the subject having the sensation. Disagrees with Malcolm over interpretation of a passage in *Inv*.

J. Hintikka, 'Wittgenstein on Private Language: Some Sources of Mis-understanding', *Mind* (1969). Discusses the translation of sections 245 and 265 in Part I of *Inv*.

Leonard Linsky, 'Wittgenstein on Language and Some Problems of Philo-sophy', *Journal of Philosophy* (1957). A readable short exposition of Wittgenstein's remarks about private language. Contrasts Wittgenstein's later view of language as a tool with his earlier view of it as a picture. The reader should compare this with Kenny's interpretation in this volume.

Brian Medlin, 'Critical Notice of Ayer's *Concept of a Person and Other Essays*', *Australasian Journal of Philosophy* (1964). Contains an appre-ciative criticism of Ayer's papers on the private language argument and on privacy.

Moreland Perkins, 'Two Arguments against a Private Language', *Journal of Philosophy* (1965). Begins by setting out the argument as a formal deduction. Takes the notion of a *practice* to be crucial to the argument.

Rush Rhees, 'Wittgenstein's Builders', *Aristotelian Society Proceedings* (1959–60). Raises the question what it is to speak, and considers it in the context of Wittgenstein's examples of the builders' language-game.

M. T. Thornton, 'Locke's Criticism of Wittgenstein', *Philosophical Quar-terly* (1969). Should be read for its criticism of Locke's *Myself and Others* (see above).

Carl Wellman, 'Wittgenstein and the Ego-centric Predicament', *Mind* (1959). Produces a battery of arguments against Wittgenstein. The angle is epistemological. Criticised by J. D. Carney (see above).